LADAKH PROFILE

LADAKH PROFILE

Dr. Prem Singh Jina

Publications

KALPAZ PUBLICATIONS
DELHI-110052

Ladakh Profile

Rs. 890

ISBN: 81-7835-437-3

Published in 2005 in India by
Kalpaz Publications,
C-30, Satyawati Nagar, Delhi-110052
E-mail : Kalpaz@hotmail.com

Laser Typesetting at : Master Computers, Delhi
Printed at : Salasar Imaging System, Delhi

Dedicated to

Mrs. Manju Jina

Contents

Monasteries of Ladakh

Defence and War

Politics

Personalities

Environment

Trade and Industries

Art and Craft

Fair and Festival

Preface

'Ladakh Profile' narrates the various aspects of Ladakh viz. History and Archeology, Mummies and Royal families, Explorers' experiences, Monasteries, Defence Analysis, Trade and Industries, Art and Craft, Fair and Festival, Mountaineering, Terrorism and Politics.

My purpose in writing this book, was to fulfil the basic requirements of Research scholars, teachers and tourists of the world who want to know about the land and the people of Ladakh. There is still much to say about this region but I hope that what I have been able to recount in the following chapters will give the reader a real interest.

Dr. Prem Singh Jina

Acknowledgements

I owe a deep sense of gratitude to Prof. Maya Ram, Director Higher Education (Rtd.), Allahabad, U.P. for the encouragement given by him. I must thank Hon. Capt. Tsewang Norbu (Tarupa) and Sri B.L. Raina, Central Institute of Buddhist Studies, Leh-Ladakh for rendering help as and when required.

I would fail in performing my moral duties if I forget to mention Mrs. Manju, Principal, Hira Convent School, Haldwani, who helped me in various ways in completing this book.

I am also grateful to the authors by whose thought and works, I have benefited immensely.

At the end I am grateful to Gyan Books Publishing House for the publication of this book well in time.

Dr. Prem Singh Jina

Introduction

Ladakh has many unconquered peaks of tremendous heights, uncharted glaciers and valleys of rich vegetation. It occupies a position of great strategic importance, to its East is China and North-West by Pakistan.

Historically Ladakh is very important region. Petroglyphs in Ladakh provide information about the region's habitation in the Proto-historic period. All such information we can get through the rock and stone carvings in Ladakh and along the Karakoram mountains. It has been in the records that during 400 B.C. Sargyal established the kingdom of Ladakh and Tibet. Niathichen was the next ruler who established the rule of the dynasty. Thereafter Gyalpo established his rule in 333 A.D. One of the famous kings of this dynasty was Gyalpo Thewang Chen Izghimpo who came to power in 650 is very famous. History of proper Ladakh has been recorded from the reign of Skyed-lde-Nima-Gon, who came to power and considered the founder of Lah-Chen dynasty. The second, called Namgyal dynasty was founded by King Bagan. During Namgyal dynasty all sects of Mahayana Buddhism spread in Ladakh. The head lamas of these established their monasteries in Ladakh under the sponsorship of Ladakh Kings time and again.

Ladakh has been attracted many travellers and visitors from each part of the world. Some were fascinated by its unique geographical position as the highest elevated land in the world. Some wanted to study flora, fauna, its ethnology and anthropology. But some came only to enjoy the hospitality of the people. Fa-Hien and Ou-Kong visited Ladakh in about 400 A.D. Thereafter many Chinese travellers visited Ladakh.

In order to spread Christianity in Central Asia, two Jesuit Missionaries visited Ladakh in 1631. During nineteen century William Moorcraft and George Trebeck visited Ladakh in 1820 and gave detailed information to British officers. Alexander Cunningham of British East India Company, Calcutta visited Ladakh in 1846. He covered Ladakh History, Geography, Culture, Religion and Trade in his book.

Robert Shaw, Hayward, Younghusband, Seven Hedin etc. were some Adventurers who visited via Ladakh to many important countries in Central Asia as well as towns located along the silk route.

In the beginning of twentieth century Tsuyoshi Hino visited Kashgar via Karakoram range. During 1913-14 De Fillipi made an expedition for Ladakh, later after six year James Baily Fraser extensively travelled in Ladakh.

In 1947 Ladakh was closed for foreigners due to Indo-Pak war. It was thrown open in 1974 after a long ban of 27 years. Since then thousands of foreigners visited Ladakh. This has given a fillip to Ladakh's economy. Today Ladakh experiences all round development. Ladakhis are taken under scheduled tribe status, and are getting reservation in all State and Central Government departments, as a result. Their living standard by all means is increasing considerably. Therefore, it would be wise to say to impose tax on Hotel and Guest House owners. Gradually other related sectors should be considered for taxation. I hope under this policy State and Central Government may get some revenue in the response of their investment in the field of tourism.

1

Rock-Carvings in Ladakh

Dr. A.H. Francke was the first scholar who highlighted the Rock-carvings in Ladakh. He collected many such carvings from lower Ladakh, that is the area below the Nimu[1] towards Alchi along the Indus river upto Skrubuchan. He found various forms of carvings beyond Khalatse. I got the opportunity to see some of them, near the Alchi bridge. These carvings of stupa and ibex belong to early Buddhist period.

Besides, many such carvings scattered throughout in Ladakh. I saw such carvings right from Taru towards Alchi then along the Indus river bank upto Skrubachan. The carvings are generally found in the following shapes :

1. Lion/Snow-leopard
2. Hunting scene
3. Wild Yak
4. Ibex
5. Goat
6. Magic square
7. Symbol of sun and moon
8. Lha-tho
9. Dancing scene
10. Stupa

We can understand that all these shapes are not carved during one time span, however, are carved by the people of different period. As there was no script, therefore, expressed their feeling through carvings. Moreover, when people got civilized and started writing, expressed their views accordingly. However, such carvings were based on Buddhism. According to the Ladakh chronicle these figures can be categorised in the following way :[2]

(i) Ancient traveller's record
(ii) Hunting and dancing scene
(iii) Around the fifth century A.D.
(iv) By the ninth century
(v) Influence of Nestorian
(vi) Dogra period.

Ancient Travellers' Record : The shapes of wild goats or ibex, leopards and yaks which are scratched into the rocks are often the only physical records of people travelling along the great Himalayan rivers two or three thousand years ago.[3]

During the third and early second millennium B.C. Okunoid tribes of Minusinsk Basin moved east and southern Central Asia as herdsmen and cattle breeders spread to the periphery of agricultural societies, later reached south of the Kunlun-Karakoram mountain belt. Okunoid culture is attributed mask-like human faces. In Zanskar[4] and Gya[5] of Ladakh region found such carvings (Drawings)[6].

In Nubra, Rohit Vohra found Mythical Animal style rock carvings. According to him :

> "There is the interesting carving of a mythical wild cat-Dragon. The paws with their crescent claws are overemphasised in their ferociousness, as is the long bushy tail. The face is similar to that of a panther. One of the most characteristic is the feline with heart-shaped ears and crescent claws. The back of the mythical wild cat-Dragon is decorated first with three jagged scales which develop into smooth curves and terminate in a ball. These elements demonstrate the mythic imagery overriding nomadic stylistic forms. Then there is the representation of a mythical bird with similar exaggerated crescent claws and a flared tail. Both these 'Fable Animal Style' carvings may date from the mid-first millennium B.C.[7]

Folke Bergman, during his archaeological research in Sinkiang, found many rock carving on the rocks on Buyantu-bulaq, Guruq-tagh. In the group of carvings he saw various kinds of animal figures such as—double hamp camel, birds, horse, wild goat. I didn't find such carving however, Scytho-Siberian Animal style drawing of a horse in this group of mid-first millennium B.C. is found on the rump from Diskit in Nubra.[8]

Francke collected some old rock carvings of Animal style pictures from Donga village[9] near Shimsha Kharbu[10] about midway between Srinagar and Leh and said to be offerings to the mythical pre-Buddhist King Kesar, made in gratitude for the birth of children.[11]

Folke Bergman with his assistant Henning Haslund Christensen visited to the Donga village which is now Muslim dominated. He saw two more bucks than appeared in Francke's reproduction. Through these Folke understand that the people still embellished this rock with carvings of the same kind as those already existed.[12]

In another case the representation of ibex carving considered as 'the old big stone-buck personification of the rock' by Francke. But Folke made his clarification as—"not all of Francke's buck figures must necessarily be connected with human fecundity. When two goats are depicted, one of them with a small goat within, denoting pregnancy, this is better explained as a prayer for increase in the stock of goats."[13]

During research I came to know that if a person does not feel well and his disease is not removed by MBBS doctors/Amchis, he then goes under the shelter of a lama who perform rituals and offer ibex made by sattu to a spirit. It is said that after such rituals he gets improvement in his health.

A.H. Francke during his research tour in 1902-03 recorded the following Animal style carvings from Ladakh :[14]

1. A yak cow (Digmo), charging a snow-leopard and a mask deer from the Khalatse Fort.
2. A wild yak and wild goat. From stone near Khalatse.
3. A snow-leopard leaping and a wild goat. From stone near Khalatse.
4. Wild goat. Attached with ancient Tibetan inscription. Romanized : Staggi lo la stong (d) pin rgyalba yeshes. Translation : (was erected) in the tiger year by 'colonel' (chief of one thousand) rGyalba yeshes. From the ruined castle, saspola bridge, left bank of Indus.
5. Lower end of the Namchag Valley near Khalatse. The lioness with the locks.

The carvings of Animal style as cited above reveal that they are very similar to the primitive carvings and may be dated in between 7th to 10th century A.D.

Hunting and Dancing Scene : One can often see hunting and dancing scene carvings on the boulders in many parts of Ladakh ; some of them may attributed second and third millennium B.C.[15] Francke also saw such carvings from the lower Ladakh. Here follows the details :

1. Horseman foreshortened from the front. It is more likely that the figures represent men riding on the shoulders of others.

This sport is exercised at the occasion of sowing-festival, for instance, at Garkun. From stone near Khalatse Fort.

2. Dance near Da : Dance in honour of the gods (lha) ; fourteen dancers, one leader.
3. Near Khalatse : A man with a bow.

These carvings reveal that they may be between B.C. 500—A.D. 800.

Around the Fifth Century A.D. : Around the fifth century A.D., as Buddhism begin to replace by chortens related to Kushan or early Gupta art in Kashmir.

By the Ninth Century : Under these carvings we can group those chortens which were engraved on the rocks or boulders of earlier Tibetan style with old Tibetan inscription in ancient *'dbu med'* (headless) character; they are probably the oldest one. However, the other groups are : those erected *stupas*, which have no inscription. These *stupas* were probably erected by illiterate people. The kind of *stupas* consist an inscription, giving the name of the erector, and the date of eraction. Dr. A.H. Francke found ancient stupa with flags near ruins of a castle, Saspola bridge, left bank of the Indus. This engraved stupa had ancient Tibetan inscription. Romanized : Sangto Chakonggis mon rkuspa sdig sbyod. Translation : (was erected) by Sangto Chakong. The mon (a low-caste man) the thief of sinful behaviour (sbyod is a mistake; spyod was meant). The erector of the stupa probably only wrote his name in the instrumental case ; another person, his enemy, may have added the second part of the inscription.[15]

These carvings seen to have been left an army of the Central Tibetal Yarlong dynasty which marched through Zangskar and was garrisoned in Ladakh.[16]

Influence of Nestorian : A.H. Francke found a carved cross-shape *stupa* on a rock near Domkhar. This carved stupa showed the influence of Nestorian art and would be in between 9th-10th century A.D. Francke read the Tibetan inscription carved below this stupa as : Text. phaggi lo la. Translated : (Erected) in the pig year.

Dogra Period : A.H. Francke found some latest carvings on a rock in Lower Ladakh. These carvings show the battle scene in which troops of Maharaja Gulab Singh or one of his successors is meant with Ladakhi troops/tribes. Here follows the details :

1. A fight between men armed with guns against men armed with bows and swords, cavalry on both sides. Dogra troops and local tribes. One of the tribes men with a sword is killed.

2. The horseman has no reins, but a whip. The large round circles near the heads of the men are explained to be shields.
3. From that of the horseman one might assume that he is a.Dogra soldier.
4. The ibex is probably older than the battle scene.

In conclusion the carvings on rocks and stones or boulders are very important in the historical point of view and many of them show the Ancient Buddhist art and culture of the inhabitants of Ladakh. These are the beautiful art work of ancient period. Therefore, we should collectively look into this matter seriously and tried to preserve this prestigious heritage. The following figures show the details :

Mask from Char Zanskar in Ladakh After : Francfort : 1990

Mask from Gya, Ladakh Vohra, Rohit : 1993

Vohra, Rohit ; op. cit. : 1993

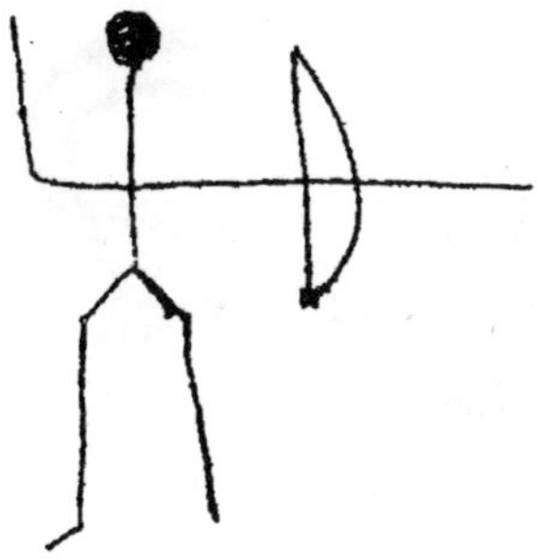

Francke, A.H., Indian Antiquary, Vol. XXXII, 1903

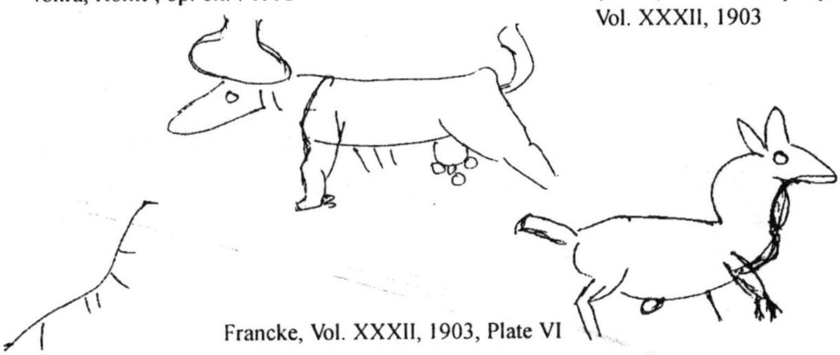

Francke, Vol. XXXII, 1903, Plate VI

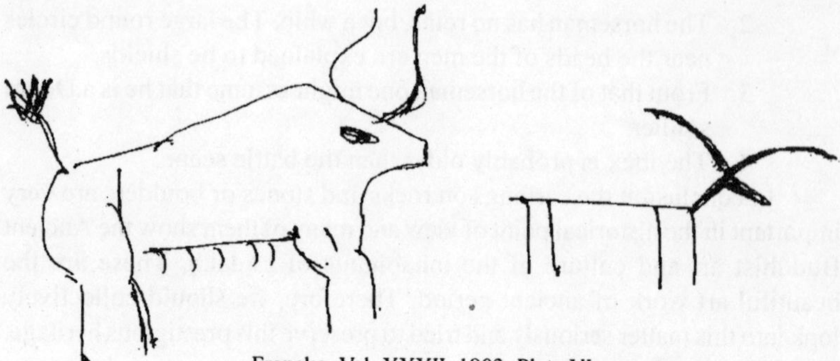

Francke, Vol. XXXII, 1903, Plate VI

Francke, Vol. XXXII, 1903, Plate VI

Francke, Plate VII

Francke, Plate VII

Plate VII, Francke, op. cit.

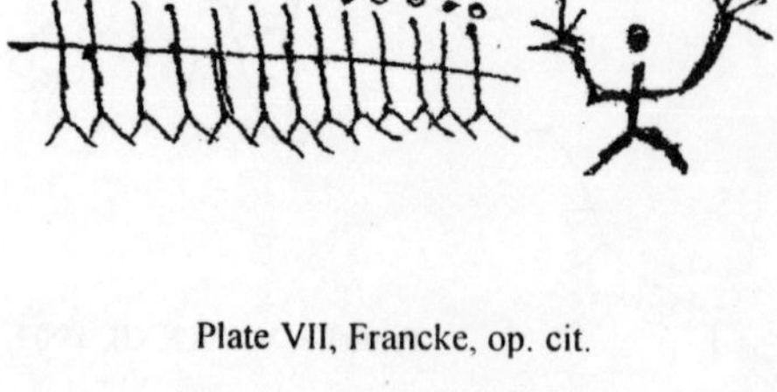

Plate VII, Francke, op. cit.

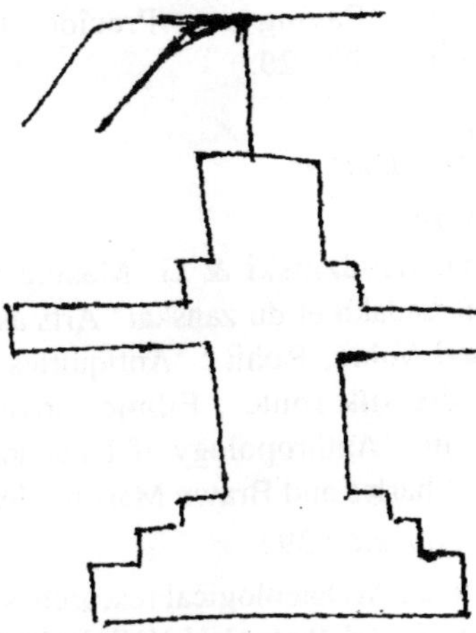

Francke, op. cit. , Plate VIII

Francke, op. cit. , Plate V

References

1. Nimu : Nye-mo or Neemo or Nyemoo.
2. Linrothe, Rob : 'Paving over Precious Heritage; Ladags Melong; Spring 1997 : 20.
3. *Ibid.*
4. Zanskar : Tib. Zangskar
5. Gya : Tib. rGya
6. Francfort, D. Klodzinski & G. Mascle : 'Pe'troglyphes archaique du Ladakh et du zanskar' Arts asiantiques ; 1990, 45 : 5-27 and Vohra, Rohit : 'Antiquities on the Southern Arteries of the silk route ; Ethnic movements and New Discoveries' In : 'Anthropology of Tibet and The Himalaya' Ed. Ramble, Charles and Brawn Martin; 1993 : 38.
7. Vohra, Rohit, *op. cit.* : 392.
8. Bergman, Folke : Archaeological researches in Sinkiang, Vol. II, Stockholm, 1939 & Plates XV, XVI, XVII & XVIII & Vohra, Rohit; *op. cit.* : 392 & Plates 4 & 7.
9. Donga village : It is a village in Lower Ladakh.
10. Shimsha Kharbu : It is also in Lower Ladakh.
11. Bergman, Folke; *op. cit.* : 192.
12. *Ibid.*
13. *Ibid.*
14. Francke, A.H. : 'Some more rock-carvings from Lower Ladakh', Indian Antiquary by Swati Pub., Delhi, 1985) : 361-363, Vol. XXXII, 1903.
15. *Ibid.*, 362.
16. Linrothe, Rob. ; *op. cit.* p. 20.
17. Francke, A.H. : 'Some More Rock-carvings from Lower Ladakh', *op. cit.* : 361.

2

King Drag pa Bum de (Tib. brags pa 'abum lde) of Ladakh and His Contribution towards Buddhism

Thri cug de[1] had two sons : Dragpa Bum de and Drag pa Bum. Dragpa Bum de was popularly known lde, whereas Dra pa Bum as Dragspa. Dragpa Bum de was elder son and ought to have been king alone of Ladakh, Dragspa would not yield, and took possession of part of the kingdom.

Social Justice : Drag pa Bum de was a simple and kind hearted king, had always mild and merciful heart for poor and downtrodden people. He believed in equality, therefore, gave equal opportunity to rich-poor, higher-lower cast people among his subjects.[2]

Construction of Religious Buildings : He constructed many religious buildings, here follows some of them :

(i) *Red Chapel*[3] : It was constructed behind Leh palace. In this Chappel he erected three statues : Maitreya, Manjushri and Vajrapani.[4] The wood and clay Maitrey statue is about 25 feet high, in a sitting posture.[5]

(ii) *Triple temple in Zangskar :* In Zangskar, he built a triple temple one surmounting the other. It had same design and architecture as Tholing temple had.[6]

(iii) *Ti-Su-Ru Chorten :* He constructed a huge chorten near the present Santi Stupa in Leh. It contained·108 temple shrines. It is said that the above chorten was constructed on the base which had 521 steps, each of 2 feet high from the land.[7]

The chorten had four main doors and placed many Buddhist statues. Today we can see this chorten in ruined shape. In 1987, Archaeological Department, government of India, New Delhi had taken this chorten under its control, later renovated.

Spitug (or Spituk) Monastery : He built this monastery. But, some historians believed that this monastery was miraclely established. However, we can trace an interesting storey in this regards :

> "During fourteen century Tsongkhapa made Tse-pag med statue from the blood of his nose. Later he handedover to his disciples, and said them to give it to the king of Ladakh. Thus the embassy from Tibet arrived in Ladakh. Cang sems shes rab zangpo was the main disciple. In Ladakh they first went to Nubra, Dragspa Bum was there. He didn't deign to look at it with so much as one eye. They then returned to Leh and appeared before king Dragpa Bum de. King rose and went to meet them. Cang sems shes rab zang po presented Tse-pag med statue. King delighted to receive the statue. Later he constructed Buddhist temple on the hillock of Spitug village and placed this statue there in a chorten."[8]

Subsequently after his inspiration Lama lha bang lo dos built the Spitug monastery.[9] In 1440 king died. Before his death he was satisfied with his religious works and said : "If I die now it matters not."[10]

Notes and References

1. Tri cug de : Tib. Kri gtsug lde.
2. Francke, A.H. : 'A History of Western Tibet', Reprinted by Asian Educational Services, New Delhi; 1995 : 75.
3. Red Chapel : A.H. Francke called it 'Red College'.
4. According to Francke : "The Maitreya statue on Namdyal temo hill, the head reaches through the ceiling of the first storey. But the statues of Manjushri and Vajrapani, which are said to have been on the right and left, are no more, although there are traces of the pedestal of at least one of them." Cf. Francke; *op. cit.* : 75-76.
5. Francke, *op. cit.* : 76.
6. *Ibid.*
7. Sonam Phuntsog : 'Ladakh' ; 2000 : 123-24. According to Francke 'Ti-Su-Ru-' could be spelled as 'Teu trashi od to' Lama Thupstan Paldan called it 'Yellow Te'u Demon'.

8. According to Francke : "The great Tsongkapa, having in his possession a Tsepag med about a finger-joint, which originated from the blood of his nose, I believe that it was a short summary of his doctrines, perhaps written with his own blood, entrusted the same to the two ascetics and said : Give it either to the one called Dragspa, or to the one called lde'. Cf. Francke ; *op. cit.* : 77.
9. lha bang lo dos was the disciple of kha dub je, the main student of Tsongkhapa.
10. Francke, A.H. ; *op. cit.* : 77.

3

King Drags pa bum (Tib. grags pa 'abum) and His Contribution towards Buddhism in Shyam Region of Ladakh Himalaya

Dags pa bum was the younger brother of Drags pa bum de. He was fierce, gloomy, and inconsiderate character didn't bother the future of his state.

He ruled over the Shyam province.[1] His principal seats were the villages of Basgo, Teya and Tingmogang. It is explained that earlier to him, there was Tingbrang village under the control of Dards. He put his full control over Tingbrang and gave new name Tingmogang.[2] Later he developed it as town. Besides, built a castle above the town and fortified it in its own way. Finally he named castle as Sing ge zing.[3]

After sometimes he built a red temple nearby to castle. In this he placed the Maitreya image along with blessed image of Avalokitesvara which brought here from Kamrup.[4]

He started the tradition to celebrate Tuschen[5] every year, which is still in practice. On this occasion Ladakhi Buddhists from surrounding villages attend the function.

King Drags pa improved the ancient fortifications at Basgo, to make them a stronghold of the first rank. Besides, it is said that he erected a palace at Leh.[6]

He ruled Shyam area for about five years. When Tsongkhapa embassy arrived in Nubra. He was there, Francke explains :

> "We heard that Dragspa was in Nubra at the time of Tsongkapa's embassy. I believe, however, that he went there to draw the local chief of Nubra over to his side, in order to make himself supreme king."[7]

In conclusion Dags pa bum was not a strong king. His main contribution was his interest to develop Tingmogang. However, his fortifications at Tingmogang and Basgo was praised by the following Kings of Ladakh. He died at a young age in 1455.[8]

Notes and References

1. Shyam province : It belongs to the area in Lower Ladakh below Nimu village towards Khalsi (or Khalatse).
2. Tingmogang : Tib. gting sgang.
3. Sing ge zing : Tib. seng ge dzeng.
4. Kamrup : It would be Assam. The statue of Avalokitesvara is made of marble in sitting posture, and at present placed in the new temple of modern designed building. On its left and right you can see 1000 eyes, hands clay statues of about 6' height of Avalokitesvara.
5. Tuschen : Tib. dus chen.
6. Francke, A.H. : 'A History of Western Tibet', Reprinted by Asian Education Services, 1995 : 80.
7. *Ibid.*
8. Sonam Phuntsog : 'Ladakh', 2000, 125 & Thupstan Paldan : 'Guide of Ladakh Gonpas', 1974 : 4.

4

King Bagan (Tib. ba rgan) of Ladakh, the Founder of Namgyal Dynasty

He was the son of lha chen bha ra. Later with the people of Shey village,[1] he formed an alliance, revolted against king Ladros Chog ldan, deposed him and ruled Ladakh kingdom from Basgo village.[2] Thus Lodros Chog ldan, who conquered many neighbouring countries didn't know what was happening within his kingdom, and lost his power by his internal foes.[3]

Founder of the Namgyal Dynasty : King Bagan was the founder of Namgyal dynasty, the second dynasty of Ladakh, lasted down to the end of the empire. It is said that he called his two sons namgyal.[4] Subsequently 'Namgyal' combined with his successor kings' name.

Invasion on Zangskar : Like king Lodras Chog ldan in his later years he decided to extend the boundaries of his kingdom. Thus invaded Zangskar. In those days Zangskar was ruled by Vassal chiefs. Rinchen Chen spalde[5] was the king of Zangla[6]; whereas Tsewang[7] was of Padum. Besides, on his way towards Zangskar he fought bravely and defeated king Hasan of Kha che. As a result he was known Kunga Namgyal.[8] He ruled Ladakh for thirty years from 1470-1500.[9]

Notes and References

1. Shey Village : It is about 15 km far away from Leh town towards south, south-east Leh or on the Leh-Manli highway.
2. Basgo village : It is about 43 km far from Leh towards Leh-Srinagar highway.
3. Francke, A.H. : 'History of Western Tibet', Reprinted by Asian Education Services, 1995 : 82.

4. Namgyal : It means perfect victors. Cf. Francke; *op. cit.* ; 82.
5. Rinchen spalde : Tib. rin chen dpa lde.
6. Zang la : Tib. bzang lad.
7. Tsewang : Tib. Tse dbang.
8. Kun ga Namgyal : Tib. Kun dg'a rnam rgyal.
9. According Sonam Phuntsog he died on 1497. Cf. Sonam Phuntsog : 'Ladakh' ; 2000 : 127.

5

Tashi Namgyal (Tib. bkra shis rnam rgyal) : A Crafty King of Ladakh

Bagan had two sons Lhawang Namgyal[1] and Tashi Namgyal. Lhawang Namgyal, the elder brother had bodily heavy strength; whereas Tashi Namgyal was very crafty. In order to attain the throne of Ladakh Kingdom, he played a crafty trick and plucked the eyes of his brother, later sent him to Lingshet jail.[2]

Subdueded Vassel Chiefs : Tashi Namgyal was a brave soldier. He conquered the country side's small states, and subdueded the vassel chiefs. His principal aim was to bring ponies in great quantities. For some extent he succeeded in his mission.

Construction of Royal Palace : It is not clear that whether King Tashi Namgyal further developed the palace as erected by King Drags pa bum, or after the dismental the earlier ruined place, rebuilt it on the top of the Namgyal Tsemo hill.[3]

Mirza Heder Invasion and Erection of Tsemo Monastery : Mirza Heder invaded Nubra valley on 1531, later he entered Leh. King Tashi Namgyal sent his army to Nubra to defend the country side. But unable to do the same, however, fought bravely and killed many Turks. Later he ordered his Army soldiers to bring the corpses of the Turks to Leh. Thereafter, under his direction all these were brought to Namgyal Tsemo hill and placed under the image of the Mahakala erected Namgyal Tsemo temple devoted to the guardian deities. The idea was behind that evil spirits were crushed and in future no further attack from the border would be taken place.[4]

Invasion on Zangskar, Khapulu and Shigar : In 1535 King Tashi Namgyal went to Zangskar with his Army to conquer the country. When he conquered Zangskar, moved towards Khapulu and Shigar. Here also he became more powerful than the Kings of these countries. As a result King Beram of Khapulu and King Garzi of Shigar welcomed him in their kingdoms, offered present in great quantities.[5]

Built a Lamasery in Phyang Village : On the advice of great lamas of his kingdom, he built a Lamasery at Phyang village, placed a long prayer flag. After the construction of Lamasery, he made a rule to send children to the Lamasery from every village at the surrounding of Leh. According to his order, every family who had more than one or two male children had to give up one, not the eldest, to be made a lama.[6]

Repairing of Alchi Choskor : The Alchi Choskor was built during 10-11th century, being destroyed some or the other reasons. He, therefore ordered his painters to repair it. Besides, he sent golden ink to Gadan (Tib. dg'a ldan), Shaskya other important monasteries to write Kangyur and Stangyur pothies.[7]

Remained without Children : King Tashi Namgyal had no children, it was a great danger to Ladakh Kingdom. There was a question before the kingdom that who would become king after him. At last on the advice of his kingdom's great lamas, he gave his wife to his brother. Subsequently after his death, Lhawang Namgyal's son became the King of Ladakh, who later gave full honours to his father Lhawang Namgyal and ruled Ladakh kingdom according to his desires.[8]

Notes and References

1. Lhawang Namgyal : Tib. lha dbang rnam rgyal.
2. Francke, A.H. : 'A History of Western Tibet', Reprinted by Asian Education Services, New Delhi, 1995 : 83.
3. *Ibid.*
4. *Ibid* & Sonam Phuntsong : 'Ladakh', 2000 : 128.
5. Sonam Phuntsog : *op. cit.* : 128.
6. Francke, A.H. : 'A History of Western Tibet', *op. cit.* : 84.
7. Sonam Phuntsog : 'Ladakh', *op. cit.* : 128.
8. Francke, A.H. : 'A History of Western Tibet', *op. cit.* : 84.

6

King Tsewang Namgyal (Tib. Tse dbang rnam rgyal) : An Able Administrator of Ladakh

Blind king Lhawang Namgyal had three sons :

(1) Tsewang Namgyal (Tib. Tshe dbang rnam rgyal).

(2) Namgyal Gonpo (Tib. rnam rgyal mgon po), and

(3) Jamyang Namgyal (Tib. 'ajam dbyangs rnam rgyal).

Tsewang Namgyal was the eldest son, therefore ascended the throne of Ladakh in 1535.[1]

War against the Princely States : As soon as Tsewang Namgyal became the king of Ladakh, the vassel-chiefs declared themselves free from Ladakh Kingdom and became independent rulers of their respective states. Hence, king Tsewang had to go to war against them. As he was a able administrator and had a good knowledge of war technique, so easily conquered the whole Ladakh and subdueded all vassel chiefs. He even conquered a portion of Baltistan.[2]

Withdrew the Decision to go to War against Turks : After conquering the whole Ladakh he got full confidence upon his army, therefore decided to go to war against Turks. But the people of the Nubra province requested him, not to go for war as Ladakh trade with Central Asian countries would suffer, indirectly Nubra's economy would be harmed. King accepted their logic and withdrew his decision. As a result he was known good administrator.[3]

War against Guge : When king abstained from the war against Turks, he decided to do some constructive work. So, in 1533 he made Leh as the capital of Ladakh and developed it accordingly. After sometimes he went on war against Guge. Later received the following items from Guge[4] :

(i) 900 gm gold annually.[5]
(ii) From Rutog (Rudog ro Rudok) 750 gm gold annually.
(iii) One hundred sheep every year for three years.
(iv) One horse.
(v) Ten tanned skin-bags.
(vi) Rs. 100/- tsod khul (Tib. gtsod-khul)[6].

Extended the Boundaries of His Kingdom : King Tsewang Namgyal was a brave soldier, he didn't want to take rest and always think how he could extend the boundaries of his kingdom. Later succeeded to extend his kingdom upto the outskirts of Lhasa. He conquered Shigar, Kharko and divisions of Baltistan[7].

Generous King : He was a generous king of Ladakh. After conquered the whole Ladakh he never dethroned the sudued rulers, but allowed them to rule his domain and authority.[8]

Development of Infrastructure : King Tsewang Namgyal believed that if he could develop the infrastructure of Ladakh, the living standard of his people would be increased, and his relationship with them would become closer. Thus built many roads and bridges. The popular among them are[9] :

(i) Hanu—Baltistan road, called Hanu-Chobarla road.
(ii) Zangskar road at Hanupata.
(iii) Hanupata bridge.

Contribution towards Buddhism : The Namgyal Tsemo temple though was erected by his ancestors, he renovated this and converted into a grand temple, decorated it with many Buddhist images.

Entrance of Kashmiri Muslims : It is said that in 1553 some Kashmiri Muslims called 'cagges' entered into Ladakh via Hanu-Chobar la, and reached upto Timogang. Like other Muslim invaders of India they destroyed some statues of Timogang monastery. The important among them are[10] :

(i) Buddha.
(ii) Dorje Chang (or Vajrapani), made of gold.

Later they returned without any harm to public. When king came to know about this happening, he felt sorry, and repaired the monastery as well as built a big chorten there.

In conclusion King Tsewang Namgyal was a kind hearted person, brave soldier and famous for his work for public utility. He died in 1557.[11]

Notes and References

1. Francke beliefed that he came on throne in 1530. Cf. Francke, A.H. : 'A History of Western Tibet', Reprinted by Asian Education Services, New Delhi, 1995 : 86.
2. *Ibid.*
3. *Ibid.*
4. *Ibid.*
5. King Tsewang Namgyal fixed the price of one tola gold Rs. 187.50. Cf. Sonam Phuntsog; 'Ladakh', 2000 : 129.
6. Tsod-Khul : It was then made of Pashmina.
7. Sumi, Tokan, D., Oki, Masato & Fida M. Hussnain : 'Ladakh : The Moonland', Light & Life Pub., Delhi, 1975 : 7.
8. *Ibid.*
9. Francke, A.H. : *op. cit.* : 87.
10. Sonam Phuntsog : 'Ladakh', 2000.
11. Sumi, Tokan D. Oki, Masato & Fida M. Hussnain ; *op. cit.* : 7.

7

Royal Families at Stok Palace of Ladakh

During the beginning of nineteen century A.D. Ladakh was ruled by weak Kings. After the death of Tsetan Namgyal, Tsespal Tondup Namgyal came to power in 1820. After sometime he directed his craftmen to construct Royal palace at Stok village in order to keep away from the royal administrative activities, as he was a weak ruler and had no capacity to face incurisions from Himachal and Jammu. He was succeeded by his son Tsewang Rabstan, who spent his time in merry making and married with three queens (Fig. 7.1)

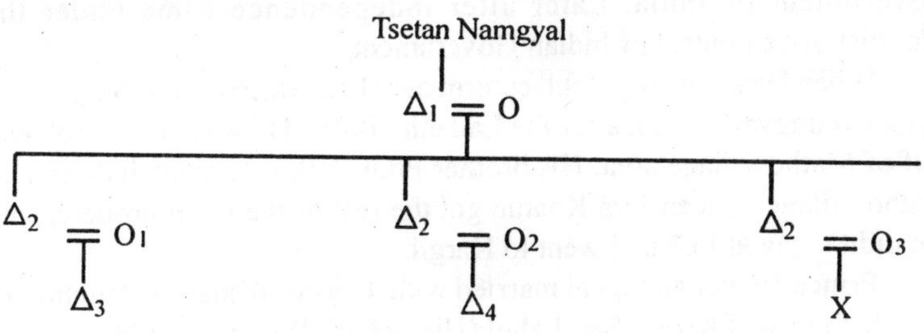

Fig. 7.1

Δ_1 = Tsespal Tondup

Δ_2 = Tsewang Rabstan

O_1 = Queen Skalzang Dolma, daughter of Tsewang Tondup, Ayu Kalon, Zimkhang Ningpa

O_2 = Queen Sonam Palkit, belongs to noble family of Piyu Pangpa village, located near Chemde-Sakti side

O_3 = Jera Khatun, daughter of noble family (Co of Pashkyum), Kargil

Δ_3 = Jigmet Namgyal

Δ_4 = Phunchok Yurgyal

Like his father Tsewang Rabstan was weak in administration, as a result Ladakh state affairs fell to disorder, others therefore got chance to interfere in state affairs. Zorawar Singh took this opportunity and invaded Ladakh. As his army entered Chushot village; king Tsewang Rabstan was enjoying at a party in Shey. When he came to know about the Dogra troops marching towards Leh; he ran away towards Lahul alongwith his two queens and mother. Queen Skalzang Dolma was pregnant, remained at Shey palace, later gave birth Jigmet Namgyal. On the way Tsewang Rabstan's second Queen Sonam Palkit also got sever pregnant pain, she stopped at Tangche village and gave birth to Phunchok Yurgyal. Finally King Tsewang Rabstan along with his queen Jera Khatun and his mother went to Lahul. After sometimes king died there and Queen Jera Khatun returned to Leh. She had no child.

In the meanwhile General Zorawar Singh got his full control over Ladakh. He constructed a new fort near Leh and garisoned with Dogra soldiers. The king of Ladakh was dethroned and Royal property was divided among king's two sons and Queen Jera Khatun. Thus king regime came to an end. Ladakh became a part of Jammu and Kashmir state, which had come into existence by the treaty of Amritsar, with the then British Government of India. Later after independence came under the administrative control of Indian Government.[2]

When Dogra army got full control over Ladakh, Zorawar Singh asked Jigmet Namgyal to look after the Ladakh affairs. He was given Stok and half of Matho village area. His brother Phunchok was given half area of Matho village. Queen Jera Khatun got the rest of the royal property; but she didn't stay at Leh and went to Kargil.

Prince Jigmet Namgyal married with Tsering Wangmo, daughter of a noble family of Khang Sar, Lahul (Himachal). When no child was born from her; Jigmet Namgyal got second marriage with Norzin Wangmo; daughter of Tsering Tashi of Rupshu (Fig. 7.2)

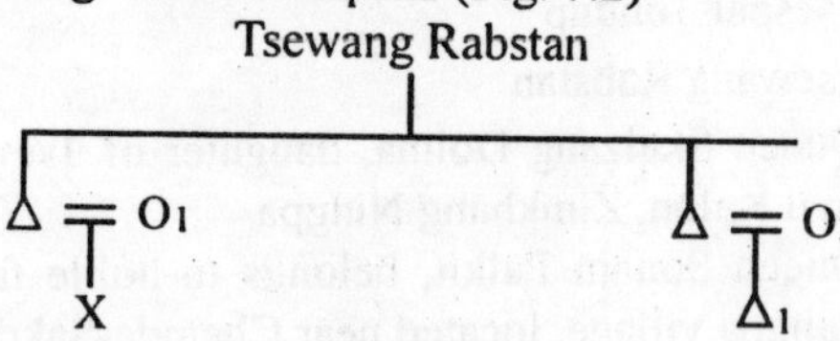

Fig. 7.2

Δ = Jigmet Namgyal

O_1 = Tsering Wangmo
O_2 = Norzin Wangmo
Δ_1 = Sonam Namgyal

Norzin Wangmo gave birth Sonam Namgyal in 1866. To know this fact Queen Tsering Wangmo jealously made a plan. She called Norzin Wangmo at her private room and said :

"I don't want to stay more at Stok palace, as no one is in Shey palace, so I'll have to go there."

Norzin Wangmo didn't make any remarks and returned to her room. Later Tsering Wangmo thought :

"Tomorrow Sonam Namgyal will get Stok property, thereafter she would unable to have control over Royal precious things viz. Youpjur, Serab Rari and Je cun Mila[3], so she has to carry these to Shey palace."

According to her plan Tsering Wangmo took the above things and in the next day departured to Shey palace. Serab Rari and Je cun Mila statue were not heavy but Youpjur box was very heavy and difficult to carry.

However, she didn't mind. In the mean while Nilza Wangmo passed through, as she saw this, got doubt and thought :

"What the use of Youpjur box at Shey palace?"

She immediately called her servant and order him :

"Immediately go behind Queen Tsering Wangmo and to find out where is she carrying Royal property-Youpjur?"

The servant ran after her, as soon queen Tsering Wangmo reached near the Choglamsar bridge, servant asked :

"Maharani Sahiba, where are you carrying Youpjur box?"

To listen servant voice, she frighten, threw the Youpjur box and went to Shey. Nilza Wangmo's obedient servant carried Youpjur box to Stok palace. Tsering Wangmo then had to satisfy with two royal things, that is, Serab Rari and Je cun Mila statue. After staying a few years at Shey palace she went to Lahul.

In 1873, Sonam Namgyal succeeded his father. He married with the princess of a noble family of Barbok, Lahul (Fig. 7.3).

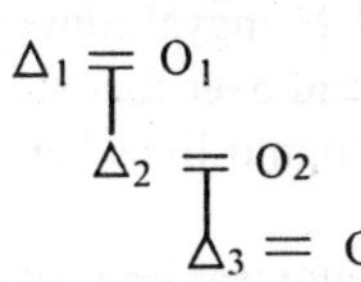

Fig. 7.3

Δ_1 = Jigmet Dadul

O_1 = Queen Nilza Wangmo
Δ_2 = Sonam Namgyal
O_2 = Queen from the noble family of Barbok
Δ_3 = Jigmet Dadul
O_3 = Queen from the noble family of Gurang palace

After sometime of his marriage Sonam Namgyal got son, Jigmet Dadul who in 1896 married with the daughter of noble family, Gurang palace, Lahul (Fig. 7.4)

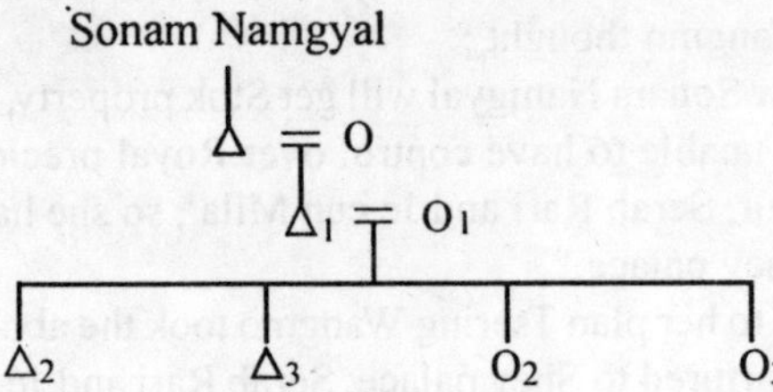

Fig. 7.4

Δ = Jigmet Dadul Namgyal
O = Queen Nilza Angmo from Gurang palace
Δ_1 = Kunzang Namgyal
O_1 = Gyalmo Diskyit Wangmo
Δ_2 = Jigmet Wangchok (Elder son)
Δ_3 = Skarma Konchok Namgyal (Son)
O_2 = Jigmet Wangmo (Elder daughter)
O_3 = Rinchen Wangmo (Daughter)

Jigmet Dadul Namgyal had son Kunzang Namgyal from Queen Nilza Angmo, who was born in 1926. He married with Gyalmo Diskyit Wangmo on 26th August 1950. Gyalmo belongs to a noble family, Khangsar palace, Lahul. Gyalmo Diskyit Wangmo later gave birth two daughters and two sons. King Kungzang Namgyal died on 16th October 1974 at Leh General Hospital. He was later succeeded by his elder son Jigmet Wangchok Namgyal.

Today, Jigmet Wangchok Namgyal converted Stok palace to museum. This palace has 77 rooms spread over four storeys. The present Queen of Ladakh, Gyalmo Diskyet Wangmo lives here in her private quarters of twelve rooms.

Later, Stok palace Museum was opened for public in 1980 after the opening ceremony by his Holiness Dalai Lama. The following precious things of royal family are displayed in various rooms of Stok Museum.

Zimchung Kelma Room

1. Royal caps[4]
2. Gzi necklace[5]
3. Key ring[6]
4. Baltistan necklaces[7]
5. Necklaces of turquoise & coral[8]

Murals in this Room

1. Man of long life[9]
2. Good luck figure
3. King of Ladakh[10]

Second Room

1. Necklaces of Gyalmo Diskyat Wangmo[11]
2. Necklaces of former queens[12]
3. Parag[13]
4. Youpjur[14]
5. Diplomatic letter[15]
6. Ceremonial teapots[16]

Room Across the Courtyard

In this room the following stuffed animals have been displayed.

1. Yak[17]
2. Marmot
3. Martan
4. Snow leopard
5. Yakskin bucket[18]
6. Carrying cases of bows and arrows

Room for Thankas

1. Five large Thankas of Padmasambhava[19]
2. Nine Thankas of Padmasambhava[20]
3. Namgyalma Thanka[21]
4. Teapots
5. Chhang pourers
6. Trumpets and masks[22]
7. Personal objects of the royal family[23]

Room of Two Glass Cases

On the opposite side of the courtyard and through a door with enchanting wooden carving is a Mongol suit of arms and helmet. The room of two glass cases is opposite of the wooden carving. The following objects are displayed in this room.

1. Glass cases charm boxes
2. Official seals and rings
3. Thankas[24]

Room for Thankas of Jataka stories

1. Thankas[25]
2. Court robes made of Chinese silk[26]
3. Late King's throne[27]
4. Wood carving[28]

Room for Chorten

1. Chorten decorated with turquoise etc.[29]
2. Two couch shell trumpets[30]
3. Ritual objects[31]
4. Telescopic trumpets[32]

Prayer Room

1. Padmasambhava Thanka[33]
2. Seat-couch[34]
3. Avalokitesvara statue[35]
4. King's crown[36]
5. Prayer box[37] and eight auspicious emblems[38]
6. Prayer book[39]
7. Gold and Silver tea cup, a dorje and tilbu[40]
8. Daru[41]

Lakchang

1. Three red sect lamas[42]
2. Tara statue[43]
3. Case of statues[44]
4. Sakyamuni statue
5. Case of statues[45]
6. Padmasambhava and four statues of Namgyalma
7. Small case of statue
8. Red-hat sect lama statue
9. Case of butter images[46]
10. Brass and Copper metal statues[47]
11. Padmasambhava, Sakyamuni & Vajrapani; three big statues[48]
12. Chakmen statue[49]

Chorten in front of Lakchang

This chorten is decorated by precious stones.[50]

Library

1. Complete set of Ka-gyur[51]
2. Hayagiva image[52]
3. Padmasambhava image[53]
4. Vajrapani image[54]

In conclusion I may say, Stok Museum is the first Museum, in which one can sees Ladakhi old tradition and culture.

Notes and References

1. Two queens : Sonam Polkit and Jera Khatun.
2. Sumi, Tokan D : Oki, Masato and Hussnain, F.M. : 'Ladakh : The Moonland', Light & Life Pub., New Delhi, 1975 : 10.
3. (i) Youpjur : The queen's crown date 650 A.D. It is said that this crown have come from the legendary Kangcho, the Chinese Princess who married with the famous Tibetan emperor King Srong Tsan sgampo.

   (ii) Serab Rari : Royal sword

   (iii) Je cun Mila : Famous Buddhist saint.

   The above three things were very important for royal family and were regarded as the royal symbol of Ladakh Kingdom.
4. Royal caps : These are the specimen caps worn by the royal children and kings. These caps have come from India, Sikkim and Tibet.
5. Gzi necklace : (Gze - Tiger's eye) necklace belongs to queen of Ladakh.
6. Key ring : It is attached with Gzi necklace.
7. Baltistan necklaces : They are two in number and belong to queen Gyal Khatoon, mother of Senge Namgyal who ruled Ladakh in 17th century A.D.
8. Necklaces of turquoise and coral : These necklaces belong to queen of Ladakh.
9. Man of long life : This mural is depicted opposite to the case of ornaments alongwith good luck figure.
10. King of Ladakh : This mural is next to the case in which king of Ladakh flanked by small figures of the queen and a brave guardian, a warrior. It contains the 'seven gems' the queen, the

Minister, the General, wheel of power, elephant, horse and jewel.

11. Necklaces of Gyalmo Diskyut Wangmo : These are displayed on the left side of second room, two pictures of the present queen wearing some of the jewellery also displayed in this room.
12. Necklaces of former queens : These are displayed on the right side of the room.
 The necklaces of Gyalmo Diskyit Wangmo and former queens are made of gold, turquoise, seed pearls, coral and amber.
13. Parag : It is displayed on the right side of the room. It is the head-dress and placed alongwith queen's ear rings.
14. Youpjur : It is queen's crown as said earlier displayed alongwith face veil of pearl known to the Ladakh as Mutigi Chhala which the queen used to wear on rare ceremonies. Below this are ear-rings called Kakul made of pearls, turquoses, gold, garnet and coral.
15. Diplomatic letter : It is next to the jewellery case. Here collection of diplomatic letters which were sent by a Tibetan ruler to the king of Ladakh in 18th century.
16. Ceremonial teapots : These are displayed on either side of the above said room. These teapots were used by king and queen during ceremonies.
17. Yak : The animal is called Dong by the Tibetians. An old bull appears a mass of black hair which flow down from the body, shoulder sides and chest.
18. Yakskin bucket : It was used for storing chhang, the locally brewed barley bear.
19. Five large thankas of Padmasambhava : These five thankas are hanged near the entrance of the room. The thankas depict the life story of the great Acharya Padma Sambhava from Western India who played many pioneering roles in introducing Buddhism in Tibet in 8th century A.D. These thankas were made in Tibet in 15th century with the natural colours of the five precious stones; gold, silver, turquoise, coral and lapis lazuli.
20. Nine Thankas of Padmasambhava : These thankas were made in Tibet in the 14th century of these precious stone colours

depict the nine different forms of Padma Sambhava who had to play a distinct role at each important event of his life.

As one enters in the Thankas's room, one can see a beautiful painting of Gesar's epic which is popular throughout in Central Asia including Ladakh.

21. Namgyalma thanka : It is hanged on the right wall of the room. White colour is the goddess of longevity has four heads, twelve arms and a stup head-dress. She holds a vajra (or thunderbolt) in her hand which symbolizes truth as indestructable.
22. Trumpets and masks : These are hanged through the central pillars and belong to Yamantaka.
23. Personal objects of the royal family : These comprise lovely brass and copper statuettes and different types of jads and porcelain tea cups.
24. Thankas : These are of 13th century, depict one hundred old Jataka stories, the life stories of previous incarnations of Sakyamuni Buddha; were brought from Tibet and done exclusively from colours ground from various stones.
25. Thankas : These Jatakas stories thankas are made of natural colour and brought from Tibet.
26. Court robes made of Chinese silk : These are displayed on the right side wall of the room and belong to king and queen.
27. Late King's throne : This room has a small sanctuary at the far, set up with the late king's throne.
28. Wood carving : In front of the above said king's throne a Ladakhi table is a master piece of Ladakhi wood carving. On this table a rare tsampa bowl, a covered gold and silver teapot on stand, and a prayer wheel are placed.
29. Chorten decorated with turquoise etc. : This chorten decorated with turquoise, coral, gold, quartz and pearls. It contains the relics of the late king's grandfather.
30. Two couch shell trumpets : The case on the left wall of the room has two couch shell trumpets (a male and female pair, the sex depending on the direction of the shell's spiral) with intricate work of silver, gold and semi-precious stones.
31. Ritual objects : These consist : a holy water dish, alms bowl, the queen's rosary, cymbals, flutes, etc.
32. Telescopic trumpets : These are placed next to the ritual objects.

33. Padmasambhava thanka : It is a large thanka, and a copy of the larger one at Hemis Gonpa that is displayed once in a period of 12 years. This thanka is made of brocade applique decorated with pearls and turquoise.
34. Seat-couch : Over the seat-couch hang two hats; one for summer and one for winter.
35. Avalokitesvara statue : It is old statue of 7th century A.D. made in India.
36. King's crown : Next to the above small statue king's crown is placed. It looks like a large turban.
37. Prayer box : It is in front of the king's crown.
38. Eight auspicious emblems (Tib. Tashi rta-gyat) : The eight auspicious symbols are : umbrella, fishes, couch shell, flower, vessel, love knot, banner and wheel. These symbols represent the following parts of human

(1)	Umbrella	:	Head
(2)	Fishes	:	Eyes
(3)	Conch shell	:	Teeth
(4)	Flower	:	Tongue
(5)	Vessel	:	Neck
(6)	Love Knote	:	Waist
(7)	Banner	:	Whole body
(8)	Wheel	:	Feet

These above Buddhist culture emblems are arranged on both sides of the front of this box.
39. Prayer book : In front of the Avalokitesvara statue, prayer book is placed. This book is unusual and valuable because it is written in gold ink on black paper.
40. Gold & Silver tea cup, a dorje and tilbu : These ritual items are placed on a table in front of the seat-couch.
41. Daru : A small double drum known as 'Daru' also placed on the above table along with ritual things.
42. Three red sect lamas : The statue of these lamas are placed in the prayer shrine. They belong to Himis and other two to Chemre Gonpa.
43. Tara statue : It is placed opposite to the entrance. This large statue is also known as female Budda among Buddhists.
44. Case of Statues : To the left of above large Tara statue, a case with statues of Tara, Amitabha and Namgyalma are placed.

45. Case of statues : In this case the following statues are displaced:
    (i) Amitabha
    (ii) Hayagirva
    (iii) Amitabha
46. Case of butter images : These are at the left side of the prayer room and are made from butter and barley flour.
47. Brass and copper metal statues : They are at the right wall of the room.
48. Padmasambhava, Sakyamuni and Vajrapani statues : These statues are comparatively large. Vajrapani in a fierce manifestation.
49. Chakmen : It is in a separate case on the far right of the room, Chakmen is a Dharmapala of Dukpa school.
50. Chorten : It is near the front of the room, decorated with coral and turquoise, contains the relics of the late king's grandmother.
51. Kangyur : It has 109 volumes of Buddha's teachings. This valuable set is printed on vellum rather than the more usual paper.
52. Hayagirva : A tantric Buddhist deity.
53. Padmasambhava : He was the great master of Tantra. He established Ningma order of Buddhism.
54. Vajrapani : He is the god of energy and power.

Bibliography

1. Booklet on Stok Palace Museum.
2. Jina, Prem Singh : Thiksey monastery of Ladakh Himalaya, Sri Satguru Pub., New Delhi.

Appendix

Tsetan Namgyal
↓
Tsespal Tondup Namgyal
↓
Tsewang Rabstan
↓
Sonam Namgyal
↓
Jigmet Dadul Namgyal
↓
Kunzang Namgyal
↓
Jigmet Wangchok Namgyal

8

Mummies in Ladakh and Spiti of Himachal Pradesh

In Ladakh and Spiti one can find mummies in the monasteries. They are preserved either in the chortens or in natural sitting posture after pasted with clay. In Ladakh they are preserved in the following forms :

1. Placed whole body inside the chorten.
2. The body remained in the natural form.

Mostly important chortens in Ladakh are constructed on the ashes of well known lamas. In Thiksey monastery at Kudung temple, two lamas' body have been preserved in silver chortens.

In another case a lama body has been preserved in a Chumoor Gonpa in Chang-Thang sub-division of Leh district, Ladakh.

Chumoor (Chumar) Gonpa belongs to Nying ma pa sect of Buddhist order. The Lama's dead body has been preserved in the tsangs-khang[1] temple (Fig. 8.1)

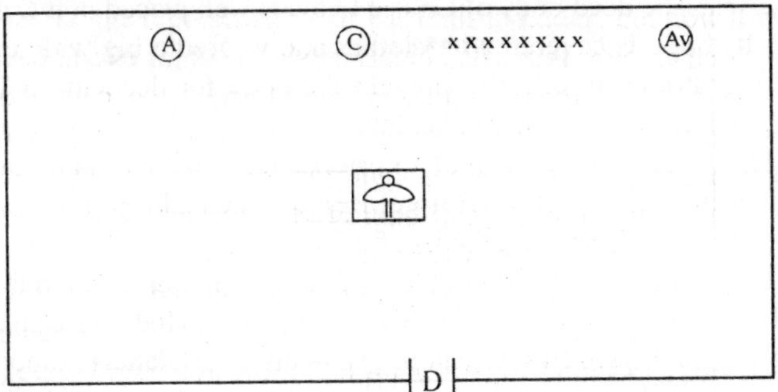

Not to scale

Fig. 8.1 Statues and mummy in tsangs-khang of Chumoor (Chumar) monastery

 : Mummy

xxxxxxxx : Eight kinds of chortens

Ⓒ : Centre statue of Guru Padmasambhava of 6 feet in height

Ⓐ : Amitaus of five feet in height

(Av) : Avalokitesvara (Thousand hands and eyes) 3-4 feet in height.

It is said that there was a *dayan*[2] looked very beautiful lady, and whoever came in contact with her, she offered a proposal of marriage before have had any kind of sexual enjoyment. After marriage she enjoyed sexual intercourse, later killed them. In this way she married with nine men. All of them she ate and killed.

Later, in a couple of decade ago a tantric lama visited to Chumoor[3]. Immediately as usual the *dayan* appeared before him. Lama with his spiritual power came to know that this beautiful lady would not be a simple lady, but a *dayan*. As the lady asked for sexual enjoyment. Lama said, wait him for sometime. Then he went for meditation. But, the lady didn't allow him to go for meditation. She came to him for sex, lama was well awared, he took the opportunity and cut down her both hands and killed her. Today her hands[7] are hanged through the ceiling of Tsangs-khang of the Chumar monastery. This temple is decorated by paintings of old tradition in black and white character. The painting of Changman, the protected deity of the monastery is depicted alongwith Padmasambhava.

According to local Buddhists the dead body of tantric lama was actually the reincarnated Chorje Lama. This time his incarnation is lived in America. The dead body of Chorje Lama is well placed in the Tsangs-khang. Its body is covered with clothes and weared a big wide cap and sited on a throne. In order to prevent the body for decaying only clay paste is being used instead of chemicals.

The preserved mummy of Chorje Lama's hair and nails increase like other human beings. Therefore, Reincarnated Chorje Lama usually called, who cut the hairs and nails of it.

Mummy at Gyu monastery in Spiti : Gyu Gonpa is 35 km far away from Tabo monastery near the Chinese border, close to Indo-Tibetan Border Police and Intelligent Bureau camp. The mummy of a lama is supposed to be 200 years old[5]. Mummy is preserved in the natural form without using any kind of paste. As a result we can see holes in place of eyes and its face is twisted because of dryness. The skin of the mummy is completely dryed and does not exit any kind of bad smell.

Notes and References

1. tsangs-khang : Tib. ltsags dman khang.
2. Dayan : Evil spirit lady. In Hindi we simply called *curel* or goblin.
3. Some scholars have an opinion that the tantric lama or Chorje Lama visited Chumoor Gonpa 50 years ago.
4. The hands of evil spirit lady cut down by Chorje Lama and only her hands below ankles are hanged through ceiling of Tsangs-khang.
5. Some scholars belief that the mummy was recovered after digging the site, that time labours informed that the mummy of a lama had blood, as he was recently being killed. Later nearby lama scholars informed that the dead Lama possibly went for meditation, it usually happens when lama goes for meditation his chitta sometimes not remain in body hence, under such circumstances does not feel heat or cold and remain as such as in meditation posture.

9

Jesuit Missionaries Appearance in Ladakh during the First Half of Eighteenth Century A.D.

Jesuit Missionaries visited Central Asia during the first half of eighteen century A.D. for the purpose to spread Christianity. During their mission Desideri and Freyre visited Leh in the autumn of 1714 via Kashmir.

Crossing Pir Panjal Range : In the beginning Jesuits decided to visit Tibet and establish there a church, later while crossing Pir Panjal range which was then difficult to cross, they decided to take halt in Kashmir rather than a direct approach to Tibet. Perhaps the other fact was that—Desideri was over the Pir Panjal mountain range, suffered by cold fever in his cough blood was started coming; so the two Jesuits decided to spend winter in Kashmir, instead of pressing on directly into Baltistan and Ladakh—then known as little Tibet and second Tibet.[1]

Expedition over Horrible Zoji Pass : In the early of the following summer Jesuits made expedition for Ladakh. They moved westwards of Srinagar and crossed horrible—motoriously treacherous Zoji la. According to Desideri :

> "... Crossing the motoriously treacherous Zoji pass only with the greatest difficulty. By Himalayan standards it was not a high pass but its extensive snow fields made the crossing a slow and exhausting business. Snow-blindness was another unexpected hazard."

Temporary Blindness : Travelling in the middle of dry weather and snowy mountains, it is sometimes difficult for travellers to move ahead.

Freyre describes how he woke one morning after sheltering in a cave to find that Desideri had temporarily gone blind :

> "When we were looking at the first rays of the dawn Father Hyppolitus and one of our Christian servants found that they could not distinguished them; and we saw then that their eyes were running with water from the glar of the snow."

Leh in 1715 : On 20 June Jesuit party finally stumbled into Leh, the capital of Ladakh. The residence of the chief Lama and the palace of the king were the fine buildings; and were defended by gates. Desideri made the following description :

> "It is situated in a wide plain entirely surrounded by mountains and studded with villages. The city extends up the slope of a mountain to the residence of the chief Lama and the palace of the king, both large and fine buildings. The whole is crowned with a large fort close to the summit and another fort on the summit. Below and on its flanks the town is surrounded by walls and defunded by gates."

Lama Land : Ladakh region itself dry and horrible for visitors and stay long, particularly during winters when temperature goes down –30°C to –60°C in some places. Desideri also agreed with this statement. However, he found Ladakhis behaviour was simple and kind. The Lamaist inhabitants to be 'kindly, cheerful and courteous'.

Guest as Fruitless : Freyre, who was officially leader of the expedition had very different ideas about Ladakhis. He regarded them as fruitless and even distrusted the rulers of Ladakh. His only concern was to get out of this benighted country and back to India, not by way of the dreadful pass over which they had come. However, there was no alternative. Desideri then requested him that if he was determined to return to India without recrossing the Zoji-La, it would have to be done via Tibet.

Journey Continue to Third Tibet : Freyre when fully convinced by the Desideri, then they together prayed to god for guidance and decided to continue their journey to Third and Principal Tibet.

Trade Route to Gartok and Lhasa : Ippolito Desideri and Freyre in August 1715 set out for Tibet, riding on horseback along the ancient trade route that runs alongside the Indus river and then climbing up and out onto the great Tibetan plateau. The route was terrible, full of desert, too cold and too arid to provide more than the meanest of existences; an unexplored wilderness of thin scrub and salt flats broken by mountain ranges, grazed over by yak and antelope and herds of wild asses—and occasionally they came acrossed Dokpas called Changpas, who dwelt in their black tents, with their herds of domesticated yak, sheep and long-haired goats. Finally they along the trade route that led from Ladakh up the Indus valley to the trading centre of Gartok and then on eastwards down the Tsangpo valley to Lhasa.

In 1717, Emanoel Freyre left to Nepal then to Agra and after two years joined Indo-Portuguese community in Goa; whereas Ippolio Desideri stayed in Tibet for five years. In April 1722 he via Nepal arrived Jesuit college in Agra then returned to Rome.[2]

Notes and References

1. Jina, Prem Singh : 'Famous Western Explorers to Ladakh', Indus Pub. Co., New Delhi, 1995.
2. *Ibid.*

10

James Baillie Fraser's Study Tour in Ladakh during 1814-15

James Baillie Fraser made extensive tour through snow range of Himalaya during 1814-15. During this period he had closely studied economic and social activities of Ladakhis and other concern. His research work came out in the form of book and published the same under the title 'The Himala Mountains' for London in 1820.

Fraser's research work enables us to catch a glimpse of the vanished glories of the bygone days, apart from this his study on Ladakh helps us to know the distribution of flora and fauna in the said region.

Fraser came Ladakh on June 1815 as a political agent for the Army of General Martindale. He entered in Chang-Thang sub-division of Leh district and took rest at Korzog.[1] Here he saw a lake which is formed by snow melted water, he describes :

> "We here no more of Para river which was left far on the left hand, on which side also, it seems by inference, that the lake is left. As the right hand hills are represented as all along coming pretty close, and the only place on the lake noticed at all is on the left, the Para river being fresh water, does not probably rise in the lake, but must likely has its origin in the streams that flow from the snow-capt mountains on the left hand; among which, probably, also the lake retreats and from whence it draws its supplies."[2]

Chang-Thang has Low Hills with Pasture Grounds : In Chang-Thang region Chang-pas called Bhoteas[3] lead their nomadic life depending upon livestock wealth. Here follows Fraser's views :

> "The road is good and proceeds over level soil among low scanty grass. Low hills are seen on both sides to the right about

a cos[4] distant, on the left hand from two to three distant. They are not rocky, but of red soil covered with thin grass, but there is no wood or jungle; their tops are even without peaks or precipices. In summer the Bhoteas bring sheep, goats and sooragooees (or yaks), to pasture; they have none of the common cattle. There are no habitations to be seen. Chucksung itself is a place of five or six Bhotea tents."[5]

Thoggee Chunmo has salt-water Lake : Thoggee Chunmo[6] is a halting pace for Chang-pas as their livestock could get water and sufficient grass. Fraser says :

> "Proceeding along a valley about two cos broad; it is sandy and grassy. On the left hand side the hills are very lofty, but there was no snow on them. Those on the right-hand are low formed of very red soil, so that the scanty grass is scarcely seen. There is no wood, nor do rocks or stones prevail. Thoggee Chunmo is a spot where there are five or six Bhotea tents with their flocks, but no cultivation. There is also a salt-water lake, two cos long, and about a gunshot broad."[7]

Lursa[8] on the Hill Thuglung[9] : The road towards Tag-lang base from Thoggee Chunmo was plain and good like Indian plains. Fraser described it as fit for treaverse by horse riding, here he says :

> "... to Lursa Thug-lung; course nearly the same. The road plain and good lies along a valley from half a cos to a cos broad, of good black soil. The hills on either hand are of moderate height; the soil of which they are composed, as well as the rocks, are red, and far from rugged; described as fit to be traversed in all directions by horses. There is no water to be found in all this march; but snow or ice is to be hand to supply its place in a deep dell about a cos from Lursa, which is desert place on the hill Tunglung."[10]

Gia is a Safe Place during Trouble : It is a big village has one fort. It is said during trouble at Leh King of Ladakh or his family members used to hide here till the situation comes to normal. Fraser explains about this place in the following way :

> "Geeah[11] is a large village of thirty houses on the left hand bank of the nullah; opposite is the fort of Geeah, in which in times of trouble the people place their families and valuables."[12]

Cho's Residence at Miru : In olden days king of Ladakh often gave independent charge to his subordinates known Khalon, Lonpo, Cho etc.[13] who had full control over the alloted areas. The Miru would be the area of Cho who had independent administrative charge. Fraser remarks :

> "Meeroo[14] is a village of fifteen or sixteen houses, where there is an old fort. Both here and at Geeah once resided two petty independent chieftains, called in the language of the country, 'cho', but they have both been reduced by the Ludhak[15] Gealbo or Rajah[16] and the country absorbed into his dominions."[17]

Upshi has Highly Cultivated Land : Upshi is famous for goat and sheep rearing centre. In olden days it had highly cultivated fields. Fraser gives the following information about this village :

> "The village of Oopsehee[18] is a little further on the left side of both. The road is good to Oopsehee. The river runs in a valley, said here however to be no more than two bowshots across, but highly cultivated with wheat, barley and rye, watered from canals raised from the river. The hills on each side are lofty, and continue their red colour."[19]

Tagna, Thiksey, Chu-shod and Shey are Rich Cultivated villages near Leh : Tagna to Shey on one side of the Shindu river and Chu-shod along the left bank are cultivated fields like plains in India. Fraser also agrees with this statement, he says :

"At Heemea[20] cross the Sing-Kechoo[21] on a wooden bridge and proceed along the right bank of the river through rich cultivation with thickly strown villages, and planted with Chiloona—trees, which border the road : the valley gradually widens to Sheh[22], where it is from three to four cos broad, of the villages on the same side, as Heemea (the left bank), Chunga is one cos further on Tungna[23] three cos, ooshat one cos more. From Sheh, the capital Leh, Leo or Le is but three cos and a half distance. The royal residence is about two cos from the river. The country around is thickly inhabited and well cultivated."[24]

A Fort of Ladakh in Basgo : It is said that King Sing-ghe Namgyal's mother Gyal Khatun resided for many years at Basgo palace, probably a fort was also built to protect the palace and royal families. Fraser did not say anything about this fort, but said only geographical location of it, he remarks :

> "Busgee[25], a fort of Ludhak, nearly a whole day's journey along the same valley, on good and even road, say eighteen miles, direction more westernly, south-west by west. There are apricots found on this road".[26]

Lama Faith People of the Himalayan Country is called Bhoteas : Generally people who have faith on Mahayana Buddhism are known Bhoteas; Nowadays, many of them are influenced by Hinduism. Fraser has the following views in this reference :

"The word Bootan, or the country of the Bhoteas, as well as the appellation Bhotea, is used in a very definite manner by all inhabitants of the hills, even by those best informed; and instead of being applied to the circumscribed country which we know as Bhootan, it signifies, generally all the country lying behind the crest of the Himala that professes the Lama faith.[27] Not only those who are directly under the Chinese government, but those of the petty hill rajahs who exercise their own authority, either independently or as feudatories of China, are known by the sweeping term Bhoteas."[28]

Leh is a Mundi of Central Asian Traders : In olden days traders came Leh with their merchandise goods from Yarkand, Russia, Baltistan, Kashmir, Gharwal, Kumaon, Himachal and many other countries. They exchanged their goods with their respective traders and either returned to their home or moved to Lhasa or Gartok for further trade. Fraser says :

"Yarkund[29] sends to Leo in Ludhak, silver, Russian leather, called Bhul, R'hal[30], felt carpets, called 'Numbdas', coarse and fine China silk tafetas, valvets, and earthenware, satble fur, small coral beads, and seed pearls; and in return receives all manner of produce from Hindustan, Keen-kabs, embroidered cloth, baftas, and other white cloths, moultan chintz, quantities of red tanned skins of sheep, goat and kid, nerbisee or zedoary, silk manufactures of Benares[31] soongrees and all sorts of spices."[32]

With Reference to Trade Ladakh is a Tributary of both China and Kashmir : In olden days Ladakh was the centre for wool/pashmina. Traders from Tibet or Chinese side exchanged wool with Hindustani items viz. spices, consumer goods etc. Later wool was supplied to Kashmir through Kashmiri trader. Thus Kashmiris had the monopoly over wool trade, in Kashmir they manufacture carpets and other woollen items. Fraser had the following opinion in this regards :

"We were given to understand that Ludhak was in some degree tributary both to China and Cashmere.[33] This may relate more to the terms of certain commercial treaties and political relations with these two states, than to any actual assessment which it submits to pay them. There is no doubt, however, that these relations are most favourable to itself, for it seems to enjoy a sort of monopoly of the whole valuable trade in shawl wool, engrossing to itself at a fixed and low valuation all the wool that is collected in the Undes, which is disposed of to the

> manufacturers of Cashmere, from whom they receive in return the produce of Hindustan & C."[34]

On one Occasion Monopoly of Wool Trade Infringed : It is said once Kashmiri traders sold shawl wool to some stangers as a result under the agreements Kashmiri could not able to supply required consumer foodstuffs to the Chinese/Tibetan traders, thus for some period Tibetan or Chinese traders did not trust upon Kashmiri, therefore, they felt to sale wool through Ladakhis to Kashmiris.

Let us know what Fraser says :

> "It appears that on one occasion this monopoly was infringed by the sale of some shawl wool to stangers, which called forth the most rigorous enactments and threats of punishment to future defaulters from the authorities of Gara."[35]

Ladakh is a Land Fit for Grazing with Little Cultivation : In olden days there was not very hard and fast rule for shepherds to grazing their animals; they often cross the international border, as a result they could able to supply pashmina/wool in bulk. Fraser also agreed with this statement as he remarks :

> "Ludhak itself is, probably, chiefly a grazing country, and supplies much shawl wool, though the principal mart for this is at Gara. The routes through its territories describes chiefly rugged mountains topped with snow projections certainly from the Himala range, and lower hills of reddish soil, covered with short grass, representing a country fit for sheep; but little is said of cultivation until, we are brought to the valley of the Singkechoo, which seems to be the rich district of the country. This is full of cultivation and villages; here also is placed the capital of the country, Leh or Ludhak."[36]

Along the Sindhu bank, Hemis to Leh villages have fertile lands : Along the Indus bank villages are densely populated, they grow wheat, barley, Yarkhandi oal, various vegetables viz. potato, cabbage, tomato etc. In olden days farmers here too grew the above said crops. Fraser says:

> "From the village of Humee[37] to Leh, a distance, it is said of sixteen or seventeen cos, we are told that the valley widens much, and is from two to four cos broad, very richly cultivated with wheat, barley, and ol, or rye, and thickly studded with villages, the road along the river excellent, broad, and planted on each side with chiloomah trees; and this prosperous state continues for a considerable distance below upon the river's banks."[38]

300 houses reduced by 1815 at Leh : Leh was the only big town in Ladakh; as Leh becoming the centre of traders, Ladakhis hurriedly constructed two or three stories houses without knowing the fact that the lower story was built by thin walls. This finally caused cracks and falling of many houses. Fraser had the following reports in this regards :

> "The town itself once contained about 1000 good houses, but report states it to have fallen off, and it is now reduced to about 700. These generally consist of several stories, the lower storey built by uniting two thin walls of stone filled with mud between them; the upper is entirely formed of the latter material, as is the roof, which is flat, forming a terrace."[39]

Kashmiri Muslims had maximum shops in Leh markets : As said earlier Kashmiris had monopoly over pashmina/wool trade, Leh then was the best place where they could get these in an easy efforts, therefore, they had good shops in Leh market. Fraser had his following opinion in this connection :

> "There are well stocked bazars and several shops (twelve or thirteen) kept by the cashmerian Mussulmauns, but no Hindoos bunyas or shopkeepers; flour, ghee, grain, flesh, and all articles of consumption are sold in the market by the people from the country, who bring them to town."[40]

Nima Namgyal was the King of Ladakh during 1815 : In Ladakh king was popularly known by title as Gyalpo and considered the highest rank in Buddhist society. He had palace at Leh on the slope of hillock nearby. Fraser got the following information about him :

> "The palace of rajah is at Leh; we were told that his title among the people of the country is 'gealbo', which is equivalent of rajah. His name is Neema Mungreal. I believe his religion is that of the Lamas; but an universal spirit of toleration seems to prevail under his sway, for all persuasions find protection there, Hindoos, Mussulmauns, Lamas and Chinese."

Cattle slaughtation was common in Leh market : In olden days meat was the main diet, Hindus in Ladakh were in a few number; rice, sugar, ghee etc. were costly, therefore, people slaughter cattle without hesitation. Fraser writes :

> "Cattle are freely slaughtered and flesh of all sorts is publicly sold in the market. It is said that rice, ghee, and sugar are very dear; wheat and barley are also expensive, but more common. Wheat is most preferred of which, and rice, they encourage

> the importation from Bischur and Cashmere, and consume a great quantity. Barley and ol or rye is chiefly used boiled into a sort of porridge."

Sheep and goats are encouraged to rear them : Ladakh has good pasture grounds, therefore, people here prefer to rear sheep and goats rather to big cattle. Fraser says :

> "In a grazing country; sheep and goats are more encouraged and reared than horned cattle."

Three grand fairs at Leh : Fair and festivals were the important events in which people got entertainment; besides trade, also exchanged their commodities to each other. Fraser had the following report in this subject :

> "Three grant fairs are held in the year at Leh, viz. one in Kartick, or October one in Phagoon or February, and one in Bhadgoon or August. The first of these is called the Jung Dooz, and is the least the second called Dummooche, is the chief one, and the third termed Sooblas, holds a middle importance. At these fairs the concourse of Mussulmauns from Yarkunds & C, of Lamas from Lassa Degurcha, Hindoos from Imritsir and all the Punjab and of merchants from cashmere, and all other places, is said to be immense; and valuable productions of these countries seems to be used as an entrepot for their riches, exporting them again by the various natural channels to their ultimate markets."

Gartok was the big market of Central Asia : In olden days trade through Ladakh to Central Asian countries was very popular. Gartok was then the main centre of trade where about 20,000 traders from the neighbouring Himalayan countries exchanged their merchandise. Ladakhis also went there for Pashmina or other wool and latter sold through the hands of Kashmiris to Kashmir valley. Fraser made the following reports in this connection :

> "It seems that Gartope is situated in the valley of the river Eekung, which is here of considerable extent, though surrounded, it appears with hills. To this place the Ludhak merchants come to purchase the wool which is brought for sale from all the country round to a great distance, for the cashmere market; and to this place, also, do the dealers from the low country of Hindustan come to dispose of and exchange their goods. The great melah, or fair, is held annually in the month of Bhadoon, and when well attended there are seen from 12 to 15,000 people."

Conclusion : James Baillie Fraser made an extensive journey in Himalayan countries. He entered into Ladakh in the month of June 1815, but did not stay much and moved further to Tibet. In this chapter I have covered only Ladakh portion and endeavoured to explain further about the views of Fraser. Thus, trade, religion, society and custom have been widely discussed.

Notes and References

1. Korzog (= Karzok) : It is a village near Tsomariri lake on the Leh-Spiti route.
2. Fraser, James Baillie : The Himala Mountains, London, 1820.
3. Bhoteas : Inhabitants who have Mongolian breed and perhaps might be migrated from Kham side of Tibet.
4. Cos : It was local measuring unit for distance and was equal to a distance walking.
5. Fraser, James Baillee; *op. cit.*
6. Thoggee Chunmo : It is a big pasture ground in Chang-Thang.
7. Fraser, James Baillee; *op. cit.*
8. Lursa : It is place on the Taglung la or Tag-lang-la.
9. Thuglung (= Taglang) : It is a pass of about 17,500 feet high.
10. Fraser, James Baillee; *op. cit.*
11. Geeah (= Gia) : This village is located on Leh-Manali road.
12. Fraser, James Baillee; *op. cit.*
13. They were the administrators during king of Ladakh regime.
14. Meeroo (= Miru) : It is located along the Leh-Manali Highway.
15. Ludhak : Ladakh.
16. Gealbo : Gyalpo, the king of Ladakh.
17. Fraser, James Baillee; *op. cit.*
18. Oopsehee : (= Upshi) : This village is located at Leh-Manali road.
19. Fraser, James Baillee; *op. cit.*
20. Heemea : From here one may cross Indus river for Hemis.
21. Singh-Kechoo : Indus river.
22. Sheh : (= Shey) : It is a village about 16 km from Leh.
23. Tungna : (= Tagna) : It is located along Leh-Manali road.
24. Fraser, James Baillee; *op. cit.*

25. Busgee : (= Basgo) : This village is located along Leh-Srinagar road.
26. Fraser, James Baillee; *op. cit.*
27. Lama faith : Buddhism of Mahayana.
28. Fraser, James Baillee; *op. cit.*
29. Yarkund : Yarkand, which was famous for woollen carpet.
30. R'hal : Rough wool.
31. Benares : Banaras, or Varanasi.
32. Fraser, James Baillee; *op. cit.*
33. Cashmere : Kasmiri, which was famous for Pashmina shawls.
34. Fraser, James Baillee; *op. cit.*
35. *Ibid.*
36. *Ibid.*
37. Humee : Hemis, here famous Buddhist monastery is located.
38. Fraser, James Baillee; *op. cit.*
39. *Ibid.*
40. *Ibid.*

11

Moorcroft Journey to Ladakh during 1820

In 1624, the Jesuit missionary, Andrada and in 1715 Desideri appeared in Ladakh. However, didn't provide useful information. Therefore, in order to have detail information about the Trans-Himalaya, Moorcroft and his party entered into Ladakh during nineteen century and in September, 1820 reached Leh, remained here for the next two years. Here follows the details.

Barala-cha Pass : Moorcroft followed the route via Kulu, Manali in Himachal Pradesh to Ladakh. Barala cha in this route is the first pass, sometimes becomes dangerous for travellers, particularly during bad weather. Moorcroft has the following views about pass :

> "The Bara Lacha ridge[1] has elevation of sixteen thousand five hundred feet. Some of the peaks were apparently one thousand feet higher. On all the great slopes and crests of the chin the snow lay in vast undisturbed masses. The summit of the pass was tolerably level. The soil on and near the pass was swampy and soft, and strewed with fragments of rock or small stones, which although dry on the upper surface were immersed in water, and gave way when stepped upon".[2]

Yu-nam Lake : After travelling a few distance over rugged path Moorcroft came across the Yu-nam lake. It is a natural lake and has about 4 km. round. Moorcroft remarks :

> "After crossing the plain we followed the left bank of the stream by a rugged path, crossing ruins of rock opened suddenly upon its left into a lake about three miles round, called Yu-nam. Not a weed deformed nor a wave ruffled its pellucid and tranquil water, there seemed to be no fish in it, nor any bird or even a

fly in its vicinity. The river that had fallen into the lake re-issued from it, and was thence called the Yu-nam river."[3]

Borax carriers from Ladakh : Leh was a famous market for Central Asian traders. Lahuli, Kulu and Chamba traders often exchanged their goods with borax at Leh. On 11th September 1820 Moorcroft saw some Chamba trader carrying borax from Ladakh at the right bank of Sum-ghi-el or Three spring river. He remarks :

> "Proceeding along the rivulet, after crossing to its right bank, the road came to a plain, along the borders of which two streams meeting with that which we have accompanied formed the Sam-ghi-el, or Three spring river. Following its right bank we came upon a party of men, women and children, some from Chamba, carrying borax from Ladakh."[4]

Valley of Wild Sheep : On 12 September Moorcroft party passed through a valley near Ruk-chun. Here Moorcroft found many wild sheep. According to him :

> "The march of the 12th continued along the plain; there was some pasture upon it, but very little water. In one place were two or three pools, surrounded by an extensive bed of sand, from the upper part of which issued a mirage resembling waves. The valley is said to be frequented by wild sheep, and some of their horns of immense size, but injured by exposure, bore evidence of the fact. Shortly after reaching Ruk-chun, a shepherd's station, near the end of the valley, where we halted."[5]

Shooting in Ruk-chun : In olden days Ladakh was famous for wild life shooting among English people. Moorcroft in his tour found wild-life in ample proportion. He remarks :

> "We remained at Ruk-chun for two days, during which Mr. Trebeck and myself shot a few hares; they were of bluish white colour, and were not much larger than English rabbits."[6]

Tung-lung[7] : The highest pass at Leh-Manali route : Tung-lung (or Tag-lang) is the highest pass of 17,500 feet along the Leh-Manali road. This pass became difficult when snow fall occurs for travellers. Moorcroft made the following statement about this pass :

> "We moved along the rest of the valley on the 15th and on the 16th crossed the ghat of Tung-lung. The pass was about seven hundred feet above the plain; from its top the horizon was beheld everywhere skirted with sharp-peaked mountains capped with snow; the snow-clouds were distinctly observable,

travelling from peak to peak, or throwing out processes towards them, as attracted by each, and showering down a portion of their contents; lightened by the discharge, they then rose and floated in the air, until they again accumulated, and were again attracted within the sphere of the crest of the mountain. From the ghat the road descended rapidly, and was marked by a rivulet, which rose on the northern slope of the pass."[8]

Chortens near a village : Moorcroft's party after crossing Tung-lung (or Tag-lang) pass, when came at a first Ladakh village on 17th September, saw two chortens. About these he explains :

"The road, crossing a rivulet of clear water, came to two large white sepulchral buildings : they were about twenty-five feet high : a square turret stood upon a base of several steps, and terminated in a similar series of steps, on the summit of which was a large urn, ornamented with sculpture; the upper part was rounded, and a pole, above six feet long, projected from the top."[9]

Inquiry of Moorcroft Mission : As Moorcroft's party reached near Giah (or Gya), Abdul Latif came and met with Mir Izzet Ullah[10] and inquired about the Moorcroft mission, when he was convinced that his mission was strictly mercantile he gave favourable report to the Raja of Giah. Moorcroft says:

"Abdul Latif availed himself of this connexion to inquire confidentially of the Mir, what were our real character and purposes, and being satisfied on these points, engaged to conduct him on the following day to the Raja of Giah and the Khaga Tan-zin, the brother-in-law of the Khalun, or chief Vazir of Ladakh. Accordingly, on the morning of the 18th, Mir Izzet Ullah went to the city, and had an interview with those officers. They seemed to be tolerably well informed of the extent of the British power, and of our relations with Sikh ruler, and very suspicious of the real object of my journey. Satisfied, however, apparently, by the strenuous declarations of my representative."[11]

Meeting with Raja of Giah : In olden days Ladakh was divided into many princely states and was ruled by different Rajas. Tsimma Punchik[12] was the Raja of Giah (or Gya) when Moorcroft arrived at Giah. He reported:

"After entering a court-yard, we passed through a dark doorway, and ascended a steep stone staircase, feeling, not seeing our way to an open gallery, on one side of which were several doors. In one of the apartments to which they led, we found the Raja, sitting on one of two chairs which I had sent for the occasion, and the Khaga Tan-zin[13] on a campstool; on the side of the room opposite to the Raja was placed the chair intended for me. When I had taken my seat, the Raja made some civil inquiries in Tibetan, through Abdul Latif, and he expressed his hope that we had not suffered any inconvenience. A moderately large tea-pot, of gilt copper, and of beautiful workmanship, was brought in, and salted and buttered tea, without milk, handed to the company. The Raja took out of a breast-pocket, his own tea-cup of yellow China. The Khaga Tan-zin also produced his, of chestnut-wood, mounted with silver. We had come provided with our own cups. After some conversation on indifferent topics I took leave. About an hour our return, the Raja and Khaga Tan-zin[14] arrived at our tents to inspect our merchandise that the frontier duties might be levied."[15]

Small pox near Leh : When Moorcroft's party arrived at Mi-ru, they were informed that on the route to Leh, some villages were under the grip of small pox. Moorcroft says : "Khaga Tan-zin informed me he had received a letter from the vazir, desiring us to take another road to Yarkand, through Nubra, as the small pox, he said was in some of the villages on the route to Leh."[16]

Uk-shi[17] : Fifty yards breadth ahead at Giah : Uk-shi Tib. 'aub shi, or Upshi' is a village ahead to Giah (or Gya) towards Leh situated near Sinh-kha-bab. Moorcroft remarks:

"At the town of Uk-shi the rivulet of Giah fell into a deep river, about fifty yards in breadth. This was the river of Le'[18], the Yuma or Sinh Khabab[19], which may be considered as the main branch of the Indus, flowing from the province of Gardokh. Uk-shi consists of not more than ten or a dozen houses."[20]

Cluster of villages and monasteries beyond Marsilla[21] : After crossing Marsilla, Moorcroft saw good dwellings and temples till Sheh[22] village. He describes :

"Between Marsilla and Changa[23] we passed two temples, with houses of the Gelums[24] adjoining one of the right bank of the river, and one on the left, but farther off, and near the foot of the mountains. Beyond Changra we crossed a plain, and then came to the lands of other villages, the chief of which were Takna[25] and Mashu[26]. On an eminence stood a building that was considered as a sort of fortress, and several houses extended from it to the west; over the plain beneath, other houses were erected, rather in a straggling position. The Yuma river[27] separated these lands on the left bank from the small towns of Thik-se[28] (or Thiksey) and Gampha[29] on its right, the latter was inhabited by great numbers of Gelums. Opposite to the eastern end of Thik-se began the extensive valley of Chu-shut[30] (Tib. Chu-shod), the dwellings with their roofs, covered with a thick pile of firewood, and dry lucrene."[31]

Meeting with Khaja Shah Nyas : Khaja Shah Nyas was descended of Emperor Baber family of Tashkand and resided at Sheh (Shey). Moorcroft made the following details :

"We were here met Khaja Shah Nyas. He had a large turban on his head, and was dressed in a wrapper of brown cloth lined with chintz. Upon the conquest of Kashmir by Ranjit Sinh[32], the jagirs of the Khaja were confiscated, and his personal safety was endangered, so that he held it expedient to seek an asylum in some neighbouring region. He has, for the present, established himself in Ladakh."[33]

Women were the Chief Labours : Moorcroft when arrived at Chu-shut[34] village, saw women were working very hard on their fields, and most the agricultural works were been finished by them. Moorcroft remarks:

"Our route by along the valley of Chu-shut, the crops in which were cut, and the straw was piled in cones : the chief labourers in the fields were women : the men, when not busy at the thrashing-floor, were smoking and launging about."[35]

Chortens and Mani walls : In Ladakh, particularly in Buddhist dominated villages, we see sepulchral towers called chortens and pile of stones a thousand paces are called Manis. Moorcroft explained :

"On turning a narrow defile, by the side of a pile of stones, it came two large sepulchral towers, connected by a pile of stones a thousand paces long. We next came to a second pile, still longer, uniting two smaller towers, on the square sides of which was sculptured, in relief, the figure of an enormous quadruped of mythological invention, the head and breast of which something resembled those of a lion, except that the mouth was armed with tusks. Some of the monuments we have seen surmounted by a large urn, something resembling an earthen oil jar; others by a conical pillar of burnt brick. The urns had always a pole projecting above them : the pillars were crowned by double coronets of gilt copper. The upper coronet was the smallest, and had its largest circumference upwards, whilst the reverse was the case with that below. In the bowl of the upper one rose a crescent, in the concave part of which was a circle with halt sides like a cheese on its edge, with a figure like a pear having its stalk upwards, on its upper edge. These ornaments were of copper or brass, gilt."[36]

Kashmiris had endeavoured not to allow Moorcroft to Ladakh : When Moorcroft entered in the capital of Ladakh, Khalun[37], initially didn't show his interest to allow Moorcroft, as British company came in India for business, later spread its political power and finally ruled over India, therefore, the steps taken by the British traveller could see the chance to dethorn the Ladakh king. Moorcroft here made the details :

"It was evident that the mind of the Khalun was preoccupied with distrust of our professions and apprehensions of injury, either political or commercial, to the interests of Ladakh : indeed he confessed as much, and remarked that he had been told it was the practice of the English to appear at first in the guise of merchants, merely to gain a footing in the country, and that, having effected this they speedily brought it under their authority. The Mir[38] laboured especially to remove the impression that the British government entertained any designs against the independence of Ladakh, and we were fortunately able to produce some evidence to this effect which seemed to have great weight with the Khalun."[39]

Meeting with Khalun : Till the end of September Moorcroft's party remained quiet and on the 1st October 1820 Moorcroft & Trebak met with Khalun. It was their formal meeting, Moorcroft says :

"A band of music struck up as we entered. We then ascended two flights of stairs to an ante-chamber full of attendants, where the Khaga Tan-zin met me, and taking my right hand let me into the audience chamber. The Khalun was seated on some cushions at the further end of the room, on the left of a window; and on his left, sat two other persons, one of whom was the Nuna, or deputy Khalun. As I advance to him he put out his hands, took mine between them, and slightly bowed. I then took my place on a chair placed opposite to him, and a conversation chiefly complimentary ensued. He inquired after our health, hoped we had not suffered from the cold, asked our ages, our country, its situation and distance. The name of the King, whether we were on terms of friendship with the Vrins (Russians), Katha's (Chinese), and Ranjit Singh[40], whether we had ever visited Rum (Constantinople). Speaking of the small pox, I endeavoured to explain to him the advantages of vaccination, and recommended its introduction. We were then served with salted tea. The Khalun, or Chief Minister of Ladakh, whose name is Tsiva Tandu[41], appeared to be about sixty. He had lost most of his teeth, was thin, and of middle stature, with a countenance expressive of shrewdness; he was plainly dressed, in a loose brown wrapper and velvet cap, without any ornament. During the interview he smoked a hukka, small, but richly decorated. (Later) after making our presents took our leave. The Khalun and his two friends shook hands with us."[42]

Caravan of Chabbas & Yarkand in Ladakh : Traders who came from Lhasa, called Chabba mission whereas caravan from Yarkand usually brought shawl-wool, tea, silks etc. to Ladakh, then same exported to Khamir. Moorcroft remarks :

> "In the course of October, a caravan of Chabbas, as they are termed, traders from Lassa[43], arrived, with many yaks laden with tea, also a caravan from Yarkand of twenty-five horses, with shawl-wool, felts, tea, and silks. The latter was the first arrived from Yarkand for many months, and its usual delay had excited great anxiety amongst the Kashmiris. Some disputes, it was known, had arisen between Omar Khan, the ruler of Ferghana and the Chinese authorities at Yarkand, and it was feared that the chief merchants, who are mostly from Indejan, and subject of Ferghana, had left that city. Although this was true, yet the delay had rather arisen from the depressed state of the market at Yarkand, in consequence of which the caravans had proceeded to Bokhara. Thus caused for delay in Ladakh."[44]

Deep Canvassion upon the Moorcroft mission : As soon as Moorcroft's party arrived in Ladakh, Khalun got cautionary letters from the neighbouring countries, adviced him not to allow Moorcroft in Ladakh. Moorcroft reported :

> "Khaja Shah Nyas having came to the vicinity of Le'[45], was visited on the 21st by the Khalun, the Nuna Khalun, the Khaja Tan-zin, one or two other officers of Ladakh, Mohsin Baba, a merchant of Turan, and Abdul Latif[46], and a conference ensued, in which our character and objects were again canvassed. The Khalun said that he had received cautionary letters from Gartok[47], and that an officer from Lassa had come there to inquire what was meant by the visit of Europeans to the frontier. That the governor of Kashmir had intimated to him that Ranjit Sinh would take offence if he gave us encouragement; that Ahmed Shah, the malik of Balti, had written to him to know who and what were; and advices came from the Bisahar frontier of the approach of a European party. These circumstances, he said, had very much shaken his confidence in us, and he was at a loss what to decide. The Khaja repeated the arguments he had formerly used in our favour, and appealed to the Khalun's knowledge of his friendship for Ladakh in proof of his not being likely to give advice detrimental to the interests of the country. He reminded the Khalun that Ladakh was not dependent either upon Lassa or Lahore; that the English, a much more mighty power than any other, were, by the possession of Bisahar, quite as much his neighbours, and still more to be conciliated; and that the establishment of a commercial intercourse especially must be highly beneficial to Ladakh."[48]

Trade proposal made by Moorcroft : Finally Moorcroft assistant Mir Izzet Ullah convinced Khalun of Ladakh to agree trade relations with British. Moorcroft says :

> "Mir Izzet Ullah was then summoned, and desired to state explicitly what we wished or expected, and as he was instructed, he replied, that all we sought for was; (1) liberty to trade with Ladakh, and through it to other countries; (2) moderate duties; (3) a permanent factory at Le'; and (4) the good offices of the government, with that of Gardokh (Gartok), to induce the latter to open the Niti Ghat to British commerce. The three first, after some discussion, were promised, but the Khalun expressed his doubt whether the Gardokh authorities themselves could permit access to the district."[49]

Kashmiris failed to influence Khalun : Kashmiris endeavoured to influence the Khalun against Moorcroft's mission but failed to do so. Moorcroft said :

> "As the administration of affairs was wholly in the hands of the Khalun, the Raja being little more than a cipher in the state, we now imagined that all difficulties were at an end. In this, however, we were disappointed. The Kashmiris having failed to influence the Khalun against us, had recourse to the Lum-pa[50], the governor of Le'[51] and engaged him to counsel the Raja not to accede to any treaty, but to send us off with all dispatch. Our old friend the Khaja here again assisted us, and gradually prevailed upon the Lom-pa to withdraw his opposition."[52]

Khalun's latter to favour British commerce but Gartok authority disapproved : Moorcroft medical advice to Lom-pa helped him to create favourable atmosphere in his favour, later trade agreement had been signed in presence of Raja of Ladakh. Moorcroft reports :

> "Still there was a delay, for the Khalun stated it was necessary, at least, as an act of courtesy towards the authorities of Gardokh, who were the ancient friends and connexions of Ladakh, to communicate with them before coming to any decision. A letter was accordingly written, and in a few weeks an answer arrived which disapproved strongly of the Khalun's conduct, and recommended our offended at the tone of this remonstrance, and determined to refer the matter to Lassa, until the beginning of May, when although no reply had been received from Lassa, engagements were exchanged between the Raja and Chief Officers of Ladakh on the one part, and myself on behalf of the British merchants of Calcutta on the other, calculated to throw open to the enterprise of the latter, and through them to the manufactures of Great Britain, the whole of Central Asia from China to the Caspian Sea."[53]

During 1820, Ladakh was a independent kingdom surrounded by Tibet, China, British province etc. : In 1820, Moorcroft's party arrived in Leh and found Ladakh a buffer country surrounded by small countries, Moorcroft describes :

> "Ladakh is bounded on the north-east by the mountains which divide it from the Chinese province of Khutan, and on the east and south-east by Roodokh[54] (or Rudog) and Cham-Than[55],

dependencies of Lassa : on the south by the British province of Bisahar, and by the hill states of Kulu and Chamba. The latter also extends along the south-west till it met by Kashmir, which with part of Balti, Kartakshe, and Khafalun complete the boundary on the west and north-west. The north is bounded by the Karakoram mountains and Yarkand."[56]

Indus Valley : The principal valley in Ladakh : In Ladakh Indus may be regarded as the most striking and important feature in the geography of Ladakh, therefore, Indus valley follows the course of the Indus. Moorcroft reports :

"The principal valley in Ladakh is that which follows the course of the Indus, and extends from south-east to north-west through the greater part of the country. It may be said, indeed, to be continued throughout, or along the course of the Dras river to the frontiers of Kashmir."[57]

Dry Atmosphere of Ladakh : Ladakh has many large desert fields which caused dry atmosphere. Moorcroft gave the following details :

"The atmosphere of Ladakh is in general, dry, the moisture being converted into snow in the winter, and speedily evaporated by the scorching suns of summer; there is consequently very little rain."[58]

Cultivation in Ladakh : In Ladakh farmers cultivate wheat, barley and buck-wheat. According to Moorcroft :

"The kinds of grain cultivated in Ladakh are wheat, barley and buck-wheat of various descriptions. The generic name of the first in Tibetan is To, of the second Nas, and of the third Do, in the eastern and Bro in the western parts of Ladakh."[59]

Zhos are preferred for ploughing : In Ladakh, yak, ox are common, but Ladakhis preferred to plough their land by zhos, Moorcroft remarks :

"Oxen of the common kind are not used for ploughing, the zho ox, or hybrid male between the yak, or bos grunniens, and the common cow, or the humped variety called zebu, being greatly preferred as is its sister, the zhomo, for the dairy. Ploughing is performed by a pair of zhos, driven by the ploughman without reins, but guided, when well broken in."[60]

Fodder in Ladakh : In Leh district Ladakhis mostly grow Yarkandi ole whereas in Kargil, particularly in Dras valley, they grow Prangos. Moorcroft says :

"One of the most valuable sources of fodder of Ladakh, and

perhaps of any country whatever, is a plant known by the name of Prangos, and which grows only in the western parts of the country at Imbal or Dras. There is also another variety of lucerne called Yarkandi; a biennial, which has a larger stem than the ordinary kinds. At Le' this is sown along with the perennial variety, and by its greater yield the first and second year supplies the defectiveness of the latter."[61]

Vegetables in Ladakh : Today one can see all sort of vegetables in Ladakh, but in olden days only a few kind of vegetables were grown by Ladakhis. Moorcroft reports :

"There is no great variety of vegetable produce in Ladakh, but onions, carrots, turnips and cabbages are reared in some places during the spring and summer. For winter use the leaves of the cabbages and turnip tops, or sliced turnips are dried : carraway, mustard, and tobacco are grown in a few gardens."[62]

Fruits in Ladakh : In Ladakh apple and apricot trees are found in large number; as Moorcroft says :

"The only fruits cultivated are apricots and apples, standards of which are reared abundantly in the orchards of every farm house. Of apricots there are said to be ten varieties, and they certainly present much difference in size, shape, flavour, colour, and surface. The apple trees are also numerous and of several varieties : some of them are engrafted, but the greater number are wildings."[63]

Timber trees in Ladakh : Willow and poplar are the only timber trees in Ladakh. Moorcroft says :

"The only timber trees found in Ladakh are the willow and poplar and chiefly the former. The poplars which, along with willows are planted about every village in Ladakh, are sometimes the Lombardy, but more frequently the black poplar."[64]

Domestic animals in Ladakh : Yaks, cows, zho, sheep, goats etc. are native and domestic animals. Moorcroft gave the following details :

"The animals of Ladakh of the domestic species are horses, asses, yaks, cows, the zho or yak-mule, sheep, goats, dogs &c. Of these the horses are small, but active and hardy. The yak is found only on high lands, and is inferior in appearance and strength to that of Chan-Than[65]. The zho is a hybrid, between the male yak and the cow. The native breeds of sheep, though larger than those of India, are much smaller than the sheep of Chan-Than. The dog is scarcely more perfectly domesticated than this little animal."[66]

Wild animals in Ladakh : In Ladakh wild sheep, kiang, hares etc. are found in ample quantity. Moorcroft made the following reports in this connection :

"The wild animals are not numerous; they are principally of the goat kind, which are much larger than the domestic goat, and yield a finer wool. The Ibex frequents the loftiest and most inaccessible crags; the male is called skin, and the female L'Danmo. The wild sheep (ovis anmon) is also met with and is much larger than the domestic one. In the eastern parts of the country is a nondescript wild variety of horse, which I may call Equus Kiang. Hares in some parts of Ladakh are found in considerable numbers. The marmot was seen in considerable number on some parts of the mountain passes. Among large birds is the gigantic chakar, which is much larger than the common patridge. Sparrows, linnets and robin redbreasts are numerous and mischievous at seed time and harvest."[67]

Mineral production of Ladakh : In Ladakh, Sulphur and soda are found in plenty. Moorcroft says :

"There are a few mines of sulphur in some parts, but in Chan-Than it is abundant. Soda is found in great plenty along the banks of the eastern branch of the Indus, and in the district of Nubra.[68] Lead and iron are found in pits, and other mountain districts remote from Le', and copper mines are said to have been discovered towards Kashmir. Gold is frequently found in the rivers of Chan-Than, and it was also discovered in the sand of the Shayuk.[69] In some parts of Chan-Than a superstitious belief prevails, that lumps of native gold, occasionally found in the mountains, belong to the Genii of the spot, who would severely punish the human appropriation of their treasures."[70]

Population of Ladakh : Ladakh is divided into two districts, Leh and Kargil. Leh is dominated by Buddhists whereas Kargil is by Shia Muslims. In 1820, when Moorcroft visited Ladakh, he estimated Ladakh population in between 1,50,000-1,80,000 as he remarks :

"The population of Le', as of the country at large, is of the Tibetan stock, but a very considerable number of Kashmirians are domesticated at Le', and a mixed race has originated from them and the women of the country, tend Argands[71]. The Kashmiris and their descendants are engaged in commerce, and the lower orders follow the business of butchers, cooks, and petty retailers. There are also some Turani merchants, and in the lands of Chushut[72] a colony of Balti Mohammedans is established. The whole population of Ladakh may be between one hundred and fifty thousand and one hundred and eighty thousand of which two-thirds, at least are females."[73]

Custom of Ladakh : In Ladakh, polyandary was prevalent in the past among Buddhists, now this practice has been gradually stopped in urban areas, however one can acknowledge the same in remote villages of Ladakh. Moorcroft made the following report :

"They have some singular domestic institutions. When an eldest son marries. The property of his father descends to him, and he is charged with the maintenance of his parents. They may continue to live with him if he and his wife please, if not, he provides them with a separate dwelling. A younger son is usually made a Lama. Should there be more brothers, and they agree to the arrangement, the juniors become inferior husbands to the wife of the elder : all the children, however, are considered as belonging to the head of the family. The younger brothers have no authority, they wait upon the elder as his servants, and can be turned out of doors at his pleasure. On the death of the eldest brother his property, authority and widow devolve upon his next brother."[74]

Dress and ornaments of Ladakhis : Ladakhi Goncha is a common dress. Regarding ornaments, Ladakhi men do not wear many ornaments, however, women wear various kinds of ornaments. As Moorcroft made the following details :

"The severity of the climate renders the use of warm clothing. The men wear close dresses of cloth made in the country. The Lama wear red or yellow[75]. The poorer classes wear the cloth as it comes from the loom. The men wear caps of the same general shape for all ranks, and differing in the material only. That of the Khalun, as of the other chief officers, was made of velvet-silk velvet of Russian fabric. The caps of the lower classes are generally made of black cloth; they are shorter, and the tops fall over one side or other, whilst those of persons of rank are erect. The dress of the women consists of a jacket with sleeves fitting, though loosely, to the shape, with a collar half way up the neck. Continuous from the jacket fall bands forming the frame-work of a petticoat, the spaces between being filled up with narrow stripes of various colours. Both sexes wear stockings, boots, the soles of which are of thick leather, like those of the Chinese, whilst the leg part is either of leather or of strong stiff cloth.

The men do not wear many ornaments—the principal consisting of large ear-rings and a small box of gold, containing some sacred text, which is suspended from the neck. The women are more gaily decorated, but their chief ornaments are the head, lappet, a stiff necklace, ear-rings."[76]

Ladakhi diet : Ladakhis in general have nutritious diet. Tea has an important role which they take three times a day with or after meal. According to Moorcroft :

> "The diet of the Ladakhis, and the Tibetans[77] generally, is nutritious and wholesome, and is remarkable for the prominent share which is taken in it by tea. All classes of Tibetans eat three meals a day. The first consists of tea, the second of tea, or of meal porridge if that cannot be afforded; the third of meal, rice, vegetables, and bread by the upper, and soup, porridge, and bread by the lower classes. The Tibetans never drink plain water. The wealthier drink grape juice and water, or sharbats; the poorer a beverage called Chang, which is made from barley."[78]

The Government of Ladakh : Raja had real power, Khalun—Prime Minister, Nuna Khalun—Deputy Prime Minister, Lom-pa—Chief Municipal and Governor of Le'[79], Chug-zut—treasurer etc. all these look after the administration. Moorcroft says :

> "The Raja is an individual of real power. The business of the government is administered by the Khalun, or prime minister, assisted by the Nuna Khalum, or deputy, the Lom-pa, or chief municipal and military officer, and governor of Le', the Chug-zut, or treasurer, who is a lama, and the Banka, or master of the horse. The administrator of the districts and town is entrusted to inferior Khaluns or Tan-zins or Rajas. A second Chug-zut is the superintendent of customs, and the business of the magistracy is discharged by officers called Nar-pas, and by the head men of the villages."[80]

Religion of Ladakh : In Ladakh Buddhism is the main religion, however Islam and Christianity both are flourishing very well. Moorcroft describes :

"I must refer for an authentic view of the religion of Ladakh, which, like that of Tibet worship Buddha, under a peculiar hierarchy. Every family in which there is more than one son furnishes a Lama or Gelum[81], who is at once a coenobite and a family priest, attached to a monastic institution under a Lama, and ordinarily living amongst the people, and conducting the rites of their daily worship in their own houses, in which a chamber is usually appropriated to an image and an attendant priest. The chief Lamas are appointed from Lassa[82]. There are also establishments of religious females, called chumas or Anis[83]. They by no means confine themselves to strictly religious duties, but take an active share in cultivation of the lands, the rearing of sheep, and goats, and the fiscal and political administration of the country."[84]

Shawl Wool : An Important article for Trade of Ladakh : Today Pashmina or fine shawl wool is exported from Ladakh to Kashmir and its neighbouring states. In olden days hundred loads were annually exported to Kashmir and small part was exported to Lahul, Chamba, and Kulu. Moorcroft remarks :

"The commerce of Ladakh is of no great value. Its chief consideration, however, arises from its centrical situation, by which it becomes the great thoroughfare for an active commercial intercourse between Tibet, Turkistan, China and even Russia on one hand, and Kashmir, the Panjab and the plains of Hindustan on the other. One of the most important articles of the trade of Ladakh is shawl wool, of which it forms, in some degree, the source, but in a still greater. The extrepot between the countries whence the wool is chiefly supplied, Rodokh (or Rudog) and Chan-Than[85] and that in which it is consumed, Kashmir."[86]

Hot springs in Nubra valley : In Nubra valley at Panamik village one my see hot springs. In Tibetan medicine it is used for patients who have body pain. Moorcroft describes :

"The hot springs, issued from the face of part of the mountain ridge. The openings were small, and the water flowed gently and equably; it was quite clear, of the same temperature, of 167°, at mouths distant two hundred yards from each other : each vent was surrounded by a bed of tufa, lined with a yellow crust. A leathery conferva grew in the currents where not above 110°, the upper leaves of which were covered with a yellow deposit : the water was wholly without taste or smell."[87]

Fort of Sakti : At the entrance of Sakti village one can see 'Sakti Fort' in ruined condition. It is said that this fort was dismantled by the Kalmaks[88] force in 1620 A.D. Moorcroft says :

"Moving on the 30th (July 1821) we soon came to the straggling houses which constituted the village of Sakti. On the face of the mountain, forming part of the eastern limit of the valley, stood the fort of Sakti, a pile of buildings, surrounded by a wall and towers, the whole built of granite blocks cemented with clay: the houses were unroofed, but the walls were mostly standing. This fortress was evidently intended to command the northern entrance of the valley, but it was taken and dismantled by the Kalmaks nearly two centuries ago, and has never been repaired."[89]

Lakes in Ladakh : In Ladakh one can see many small and big lakes in the high mountain range. Moorcroft says :

"Beyond the village of Muglib the river descended in two small streams from the mountains either hand, which must be the seat of its source, on the bank of a small lake called Tswar. Las Marma, this lake, about three-fourths of a mile in circumference collecting the waters of the mountains bounding the valley of Do-mo-chu gives rise to a small stream, which runs into the river of Durgukh[90] near the village of that name. The lake Pangkung[91] (had) no appearance of fish. The water was extremely salt (and) perfectly clear."[92]

Large herds of Kiangs beyond Chu-sul : In the neighbouring deserts of Chu-sul, one can see large herds of Kiangs. Moorcroft also saw these and remarks :

"We saw many large herds of the Kiang, and I made numerous attempts to bring one down, but with invariably bad success. Some were wounded, but not sufficiently to check their speed, and they quickly bounded up the rocks, where it was impossible to follow. They would afford excellent sport to four or five men well mounted, but a single individual has no change. The Kiang allows his pursuer to approach no nearer than five or six hundred yards; he then trots off, turns, looks and waits until you are almost within distance, when he is off again. If fired at he is frightened and scampers off altogether. The Chan-than people sometimes catch them by snares, sometimes shoot them. From all I have seen of the animal, I should pronounce him to be neither a horse nor as ass. His shape is as much like that of the one as the other; but his cry is more like braying than neighing. The prevailing colour is a light reddish-chesnut; but the nose, the underpart of the lower-jaw and neck, the belly and legs, are white; the mane is dum and erect. The ears are moderately long; the tail bare and reaching a little below the hock; the height is about fourteen hands. The form, from the fore to the hind-leg and feet, to a level with the back is more square than that of an ass, his back is less straight, and there is a dip behind the withers, and rounding of the crapper, which is more like the shape of the horse; his neck is also more erect and arched than that of the ass."[93]

In conclusion Moorcroft arrived Ladakh in 1820 via Manali. He stayed here for two years, during this period he visited Nubra, Chang-Thang, and many central parts of Ladakh. Later, wrote a book 'Travels in the Himalayan provinces of Hindustan and the Panjab, Ladakh and Kashmir; in Peshawar, Kabul, Kunduz and Bokhara'.

Notes and References

1. Bara Lacha ridge or called Paralassa chin, and makes its elevation 16,500 feet. Cf. : Moorcroft, William and Trebeck, George : Travels in the Himalayan Provinces of Hindustan and the Panjab; in Ladakh and Kashmir; in Peshawar, Kabul, Kunduz, and Bokhara,' Sagar Pub., New Delhi, Vol. I, 1971 (Reprinted).
2. *Ibid*; 215-16.
3. *Ibid*; 217.
4. *Ibid*; 224.
5. *Ibid.*
6. *Ibid*; 225.
7. Tung-lung : Tag-lang-la.
8. Moorcroft, William; *op. cit.* : 225.
9. *Ibid*; 226-27.
10. Mir Izzet Ullah : He accompanied Moorcroft Mission to Ladakh in 1820.

11. Moorcroft, William; *op. cit.* : 229-30.
12. Tsimma Punchik : Raja name can spelled as .... Phunchok.
13. Khaga Tan-zin : Ka-ga stan zin.
14. Khaga Tan-zin; Cf. Ref. No. 13.
15. Moorcroft, William; *op. cit.* : 232-33.
16. *Ibid*, 234-35.
17. Uk-shi - Up-shi.
18. Le' = Leh.
19. Sinh Kha bab = Singha Khabab = Indus.
20. Moorcroft, William; *op. cit.* : 236-37.
21. Marsilla - Marsilang.
22. Sheh = Shey.
23. Changa = tsang-dag
24. Gelums = Ge-longs.
25. Takna = Tag-na.
26. Mashu = Matho
27. Yuma river = Indus river.
28. Thik-se = Thiksey.
29. ampha = Gom-pa = monastery.
30. Chu-shut = Chut-shud.
31. Moorcroft, William; *op. cit.* : 240-41.
32. Ranjit Sinh = Ranjeet Singh
33. Moorcroft, William; *op. cit.* : 242-43.
34. Chu-shut = Chu-shod.
35. Moorcroft, William; *op. cit.* : 244.
36. *Ibid.*, 244-45.
37. Khalun = Kalon.
38. Mir = Mir Izzet Ullah.
39. Moorcroft, William; *op. cit.* : 246-55.
40. Ranjit Sinh = Ranjeet Singh.
41. Triva Tandu = Tashi Tondup.
42. Moorcroft, William; *op. cit.* : 249-50.
43. Lassa = Lhasa.
44. Moorcroft, William; *op. cit.* : 252-53.

45. Le' = Leh.
46. Abdul Latif = A pupil of Shah Nyas Khan.
47. Gardokh = Gartok.
48. Moorcroft, William; *op. cit.* : 253-54.
49. *Ibid*, 254-55.
50. Lom-pa = Lon-po.
51. Le' = Leh.
52. Moorcroft, William; *op. cit.* : 255-56.
53. *Ibid.*, 256-57.
54. Roodokh = Rudokh = Ru-thog.
55. Chan-than = Chang-Thang.
56. Moorcroft, William; *op. cit.* : 258.
57. *Ibid.*, 260.
58. *Ibid.*, 269.
59. *Ibid.*, 274.
60. *Ibid.*, 272-73.
61. *Ibid.*, 288-93.
62. *Ibid.*, 295.
63. *Ibid.*, 295-97.
64. *Ibid.*, 306-08.
65. Chan-Than = Chang-Thang.
66. Moorcroft, William; *op. cit.* : 309-10.
67. *Ibid.*, 312-13.
68. Nabra = Nubra.
69. Shayuk = Shayok.
70. Moorcroft, William; *op. cit.* : 313-14.
71. Argands = Argons.
72. Chushut = Cho-shod.
73. Moorcroft, William; *op. cit.* : 319-20.
74. *Ibid.*, 321-22.
75. The Lama wear red or yellow : Lama wear yellow dress during ritual ceremonies, other time they wear red dress.
76. Moorcroft, William; *op. cit.* : 322-27.
77. Tibetans = Buddhists.

78. Moorcroft, William; *op. cit.* : 321-22.
79. Le' = Leh.
80. Moorcroft, William; *op. cit.* : 334-35.
81. Gelum = Gelong.
82. Lassa = Lhasa.
83. Chummas or Anis = Chomo.
84. Moorcroft, William; *op. cit.* : 340.
85. Chan-Than = Chang-Thang.
86. Moorcroft, William; *op. cit.* : 346-47.
87. *Ibid.*, 405-06.
88. Kalmaks = Mongol force.
89. Moorcroft, William; *op. cit.* : 426-27.
90. Durgukh = Durbugh.
91. Pangkung = Pang gong.
92. Moorcroft, William; *op. cit.* : 432-35.
93. *Ibid*, 442-43.

12

Travel Diary of Captain Knight in Ladakh

Travel diary is simply a source of enjoyment for readers, but for writer it is the description of his real adventure. Keeping in view to the above fact I am here covering the experiences of Captain Knight who visited Ladakh during summer 1860.

Contingent for Ladakh : During 1860 Ladakh was popularly known as Little Thibet. Captain Knight, therefore, used Little Tibet for Ladakh. He marched along with his contigent for Ladakh from Kashmir at the morning of 27th July 1860. His contigent was looking like a train in which he had coolies, helpers, servants etc. He himself writes about this in the following way :

> "We found that our possessions required fourteen coolies for their transport. Our own immediate effect took four, viz. bedding two, guns one, and clothes & C, one; the kitchen required four more; tent one, charpoys one, servants' reserve supply of food one, brandy one, plank for table and tent poles one, and last though not least, the twelve ducks took up the services of the fourteenth all to themselves. The rest of our train consisted of the faithful Rajoo, who came entirely at his own request to see a new country, the two servants, the sepoy, and the coolie's mate, who was to act as guide, carry small matters and make himself generally useful."[1]

Marmots near the Zojila : I several times passed through Zojila in between 1981-86, but unable to see marmots, however, saw them near Tag-lang pass and North polo beyond Kherdung la. Captain Knight was fortunate enough to come across some marmots near Zoji-la. He described about this beautiful animal in the following lines :

"About five kos on our journey we halted to let the kitchen come up, and had our breakfast on the snow in the company of a select party of marmots. The little creatures appeared to live in great peace and seclusion here, for they let us up, in their ignorance of fire-arms, to within thirty yards of them before scuttling into their habitations. They were all dressed in blacklish brown suits of long thick fur, and considering that they live in snow for at least eight months out of twelve, they appeared not the least too warmly clothed. As we went by they used to come out and sit up on their hind legs, with their fore paws hanging helplessly over their paunches, while, with a shrill discordant cry, they bid us good-morning and then hurried back to their houses again."[2]

Mud Fort in Dras : Dras is the first village on way to Ladakh. Knight reached here on 1st August 1860. Here he found flat roofed houses with a mud fort. He remarks :

"We reached Dras, a little assemblage of flat-roofed houses, with a mud fort about half a mile from it, in the valley. This was built with four bastions and a ditch scarped with paving-stones, which surrounded it on all sides except one, where it was naturally defended by the torrent. On the road we passed a curious bridge, built entirely of rope manufactured from twigs of trees. The cables thus formed were swung across the torrent, from piles of loose stones, in a most scientific way, though not one calculated to inspire confidence in any traveller with weak nerves who might have to trust himself to its support. It appeared, nevertheless, a most serviceable structure and was decidedly picturesque."[3]

Ancient Male and Female stone carved figures : There are 10th century A.D. Buddhist stone carved figures outside the Dras[4] village. Knight explained about these figures in this way :

"Outside the village, we came upon two curious old stones, standing about six feet high, upright and carved in the way we had already seen at the ruins of Pandau and elsewhere. These stones were of irregular form, and carved on three sides, and the designs, through much worn, were distinctly traceable. They represented apparently, a male and female figure, standing about five feet high, and surrounded by three smaller figures each. Like all the other sculptured figures we had seen they were innocent of clothes, with the exception of the rope, or very scant drapery, which ran across their ancles and up either side to the shoulders."[5]

Yak hair women bags carried salt to Kashmir : In olden days Ladakhis did not cut their hair and used to make pig tails from their long hairs. They covered their heads by Chinese skull-caps and often employed in conveying salt from Ladakh to Kashmir market. Captain Knight says :

"The few travellers we met during our march were flat-nosed, heavy-looking creatures, with Chinese skull-caps and pig-tails, and were employed in conveying salt to Cashmere[6], packed in bags of woven hair, and laden on cows and asses as weird and strage-looking as their owners. We also encountered an original looking gold-washing association of five, who were wending their way towards the snow with their wooden implements. They were all also weighted with bags of grain, to keep them alive during their search. Their labour consists in sifting the fine sand which comes down in the snow-torrents, charged with minute particles of gold; and the proceeds, from the appearance of 'the trade', would not seem to be very great. They say it amounts only to a few annas a day, but would probably not allow to the full amount for fear of being taxed."[7]

Primitive specimen of a smoking apparatus : After passing through Dras, Knight came across a primitive apparatus which consisted a dab of mud struck in a hole of a tree. He says :

"We saw the most primitive specimen of a smoking apparatus probably ever invented. It consisted of a dab of mud stuck in a hole of a tree, about five feet from the ground. Two small sticks, inserted in this from above and below and then withdrawn had evidently served to form the smoke passage; while the bowl as evidently had been fashioned by the simple impression of a Thibetian Thumb, the whole forming, for the use of needy travellers, a permanent and satisfactory a public pipe as could well have been devised. It had just been in requisition before we passed, for a small quantity of newly-burned tobacco lay in the bowl; and a fresh patch of clay on the mouth piece had probably been added, either in the way of general repairs or by some extra-fastidious traveller, who preferred having a private mouth-piece of his own."[8]

Chungun, a little oasis with three or four houses

After Dras Captain Knight came to a little oasis of about five acres of cultivated land. He says :

"Chungun, a little oasis of about five acres of standing barley, with three or four flat-roofed houses dotted about it in the usual Tartar style of architecture. It also boasted four poplar-trees, standing in a stiff and reserved little row, evidently in proud consciousness of their family importance among such rugged, treeless, iron."[9]

Hundas : A perfect little Oasis : Hundas village also had little cultivated land and planted in the neatest way. He remarks :

> "The village Hundas was another most perfect little oasis. It was only about five or six acres in extent, under the frowning mountain, and was terraced and planted in the neatest and most economical way imaginable. The fields were beautifully clean, and were quaintly adorned in many instances by huge blocks of rock from the mountain above, bigger considerably than the whole of the houses of the village put together."[10]

Primitive Race : Leaving Kargil fort, Captain Knight reached at Pushkoom village on 4th August 1860. Here he found natives who were collecting their crops. The ladies, he noticed wore sheep and goat skins and altogether looked, primitive race. He writes :

> "I found the natives hard at work collecting their crops of wheat and barley, and stowing them away, generally upon the flat tops of their houses. They seemed altogether a peaceful primitive race; but, although their ground appears in first-rate order, they themselves are uncultivated and dirty in the extreme. The ladies, I am sorry to say, are even rather worse in this matter than the gentlemen. The female costume consists generally of robes of sheep and goat skins thrown across the shoulders; while a long tail of twisted worsted plaits, looking like a collection of old-fashioned bell-ropes, forms the chief decoration. This is attached to the back hair, and hangs down quite to the heels, where it terminates in a large tuft, with tassels and divers ball of worsted attached to it."[11]

New Description of Monuments : Captain Knight on 6th August 1860 came to Shargol, a Buddhist village. Here he saw series of chod-tens[12] looked as tomb like buildings. He says :

> "The village of Shergol, where we halted for breakfast. Here we found ourselves fairly among the Buddhists, and saw an entirely new description of monuments connected with religion, from we had yet encountered. The most striking objects were a series of tomb-like buildings without entrances, and adorned on all sides by the most hideous effigies rudely executed in coloured mud."[13]

Shooting Tour : In those days Ladakh was famous for shooting. Every year famous hunters came here for shooting game. At Shargol Captain Knight met a hunter who was returning from a shooting tour. He explains :

> "Here we met wandering Englishman, who was wending his way back to the valley. He was returning from a shooting tour, was all alone, and appeared to have had very hard work indeed of it, if his face and hands and generally dilapidated appearance might be taken as a criterion. He appeared to be a thorough sportsman, and had bagged several head of large game, which he showed us. They were principally a kind of wild sheep with enormous heads and horns, each of his trophies being almost a coolie load in itself."[14]

Colossal figure with four arms on rock : At Mulbe one can see a massive rock standing figure of Chamba resembles to Gandhar art. Captain Knight explains about this figure in the following way :

> "At a place called Moulwee[15] we came to a curious block of massive rock standing close beside the path, with one of the red-topped houses built into its side. Above this was a colossal figure with four arms rudely cut on the face of the rock, and above all was perched an implement, something after the fashion of a Mrs. Gamp's umbrella of large proportions, together with sundry sticks and rags, which seem to be the common style of religious decoration in these parts. The figure was about eighteen feet high, the lower extremities being hidden behind the building at the base of the rock. It resembled in some measure the sculptures occasionally seen among Hindoo temples."[16]

Supreme Being : In every Buddhist village one can see Mani walls which covered by 'Om Pani Padme Hum' and other related Mantas inscribed on the stone plates at the entrance. Captain Knight also saw such Mani walls as he remarks :

> "I ascertained that the words carved upon the stones were 'Om Mani Panee'[17], and meant, as far as I could make out, 'the Supreme Being'. As the old gentleman repeated the mystic syllables, he bobbed and scraped towards a strange looking monument close by, in an object deprecatory way, as if in extreme awe of its presence[18]. Such were the quantities of the inscribed stones about this place, that in one long wall I estimated there must have been upward of 3,000."[19]

Lamayuru : A headquarter of Lamas : Lamayuru monastery belongs to Drigung Ka-gyud pa order situated at the base of Fotoola (Po tu la) pass. It is one of the oldest monastery of Ladakh. Knight explains about its location in the following way :

> "Lamieroo[20], as its name would seem to imply, appears to have been a headquarters of the Lamas and their religion. It contains a curious monastery, or Lamaserai, built upon the extreme top ledge of a precipice of concrete stone, and at its base (some hundred feet below) the habitations which constitute the village are also perched on pinnacles of rock and scattered about, often in the most unlikely spot imaginable."[21]

Temples of Lamayuru : In each temple of the monastery one may noticed that Buddhist statues and monuments are normally placed in front of the entrance door. According to Knight :

> "The temple we found a small square room with a gallery round it, from which were suspended dingy-looking Chinese banners, flowers, &c., and at one end were about twenty idols of various designs, seated in a row staring straight before them, and covered with offerings of Indian corn, yellow flowers, butter, &c. They were for the most part dressed in Chinese fashion, and in the dusky light had certainly a queer weired-looking appearance about them. The service (by particular desire) began by three of the most unctuous of the Lamas squatting down on some planked spaces before the divinities, and raising a not unmusical chaunt, accompanying themselves at the same time with a pair of cymbals, which two large double-sided tom-toms or drums gradually insinuated themselves into the melody. These were each fixed on one long leg and were beaten with a curved stick, muffled at the end. The performance of the cymbals was particularly good, and the changes of time they introduced formed the chief feature of the music, and was rather pleasing than otherwise. The service as it drew to a close, was joined by a duet upon two enormous brass instruments like speaking-trumpets grown out of all decent proportions; they were about five feet long, and were placed on the ground during the performance."[22]

Perag a woman head-dress : Ladakhi Buddhist married woman often wear curious head-dress. Captain Knight describes :

> "The women here, wore a curious head-dress, differing from anything of the kind we had before seen. It consisted of a broad

ban extending from the forehead to the waist behind, and studded thickly with large coarse turquoises. These generally decrease in size from the forehead, where there is a larger turquoise than the others, down to the waist, and where the hair ends, it is joined into a long worsted tail terminating at the heels. Some of these bands must be of considerable value, but the proprietors, although otherwise in complete rags, will not part with them for any consideration."[23]

Kha-la-tse : A village of fifteen huts : Kha-la-tse is a beautiful village consists walnut and apricot trees. Knight reached here on 9th August 1860 and explained about this as :

"Kulchee[24], a tidy little village of fifteen huts, situated in an oasis of apricot and walnut-trees."[25]

Lantza inscriptions on the Mani wall : On the Mani walls one can see inscribed stones of Tibetan and Lantza character, Knight writes :

"The character most common on the inscribed stones, and one of those now in actual use, Romeeque; the square character on the stones, is obsolete, and is called Lantza[26]; while a third character, Tyeeque. Khurjidal, would pass through the land, and inspecting these mounds of inscribed stones, would write down the names of all those who had contributed to the heap. Whatever, it was, all those who had contributed their share towards its dissemination, by adding stones to the mounds, were certain of future rewards, while those who had omitted to do so were as equally certain of punishment."[27]

Tax : When Knight visited Ladakh, he noticed that each villager of Ladakh had to pay certain amount to Maharajah Treasury as tax. Here he explains :

"Regarding the state of the people here he told me that each house paid a tax of seven rupees per annum to the Maharajah. This, for the entire village, would only give 105 rupees per annum towards the enrichment of the Treasury."[28]

City of the Dead : Knight came across the Leh, the only town of Ladakh from the distance assumed as it would be a city of the dead. He writes :

"The town of Ladakh, although in a commercial point of view by no means a flourishing-looking settlement, was, as far as picturesqueness was concerned, everything that could be desired. It was built in the style so popular throughout the country—on pinnacles of rock, and such out of the way positions as seemed, of all others the least adapted for building purposes—immediately outside the town, occupying a sort of bason among the surrounding mountains, was what might fairly be called a 'city of the dead'. It was of considerable extent, and was formed of group of the numerous monumental buildings."[29]

Buddhist Custom : Here in Ladakhi Buddhist family had a custom to offer a boy or girl to concern monastery to become monk or nun. Captain Knight writes :

"The Lamas are provided, by the custom of dedicating in every family of two or more, one to that office; should there be a number of girls in a family, all those that do not marry become nuns, and adopt the male attire of red and yellow. The nuns, however, seem to be by no means kept in confinement; they work in the fields. Among other curious information that each man is entitled to the luxury of a wife all to himself, but that a family of four or five brothers frequently have but one between them, and that the system is productive of no ill-feeling whatever among the different members."[30]

Leh Bazaar : In olden days, Leh was one of the popular mandi of Central Asian countries. Traders from different parts of these countries came here for trading purpose. Knight says :

"In the afternoon we explored the Bazaar, where we found abundance of dogs, dirt, and idlers, but little else. What little there was in the way of merchandise the proprietors seemed utterly indifferent about disposing of and after visiting a few shops we went away in disgust. The people were a mixture of Cashmeeries, Chinese, Tartars, Bangalees, and Indians of all sorts and sects, and more idle good for nothing looking scoundrels I never laid eyes on."[31]

Hemis Monastery : This monastery is built on the base of rock outside Leh town surrounded by poplar trees. Captain Knight remarks :

"The monastery we found situated in a beautifully-wooded valley, thickly planted, and having a dashing little torrent foaming through the centre. It was built as usual, on the very face of the rock, and towering above it was an airy fort. We inspected the monastery, and were waited upon by half-a-dozen Lamas who showed us through various temples of the gods. Originally containing some two hundred Lamas, its numbers had now dwindled down, by their account, to fifteen or sixteen.

They owned to having treasure in the monastery to the amount of three lakhs of rupees (£ 30,000). Some of the divinities were, however, provided with vestments of cloth of gold, and were seated upon thrones, studded with would be precious stones. Others were accommodated with large silver bowls, placed on pedestais, filled to the brim with 'ghee', or rancid butter, and unless blest with inordinate appetites, these, from their enormous size. We were altogether conducted through four temples, each inhabited by a number of Chinese figures, seated in state, with offerings of corn, flour, rice and ghee, &c., before them, and these were generally served in valuable cups of China, and precious metals. Hanging from the ceiling and the walls around were scrolls, decorated in the Chinese fashion, with figures of tightly-robed."[32]

Prayer Wheels : In Ladakh at the entrance of the monastery one can often see big prayer wheels, besides number of small one around the walls of temples. Today I have noticed one or two big prayer wheels at the entrance of each Buddhist village in Ladakh and Leh district in particular. On 17th August 1860, Captain Knight also noticed prayer wheel at Hemis monastery. He remarks :

"The most curious things in the place, however, were the praying wheels, which I here saw for the first time. They were little wooden drums, covered round the sides with leather, and fitted vertically in niches in the walls. A spindle running through the centre, enabled them to revolve at the slightest push. In one place we came upon a praying-wheel, turned by water. Sometimes the people carry portable wheels."[33]

Wild Animal : Ibex : In Ladakh in the high mountains we can see Ibex in good number. They usually graze together in a group of 6 to 20. Knight also came across a group of half dozen Ibex when he went to the high ranges of mountains beyond the Hemis monastery. He says :

"Having attained the greatest height actually attainable, we spied quietly grazing about half a mile off, some half dozen little animals, which my 'sportsman' declared to be Ibex. On attaining our hardly-earned post of vantage, however, there was no sign of our friends, but, suddenly, on the mountain below us a herd of about five and—twenty more appeared to our delighted view.

Wall painting in Lamayuru Monastery : In every big monastery of Ladakh is decorated by beautiful wall paintings. In olden days these paintings were made by stone colours. Nowadays chemical colours have been used. I have seen many monasteries in Ladakh and have come to this conclusion that the old wall paintings of many monasteries have been destroyed by rain. Therefore, necessary steps should be taken in order to preserve them instead to re-paint them by chemical colours. Knight also acknowledge such paintings in Lamayuru monastery. He says :

> "The principal decorative work was being carried on by a Chinese-looking, pigtailed artist, evidently not a local celebrity, who was embellishing the walls most profusely with scenes, portrayed in the purest style of pre-Raphaelite colouring. The figures in these had only been flourished with flesh-coloured spots where their faces were to be, and the foreign 'pigtail' was employed, seated on a high platform, in furnishing them with features and casts of expression in accordance with the spirit of scenes which they helped to composed. This he did certainly with very great skill, and the operation was a most interesting one to watch. The floor was covered with pigments and materials of all kinds, and the little community, in the midst of the surrounding apparent solitude, were working away like a hive of bees. This appeared to have a hive-like dislike also of the approach of a stranger, and one old Lama, with a twisted mat of hair erected on the top of his head-a drone of the hive-took a particular dislike to me."[35]

Statues in Lamayuru Monastery : Statues such as Padmasambhava, Avalokitesvara, Dolmas, Buddha, Bodhisattvas are the other sense of decoration. In Ladakh in every monastery one can see them at one side of temple. Captain Knight also saw these, but, he did not know the name of these, however, explained about them in the following way :

> "In the inner part of the temple was a large coloured statue, with eight arms, and two-and twenty hands. The heads were placed in trees, looking every way, in the shape of a pyramid—a single head crowning the whole. One of the hands held a bow, but the implements contained in the others were entirely Buddhist in character. Behind this figure was a star, with innumerable radiating arms from the centre, while from the points of the figures were five other rows of hands, continuing the star-like circle. These were in half relief on the wall, the figure itself standing out some feet, as if to receive and appropriate the offerings of corn, flowers oil, etc."[36]

Reception by Kardar and Thanadar of Kargil : Captain Knight and his party after visiting Leh and Hemis monastery returned to Kashmir valley. On 20th August 1860 Captain arrived at Pushkoom where he was received by Kardar and Thanadar of Kargil. In his honour Ladakhi dance was also organised by them. Here follows the description :

> "We were now received in due form by the Kardar, and Thanadar of Kargil[37], not to mention the Wazeer or Vizier of Pashkoom. This dignitary had formerly been its Rajah, but during Gulab Singh's time[38] was reduced to post of Vizier, or Prime Minister to nobody in particular, with a salary of some thirty rupees per annum. Where our last camp was pitched, we found a circle of natives congregated, some standing, some sitting on their haunches, but all accompanying to the full extent of their voices—at the same time clapping time with their hands—the efforts of a band of six or seven artists on the pipe and tabor, who kept up a quavering strain of what they doubtless believed to be music. To the united melody thus produced, a string of a dozen or so of ladies, in their full war paint, were decorously going through the monotonous evolutions of a popular dance, waving their arms about, gesticulating, and at the same time lingering, as it were, over the ground, and comporting themselves in that staid, yet fitfully lively way, they were attired most picturesquely, and evidently in their very fullest ball costume, so that we were fortunate in hitting upon such a good opportunity of seeing their gala manners and customs. They all wore caps of some kind, either of a small close-fitting pattern, like a fex, or in the shape of a large, and very ultra scotch cap, black, and very baggy; these were hung round with little silver ornaments, something in the shape of wine labels for decanters, but studded with turquoises, some of them, also, wore brooches, generally formed of three cornelians, or turquoises, in a row. The broad bands of turqoise, worn usually on the forehead, were for the time disrated from their post of honour, and were suspended instead from the nap of the neck, over a square piece of stiff cloth, embroidered with strings of red beads. Round the shoulders and hanging low, in order to show off turqoises, lumps of amber, and other family jewels, were the sheep skin cloaks, inseparable from Thibetian female costume; they were, however, of larger size than those of every day life, and were gorgeously decorated

> outside in red and blue, the fur merely appearing at the edges. Below this, everything merged in some mysterious way into the variegated sheep skin boots of the country, also decorated with red, blue, and yellow cloth patterns on the instep. These bore a very conspicuous position in the dance, as the ladies, contrary to the principles of modern art, were continually regarding and showing forth the aforesaid boots, as they glided about, and pattern the time to the well-marked music. The dance was altogether much more pleasing than the Indian nach, and the ladies, in spite of their savage jewellery, and rude manner, were more womanly and respectable than their gauzy, be-ringed and bare-footed southern rivals."[39]

Polo Game : In Ladakh Polo was very popular. This game was in fact came here from Baltistan. Ladakhis during summer season often played in Dras, Leh and in every open ground surrounding to the respected villages. Captain Knight also got chance to acknowledge this native game. Here he explains :

> "To my astonishment, some fifty or sixty Thibetians here assembled, each provided with a veritable hockey stick, not on foot, however, but each man mounted on his own little mountain pony, and prepared to play a downright game of hockey on horseback. In the centre of the battle-field, between the two 'sides', the pipes and tabors forming the band took their station, and each time the wooden ball of contention was struck off, set up a flourish to animate the players. The Thibetians, however, required no such artificial excitement, but set to work with an energy and spirit quite refreshing to behold, and the scene soon became most animated and amusing. The Thibetians, unlike Englishmen under similar circumstances appeared to think the more clothes they had on the better, and in their long woollen coats and trousers, and their huge sheepskin boots, they quite overshadowed the wiry little horses they bestrode. Besides having to carry all this weight, the ponies most unfairly, came in also for all the shinning; but in spite of these disadvantages, they performed their parts to admiration, dashing about in the most reckless manner, at the instigation of their riders, and jostling and knocking against one another in a way that would have disgusted any other pony in the world. Conspicuous among the crowd of riders, was the thirty-rupee Prime Minister, who on a most diminutive little animal, charged

about in a way he never could have condescended to do, he had the misfortune to have still remained a Rajah. Each time that the ball was sent into the goal, the striker, picking it up dexterously, without dismounting, came again at full speed down the course, the band struck up, and throwing the ball into the air, he endeavoured to strike it as far as possible in the direction of the adverse party. Behind him, at best pace, came his own side, and a desperate collision appeared the inevitable result; however, not a single man was unhorsed during the entire struggle, nor were there any violent conclusions, or accidents of any kind on either side. The men rode very short, and their clumsy boots, stuck through the heavy stirrup-irons, gave them a ludicrous appearance, which was little indicative of the firm seat and active part they displayed in the games."[40]

Bridge of Rope : In olden days Ladakh had many rope bridges some of them still can be seen in Zangskar Tehsil of Kargil district. Captain Knight gave beautiful explanation about this bridge :

"An unexpected obstacle then presented itself in the shape of a bridge of rope of a very considerable length, crossing the torrent. It was formed of the twigs of trees, and being in an unpleasantly dilapidated condition, the passage was a matter of some difficulty if not danger. To save the direct strain a number of the villagers took up their position to distend the side ropes, and having to get over the outstretched legs of these officious aids, made the affair a very much more nervous proceeding than it would otherwise have been. The lowness of the side-ropes, and the oscillation of the rickety structure rendered the feat altogether a rather more amusing performer, and I was not sorry to reach the opposite shore. On the arrival of the coolies, they all hung back, and regarded the machine with utter astonishment."[41]

Sankoo village had greenery and was good population. Here Captain found a new kind of bridge made of trees. He says :

"Arriving at Sankoo, we found it a well-wooded thinly-inhabited valley, about a kos and a half in length. Here we had a new specimen of bridge architecture to pass. It was formed simply enough of two crooked trunks of trees."[42]

Avalanches : As some villages are located just below the high rocks, sometimes were been suffered heavily by avalanches. Knight during his journey to Ladakh when came across to Tesroo acknowledged such incident, he remarks :

> "Some sixteen miles from Sankoo to Tesroo, or Sooroo, at the foot of the grandest snowy range we had yet encountered. The path led us over a gigantic fall of rocks, evidently the deposits formed by successive and destructive avalanches. In some parts the traces were quite fresh, the rocks being rent and uptorn in a wonderful way; and, in one place, we passed the ground where two villages had been entirely overwhelmed by an avalanche, the entire population of twenty five having been killed in the ruins."[43]

Blue Sky : Captain Knight enjoyed fresh air of Ladakh and beautiful scenic appearance one after the other valleys during his journey. The noble mountain of pure unbroken snow and blue sky attracted him most. He describes :

> "In the finest and freshest of morning air, we suddenly opened upon a noble mountain of pure unbroken snow, rearing its head proudly into the blue sky among a train of countries, not so noble nor so purely, whitely, clad as itself, but still arrayed in robes of glistening snow. Here the path emerged from the side of the rugged mountain torrent, and about two kos over fine turfy grass brought us to within some three miles of Sooroo."[44]

Revenue : In Ladakh, villagers grow only one crop, thus the grain produce out of that stored for long winters; for the winter subsistence they collect fire wood and store them outside. Not only this zamindars here collect revenue and pay two rupees a year to Maharajah. Knight made the following remarks :

> "The appearance of a Thibetian settlement here, as one looks down upon it from a height, is very much that of an ant-hill. The huts are built on the top of each other and generally on mounds, and the people, like ants, are busily and laboriously employed in lying up their winter store, not only of grain, but also of fire-wood, and anything capable of serving in its place, to enable them to struggle through their dreary months of captivity. Huge loads of corn and stacks are to be seen moving about, and again appearing on the housetops, where they are stacked and stored. The bundles of fire-wood being placed with the branches outside. The zamindars here pay but two rupees a year to the Maharajah, but it seems a hard case."[46]

Dogra Invasion : Through the Captain Knight travel records, one can easily understand that Gulab Singh army entered into Ladakh via Doda-Kishtawar side. Knight says :

> "Everywhere there were signs of the invasion of Gulab Singh, some twenty years ago. Houses in ruins, and forts reduced to dust and rubbish. To replace these later, a new fort had been constructed by Rumbeer Singh, in what appears about the worst possible position in the entire valley to render it of any use whatever."[47]

Traditional Thrashing System : In Ladakh farmers thrashing their agricultural products through animals, they usually tie yak, demo, zomo, cow, ox and donkeys with one rope and revolve them with a pole over the corn, wheat etc., and thrash their agricultural products. Knight remarks :

> "The people were busily employed in their fields, pulling and carrying corn, and treading it out with oxen. A team of six I saw, most uncomfortably performing this work. They were tied together by the noses, and so small a piece of ground had they to revolve upon, that the innermost animal had to go backward continually, while the centre ones were regularly jammed together by the outsiders. Two deformed natives were employed in driving these unhappy thrashing machine."[48]

Snow Valley : Captain Knight returned to Kashmir via Suru-Karchi, Zangskar and Kistwar. While travelling in Zangskar he saw snow and remains of mighty avalanches. He remarks :

> "We mounted continually towards the huge white masses of snow which so lately towered above us in the distance. Passing the remains of mightily avalanches firmly fixed across the foaming torrent, we ascended the snow valley by the side of a perfect mountain of ice and snow, the accumulations of possibly as many years as the world has existed, which had formed itself immoveably between the mighty mountain's sides. The terrific force, with which the masses of snow had come down each season, to repair the ravages in the frozen monaster's constitution caused by the melting away of his lower extremities, could be seen by the enormous blocks of stone which rested on its surface in all direction."[49]

In conclusion I may say that though during nineteen century every explorers were interested to visit Central Asian trade centres such as Yarkand, Khotan, Lhasa and Baltistan. But Captain Knight concentrated his exploration only in Ladakh. He covered most of the parts of Ladakh excluding Nubra. During his visits he covered many interesting information from Ladakh, these are equally important to us to know the past Ladakh and the cultural heritage of this country.

Notes and References

1. Knight : 'Travels in Cashmere & Thibet'; First published in 1863; Reprinted in 1992; Vintage Books, Gurgaon, India : 129-30.
2. *Ibid.*, 139-40.
3. *Ibid.*, 142-43.
4. Dras : It is a village in the Dras valley between Zojila and Kargil, and famous for heavy snow fall. During winter here temperature falls below zero degree upto –50°C; therefore, known as the second coldest place of the world. There are two stone pillars on the road side which are called "the women", because figures of women are carved on these pillars.
5. Knight ; *op. cit.* 143-44.
6. Cashmere : Kashmir, the capital of Jammu and Kashmir state.
7. Knight ; *op. cit.* 145-46.
8. *Ibid.*, 146.
9. *Ibid.*, 146-47.
10. *Ibid.*, 148.
11. *Ibid.*, 150-51.
12. Chod-tens : Tib. Dung-tens in Sanskrit termed as Chaitya or stupa. Normally dedicated to the celestial Buddha.
13. Knight ; *op. cit.* 152-53.
14. *Ibid.*, 154.
15. Moulwee : Mulbe.
16. Knight ; *op. cit.* 156-57.
17. Um mani panee : Om Mani Padme Hum meaning thereby 'Om the jewel in the Lotus, Amen!, M. Hac's account of an explanation of the formula, which he received from the highest authority at Lhassa, is as follows : "Living beings are divided into six classes—angels, demons, men, quadrupeds, birds and reptiles. These six classes of beings correspond to the syllabus of the formula. 'Om mani padme' houm'. Living beings by continual transformations, and according to their merit or demerit, pass about in these six classes until they have attained

the apex of perfection, when they are absorbed and lost in the grand essence of Buddha. Living beings have, according to the class to which they belong, particular means of sanctifying themselves, of rising to a superior class, of obtaining perfection and of arriving in process of time at the period of their absorption. Men who repeat very frequently and devotedly 'Om mani padme' houm', escape falling after death into the six classes of animate creatures, corresponding to the six syllabus of the formula, and obtain the plentitude of being, by their absorption into the eternal and universal soul of Buddha." Captain Knight, 'Travels in Cashmere & Thibet,' *op. cit.* : 373.

18. According to Turner such monuments which seem to be chod-tens are sometimes known as Dagabas or bone-holders, and are erected either over the corse of a Lama or the ashes of some person as he remarks : "The tribute of respect is paid in Tibet to the manes of the dead in various ways. It is the custom to preserve entire the mortal remains of the sovereign Lamas only. As soon as life has left the body of a Lama, it is placed upright, sitting in an attitude of devotion, his legs being folded before him, with the instep resting on each thigh, and the sides of the feet turned upwards. The right hand is rested with its back upon the thigh, with the thumb bent across the palm. The left arm is bent and held close to the body, the hand being open and the thumb touching the point of the shoulder. This is the attitude of abstracted meditation. The bodies of inferior Lamas are usually burnt, and their ashes preserved with greatest care, and the monument in which they are contained are ever after looked upon as sacred, and visited with religions." Cf. Captain Knight 'Travels in Cashmere & Thibet', *op. cit.* : 160 and quoted from Turner travel records. In this connection my opinion is that there are only a few Dagobas in Ladakh in which learned high class lamas' body being preserved. However, this tradition slowly coming to an end and normally chod-tens of high class Lamas, and VIPs erect over the ashes of concern.
19. Captain Knight ; *op. cit.* : 159-60.
20. Lamieroo : Lamayuru.
21. Captain Knight ; *op. cit.* : 163.
22. *Ibid.*, 165-66.
23. *Ibid.*, 168-69.

24. Kulchee - Kha-la-tse or Khalse village.
25. Captain Knight ; *op. cit.* : 169.
26. Lantza : Sanskrit language among the Buddhists of Nepal proper, by whom it is denominated Ranja.
27. Captain Knight ; *op. cit.* : 171-72. Cunningham describes about Mani as "The Mani—a word naturalized from the Sanskrit—is a stone dyke, from four to five feet high, and from six to twelve in breadth; length from ten or twenty feet to half a mile. The surface of the Mani is always covered with inscribed slabs; these are votive offerings from all classes of people for the attainment of some particular object. Does a childless man wish for a son, or a merchant about to travel hope for a safe return; each goes to a Lama and purchases a slate, which he deposits carefully on the village 'Mani', and returns to his home in full confidence that his prayers will be heard." Cf. Knight ; *op. cit.* quoted from Cunningham.
28. Captain Knight ; *op. cit.* : 173.
29. *Ibid.*, 182.
30. *Ibid.*, 184. Regarding the luxury of a wife with a family of more than one brother, Turner remarks : "One female associating her fate and fortune with all the brothers of a family, without any restriction of age or numbers. The choice of a wife is the privilege of the elder brother ; and singular as it may seem, a Thibetan wife is as jealous of her connubial rites as ever the despot of an Indian Zenana is of the favours of his imprisoned fair." Cf. Knight ; *op. cit.* : 184-85 as being quoted by him.
31. Captain Knight ; *op. cit.* : 185-86.
32. *Ibid.*, 191-93.
33. *Ibid.*, 192-93.
34. *Ibid.*, 195-96.
35. *Ibid.*, 212-13.
36. *Ibid.*, 213-14.
37. Kurgil = Kargil : Ladakh region has two districts viz. Leh and Kargil. Kargil district is dominated by Shia Muslim population. Kargil is the district headquarter of Kargil district.
38. Gulab Singh : Maharaja Gulab Singh of Jammu and Kashmir had sent his army to Ladakh under the command of Zorawar

Singh. His Dogra Army invaded Ladakh in 1834 and occupied it.

39. Captain Knight ; *op. cit.* : 216-18.
40. *Ibid.*, 218-20.
41. *Ibid.*, 223.
42. *Ibid.*, 225.
43. *Ibid.*, 228.
44. *Ibid.*, 228-29.
45. Thibetian : Captain Knight in his travel diary used Tibetian word for Ladakhi people.
46. Captain Knight ; *op. cit.* : 230.
47. *Ibid.*, 231.
48. *Ibid.*, 231-32.
49. *Ibid.*, 232-33.

13

Ladakh : A Robert Shaw's visit to high territory of Trans-Himalaya during 1867-68

Introduction : Till 1830 many passes and deserts of Central Asia were unexplored. Then two big countries—British and Russia had made several plans to explore these by sending their young officers. In this connection Robert Shaw on 20th September 1868 set out from Leh to ancient Silk route towns : Yarkand and Kashgar. In this paper I'll cover his visits to Ladakh where he preliminary visited during 1867.

Natives of Ladakh are seen every year in Kangra : In 1859, at the age of twenty, Robert Barklay Shaw came to India and resided at Kangra. Later he started tea plantation as a career. In those days Central Asia was a good market for Indian tea, therefore, with the intention to explore tea markets in Central Asian countries he often met with western Tibet natives as well traders from the Central Asian countries in Kangra. About the natives of Ladakh and its neighbouring countries he made the following remarks to whom he met in their tents at Kangra valley.

> "These speculations assumed a marvellous attraction as one gazed up at the mighty wall behind which their mysteries lay hid. They were nourished by the appearance of those natives of Ladakh, Zanskar &c., of western Tibet who are to be seen every year in the Kangra valley. Black tents of peculiar make appear for a few days at a time in the winter on open spaces by the road-sides, and shelter dingy families of narrow-eyed Tibetans—petty traders, who come down with their wares. They are not prepossessing in appearance, with their high cheek-

> bones, their dirt, and their long pig-tails. But they are most good-tempered of mortals, and they always greet you with a grin."[1]

Ladakh penetrated by English sportsmen : Robert Shaw when resided at Kangra valley often came in contact with English sportsmen who penetrate into the wilder parts of Ladakh bring down reports of the wonderful animals to find there and about the culture of Buddhists. He remarks :

> "Wild sheep as large as ponies, wild cattles with bushy tails like horses and long hair on their flanks reaching nearly to the ground, besides antelopes and gazelles, are to be obtained by those who toil sufficiently; while, for non-sportsmen, the curious monasteries perched on almost inaccessible rocks, with their Romish ceremonial, their prayer wheels, their gigantic images, and ancient manuscripts from the chief attraction."[2]

Ladakh was the centre for Central Asian traders : As said earlier that though Robert Shaw was resided at Kangra valley, well known about the trade situation and other related activities of Central Asia through traders. He says :

> "While Ladak was thus tolerably well known, though situate at the distance of nearly a month's march across the mountains, the region beyond it seemed to combine all the attractions of mystery and of remoteness. Some few native traders had been known to penetrate to the distant marts of Yarkand, and even Kashgar, and they brought back frightful tales of toil endured and of perils escaped. Men's lives were there said to be of no more account than sheep's, and few traders ever dared to repeat the venture."[3]

Robert Shaw visits to Ladakh to meet caravans from Central Asia: Robert Shaw in 1867 came Ladakh in connection to meet caravans from Central Asia which annually came to Western Tibet. Later he visited to Khotan, when he passed through Roopshoo, saw many nomades who had tents like honeycomb at every halting place. This whole belt is very cold. Robert Shaw explains :

> "Lying at an elevation equal to that of Mont Blanc, this plateau consists of broad valleys without water, which means a few hundred yards wide, and are really plains of many miles is extent. On either side arise rolling mountains of all shades of red, yellow, and black; the rock occasionally cropping out near the summit to break the uniformity of the long shingly slopes

of debris. Everything is bare gravel. Not a glimpse of verdure is to be seen, save in some slight depression where the eye at a distance catches a faint yellow gleam along the ground, which a nearer approach shows to be the effect of some scattered blades of a harsh and prickly grass, piercing up through the gravel like so many discoloured porcupine quills. When you begin to despair of finding those great traveller's requisites, water and wood, your guide will lead you into a recess of the hills, where a small stream derived from some distance snow-bed far up the hill-sides, has given rise, before disappearing under the gravel, to a thicket of brushwood two or three feet high, and where groups of shallow pits, surrounded by loose stone walls, each with its rough fireplace in the middle point, point out where the wandering tribes of Tibetans occasionally pitch their tents. If you are wise, you will take advantage of these sheltering side-walls, low and creviced though they be, for suddenly, in the afternoon, there will numb all the life in your body under a dozen covers, if it strike you. The Tibetan traveller cares for no roof overhead if he can shelter himself from the wind behind a three-foot wall. Hence the numerous little stone enclosures clustered together like cells of a honeycomb at every halting-place, which one side always raised against the prevailing wind. While thus sheltering himself from the cold of the afternoon, the traveller will scarcely believe he is in the same country where in the morning he was guarding against sunstroke, and nearly blinded by the insufferable glare. It is a terribly unsatisfactory country to travel in. When, after threading these interminable valley—plains, you descend again towards the inhabited country of Ladak, the first bits of village cultivation seen on an opposite hill-side have a most singular effect."[4]

Mane and Chortens near villages : In Ladakh Robert Shaw saw Mane and chortens near villages of Ladakh. Whitewashed chortens are supposed to contain the remains of sainted Lamas. He says :

"Approaching the village, you pass a long, low, broad wall, covered with flat stones, inscribed with sacred sentences in two different styles of the Tibetan character. This is a 'Mane', and not a village is without several of them. At each end there is probably a 'chorten', in form a large square pedestal, surmounted by a huge inverted te-pot all whitewashed; while crowning all is a small wooden globe or crescent support on a sort of obelisk. These erections, varying from ten to twenty feet in height, are supposed to contain the remains of sainted lamas, whose bodies have there been buried in a standing position. Little pigeon-holes at the sides are filled with numerous small medallions, looking like lava ornaments. They are moulded into wonderful figures of hundred-handed deities, venerated by this denomination of Buddhists, and are composed of clay, mixed with the ashes of other dead lamas, who are thus, in a material sense, transformed at death into the image of their gods. On reaching one of these structures, the devout Tibetan invariably passes it on his right; hence the road here always bifurcates to allow to this being done both by goers and by comers."[5]

Houses of Ladakhis : Ladakhis have normally flat-roofed, two-storied houses made of by sun-dried bricks and struck above roof by small flags and rags of coloured cotton. Robert Shaw describes :

"The scattered houses of the village are flat-roofed, two-storied, built of huge sun-dried bricks, with walls sloping considerably inwards, and finished off with brilliant white and red stucco over the doors windows. On the roofs are generally small piles of horns (either of wild animals or of domestic sheep and goats) stuck all over with small flags and rags of coloured cotton."[6]

Dress and Ornaments of Ladakhis : Lamas wear red petticoats and cover upper part of their bodies by the same colour shawl whereas ladies wear head ornament called perak. Here Robert explains :

"Fierce-looking black 'yaks' with their bushy tails and long hair hanging below their knees, and giving them a petticoated appearance, graze about the fields or grunt discontentedly as they are led in by the nose to carry the traveller's baggage. They are generally conducted by the women who wear red and blue petticoats with the stripes disposed up and down, cloth boots gartered up to the knee, tight-fitting jackets covered with a sheepskin cape (hair inwards), sometimes lined with scarlet cloth, bare heads with curious cloth lappets protecting both ears from the bitter wind, and above all a 'parak', their most precious ornament, consisting of a broad strip of leather hanging down the back from the top of head, and sown all over with rows of large false turquoises gradually dwindling away to single stones near the tip. The mean, beardless all, wear similar cloth boots, thick woollen frocks girt ground the waist and just reaching below the top of the loggings, and on their pig-tailed head a kind of black phrygian cap, like an English drayman's of which the hanging end serves a variety of purposes, being brought down either to shade the eyes from the sun or to shelter either ear from the cold blasts of the afternoon. Lama, dressed in a red robe which allows one arm and shoulder to be bare, as is also the head. In his hand he carries a prayer cylinder, which he whirls round on its wooden handle by an almost imperceptible motion of the hand, aided by a string and small weight attached to it, and assisting the rotation."[7]

Leh town with large number of Toorkee merchants : When Robert Shaw arrived at Leh to the study of Ladakhi culture, acknowledged many Toorkee merchants in Leh town. He says :

"For stalking about the streets, or seated in silent rows along the bazaar, were to be seen men of a different type from those around. Their large white turbans, their beards, their long and ample outer robes, reaching nearby to the ground, and open in front showing a shorter under-coat girt at the waist, their heavy riding boots of black leather, all gave them an imposing air; while their dignified manners, so respectful to others, and yet so free from Indian cringing or Tibetan buffoonery, made them seem like men among monkeys compared with the people around them."[8]

Meeting with Yarkandee Pilgrim : Robert Shaw during the course of his studies about the characteristics of Central Asian countries and their rulers, he came across with a Yarkandee pilgrim. About him he writes :

"On our first arrival a man approached me dressed in a felt wide-awake, a long flowered dressing-gown and high riding-boots. His beard and moustache were light brown, his face quite fair, and he stared me in the face like an Englishman. I was on the point of addressing him as one, when he turned aside and sat down by my Mussalman servants. He was Yarkandee 'Hajjee' or pilgrim."[9]

Dr. Cayley, the first British Resident at Leh : In 1867, British Resident at Leh announced a considerable reduction in duties. Yarkandee merchants were then very much happy with this announcement. Robert Shaw says :

"Dr. Cayley, the new British Resident at Leh, was able to announce to them a considerable reduction in the duties. It appeared that, some year before, the Cashmeer Maharaja, in whose territory Ladak lies, had entered into engagements with the Supreme Power, the British Government, to reduce his enormous custom duties to five per cent for merchants trading between India and Central Asia. As usual, this engagement was nowhere carried out, and after repeated remonstrances, our Government was oblidged to depute an officer to Ladak, for the purpose of watching its execution. Dr. Cayley was the first appointment to this post, and he at once reported to our Government that the reduction of duties was systematically disregarded by the Cashmere officials. On the details being brought officially to the knowledge of the Maharaja orders were sent up to Ladak to remedy this state of things, and this time these orders were attended to, as there was a British officer to watch over their execution."[10]

Bara Lacha, a pass for danger : At late October 1867 Robert Shaw returned to Kangra valley via Bara Lacha. At Bara Lacha he experienced heavy snow fall and lost his two servants, anyhow with the help of brush wood fire he removed snow, here he attracted by a Sikh merchant carried a parcel of valuable silks. This Sikh merchant also frozen his hand, but somehow survived. He explains beautifully this incident in the following way :

"I shall never forget that night's bivouac on the snow. As soon as the horse carrying the brush-wood fuel came up (it was past 12 o' clock at night), we two Englishmen made shift to light a fire against a rock, clearing away the snow for the purpose. Attracted by this, a Sikh merchant who was crossing the pass the same day, came and sat down with us. His long black beard and moustache were covered with pendant icicles which dragged down the hair by their weight. His face was haggard, and his only thought seemed to be of the fire. He was travelling quickly with all his wealth in a portable form, carried on five lightly laden horses. One the most valuable, he was in the habit of leading himself as he rode. He now told me that, finding his hand getting frozen by holding the leading rope, he had cast this treasure-laden animal adrift in the pass, and did not know what has become of him. On his own horse he had carried a parcel of valuable silks. This had slipped off a few hundred yards back, but he had not had the energy to dismount and pick it up. I advised him to walk instead of riding when the cold was so great. But I must add, in explanation, that our style of clothing had somewhat contributed to this. We wore each of the usual articles of dress about fourfold, besides a huge fur robe and a lambskin cap tying below the chin. I may add that our friend, Tara Sing the Sikh, recovered his treasures for one of my servants, a hill man, who was coming behind finding a stray horse with pass, caught him and brought him on."[11]

Journey to Leh in 1868 : On the 6th of May 1868 Robert Shaw again visited Ladakh before his expedition to Yarkand and Kashgar. This time he came across Pangong lake. He imagined this lake very much resembled to the lake in Geneva, and about eighty miles long, but four or five miles wide. He explains :

"It is altogether about eighty miles long, but only four or five miles wide. The colour of its water, the shape of its mountains, the climate, everything almost reminds me of the lake of Geneva. But there is not one blade of green. For the distant mountain view this does not make much difference. The purples and blues remain the same."[12]

Indus has the source near Mansorawar : Indus river has source near Mansorawar (Masarovar) lake and enter in Ladakh at Damchok. Robert Shaw here says more about this river :

"It rises in the mysterious and sacred lake of Mansorawar, near the source of the great Brahmaputra. It runs north-west for many hundred miles before its course becomes known. It continues in the same direction through Ladak and Baltistan, after which it again enters a mysterious and unexplored country, where it enters changes its direction, emerging at Attock with a south-westerly course through the Punjab and Sinde."[13]

Reached Leh on 6th August 1868 : When Robert Shaw reached at Leh, sent his man Diwan Baksh to Kashmir to get King's permission to go to Yarkand. Finally on 20th September 1868 he got the permission from King. In the meanwhile he came across with some Argoons at Leh. They had a monopoly of the carrying traffic. He has the following information about Argoons :

"Ladak is infested with a set of suffians called Argoons[14] half-bred between Toorkistan fathers and Ladak mothers. Like most half-castes they possess all the evil qualities of both races without any of their ventures. They also in Ladak possess a monopoly of the carrying traffic. They own a few miserable ponies, and as soon as they have made a bargain with a merchant for the carriage of his goods and received a large advance, they go and buy a few more from some brother Argoon, who has just arrived with his cattle half-dread from a journey. These ghosts of horses are then fed up for a few days till their sores begin to heal, when they are started again under loads that would break down a London dray-horse in such country. This is a favourable specimen of an Argoon's conduct. You are happy if he does not insist on getting the whole money in advance, and then get himself taken up by some convenient creditor, who will only let him go on receipt if a further sum of good money which you have to throw after the bad. With me the case was even worse. Having a home, and a wife or two at each end of their journey—both at Yarkand and at Leh—they are equally in dread of the rulers of both places. ... as the men who had good horses, after making me accept exorbitant terms of their own asking. All these troubles I will leave to the imagination, merely saying that I did not start till the 20th of September from Ladak, being compelled to trust the greater part of the goods to the tender mercies of an Argoon named 'Momin' (= the faithful one), who promised to start after me in eight or ten days when his horses should be ready."[15]

Conclusion : Robert Shaw came in India in 1859 and settled down at Kangra valley. Later started his career as a tea planter in the same valley. During the course of tea plantation he came in contact with Central Asian traders. Therefore, thought to visit Central Asian countries, particularly Yarkand and Kashgar which were then known as popular town along the silk route. In 1867 he came Ladakh and spent a few months, interacted with Central Asian traders at Leh, inquired about the rulers and tradition or customs of Central Asian countrymen. Later on 20th September 1868 he finally decided to march to the above said countries from Leh. He took the help of Argoons at Leh, they were well known about the Central Asian trade routes. Besides, he got orders from the Governor of Ladakh under which several villagers near the Pangong lake were bound to give ponies to Robert Shaw caravan for loading or unloading upto the assigned camp.

Notes and References

1. Shaw, Robert : 'Visits to High Tartary Yarkand and Kashgar', Oxford University Press, 1984; First published by John Murray, London, 1871 : 3.
2. *Ibid.*, 3.
3. *Ibid.*, 3-4.
4. *Ibid.*, 7-8.
5. *Ibid.*, 8-9.
6. *Ibid.*, 9.
7. *Ibid.*, 9-10.
8. *Ibid.*, 11.
9. *Ibid.*, 12.
10. *Ibid.*, 12-13.
11. *Ibid.*, 14-15.
12. *Ibid.*, 69-70.
13. *Ibid.*, 70.
14. Argoons : They are not only the half-bred between Toorkistan fathers and Ladak mothers, Yarkandi fathers and Ladak mothers offsprings are also known as Argoons. Robert Shaw quoted Marco Polo comments in this regards as—There is likewise a class of people called 'Argon' because they are produced from a mixture of two races; namely, those natives of Tenduk who are idolaters, and the Mohomedans.
15. *Ibid.*, 75-76.

14

H.W. Bellew's Journey to Ladakh in 1873-74

H.W. Bellew was attached with the Embassy of Kashgar in 1873-74. He made his journey from Kashmir to Kashgar via Ladakh. During July 1873 Bellew at Kashmir noticed some large caravans of *kút*[1], the roots of *kút* were collected on the hills near the Zojila pass. The root of *kút* used in making drug and had very good demand in Rawal Pindi. Annually about 240 loads or 38,400 pounds *kút* sold at Rawal Pindi market. Bellew remarks :

> "We met some large caravans of kút—the 'costum' of the ancients-bound to Rawal Pindi. I noticed three convoys, said to consist of eighty bullocks each. I learned from one of the drivers that the root was collected on the hills near the Zojila pass. The driver told me that each bullock carried two maunds of kút, and that the drug was brought by the merchants at Rawal Pindi, at the rate of a rupee per *ser*[2] of two pounds. Some idea of the quantity of this root which is annually carried out of Kashmir may be formed from the approximate data I got from this man. The 240 loads of this drug which we met on this day—and its peculiar odour loaded the air around—represent, at eighty pounds per maund, a total of 38,400 pounds of kút worth at Rawal Pindi 19,200 rupees."[3]

In fact kút is not a drug, but generally used in making incense or agarbatti and thus consume in Hindu temples.

March to Leh : After staying about one month at Srinagar H.W. Bellew and his party marched away from Srinagar to Leh on August 1873. At Srinagar Maharaja Ranbir Singh, Diwan Kirpa Ram and other his principal officers attended the farewell ceremony of Bellew and his party. On the first week of September they reached Baltal, at the foot of Zojila pass.

Zojila : the getway to Ladakh : Zojila is the pass from where one can see a beautiful Kashmir valley on one side and a dry with no tree country on the other side. Bellew says :

> "We crossed the Zojibal pass, and shortly after passed from the territory of Kashmir proper to that of Tibet. We left behind us a beautiful country, luxuriant in vegetation ever fresh in the moist atmosphere of its climate, and entered a region in the dry air of which no tree and no herb flourished away from the banks of its rivers and water-courses."[4]

Zojila is the corruption of Shivoji and forms the serious obstacle for traffic : Kashmiri says that Zojila is the corruption of Sheoji, as it is covered by snow for most of the time of the year and thus the living place of Shivoji, popularly known Zoji-bal among Kashmiris. According to Bellew :

> "The pass itself, however, is the great object of attention here, as it forms the most serious obstacle in the way of uninterrupted communication with the regions to the north. It is called Zoji-la by the Tibetans and Zoji-bal by the Kashmiris. The terminal syllable, in the language of each respectively, signifies 'hill pass', and the proper name is a corruption of Shivaji or Sheoji, one of the three great Hindu deities. The pass is closed to traffic during nearly half the year, and is entirely impossible except to post couries, and then at peril, during two months. It is crossed by two roads; one of these follows up the bed of the river, and passes over the blocks of ice and snow drift which block the narrow gorge or gap through which it flows ; and the other winds up the steep slope of the hill rising above this gap to the north. The first is seldom used owing to its dangers, and is only practicable to footmen; the other is a very fair road, as is kept in repair by the Kashmir authorities."[5]

Shia Muslims with a mixture of Aryan and Turanian race : At Dras inhabitants belong to a mixture race of Aryan and Turanian types. They are of Shia Muslims had a collection of half-a-dozen hamlets dispersed over the inequalities of a spacious basin in these close set hills. In the centre of the basin was a small square fort with a garrison of fifty men, and adjoining to this was a collectorate of the governor of Dras. Bellew made the following remarks :

> "The natives of (Dras) district are Shia Musalmans professedly, but in physiognomy resemble the Tatars we come to further on, and with whom they consort freely. Their dress is a compromise between that of the Kashmiri and the Bhot, and but for the turban some of the wear they are not to be distinguished by the stranger from the Bhot, to whose speech their own assimilates. Their complexion, however, is generally fairer than that of the Bhot, and some of them show very distinct traces of intermixture with Kashmir blood. They seem, indeed to be merely Muhammadanised Tatars forming the connecting link between the divergent Aryan and Turanian types. Few of them understand any but their own language, and they even have different names for their several villages and camping stages to those used for them by the Kashmiris. Thus they call Dras-Himbaps; Matayan-Ambuti; Pandras-Pran, &c."[6]

Zho and Zhomo are the popular animals in Dras : In Dras valley along the stream one can observe lucerne which natives pile for their cattle as winter fodder. They have hybrid between the yak and domestic cow, called Zho and Zhomo for the male and female respectively. Bellew remarks:

> "We observed many stacks of lucerne—here called *buksuk*, and at Leh *Chhumpo*—and prangos piled in the roadside fields as winter fodder for the cattle of this country—the hybrid between the yak (bos grunniens) and the domestic cow, which is called *Zho* and *Zhamo (Zhomo)* for the male and female respectively. There are several cross-breeds between the hybrid and the parent stocks, but they are not common nor so valued as the simple hybrid. The *Zho* is very enduring and docile, and is preferred in the plough and under the load to the more hardy but restive yak; whilest the *Zhamo (Zhomo)* is said to give a more abundant and steady supply of milk than the common cow."[7]

Site for gold-diggers : Next to Dras towards Kargil Bellew acknowledged a solitary police station of Kharbo. Beyond this there were some ruined walls of some huts of gold-diggers. He remarks :

> "After crossing some rough ground, rises to a small flat on which stands the solitary police station of Kharbo. Beyond the police station we came to the ruined walls of some huts, which marked the site of a hamlet formerly occupied by some gold-diggers who worked in the steep slope of the hill forming the

opposite side of the river channel. They had run a gallery someway into the hill, and used to wash the auriferons soil in the river with profit till, one day the loose earth sub-siding buried a number of their men, and the accident being looked on as an interposition of providence, the enterprise was abandoned and the colony dispersed."[8]

Kargil has no monuments of Buddhists and Muslims : On 12th September 1873, Bellew and his party reached Kargil. It was the district headquarter of Kargil which was extended from the junction of the Thangskam with the Dras river to the Photola (Po-tu-la) pass, had a fort and collectorate, but showed no monuments of Buddhists and Muslims. Bellew explained about Kargil as :

"(Kargil) is the capital of the district of the same name, which extends from the junction of the Thangskam with the Dras river to the Photola pass, and has a fort and collectorate. The latter is situated at the top of the village. The fort commands the road at the junction of the rivers, and is situated on an isolated boulder bed in the stream of the Saru river which rushes past on each side with ceaseless din. Indeed, the country so far as we have come on this side of Kashmir shows no monuments betokening the predominance or even the cultivation of either one religion or the other, and neither *masjid* and *ziarat*, nor *gonpa* and *chhorten* meet the eye to tell of Musalman or Buddhist devotee. But in the crowd of seven or eight hundred men gathered about our camp the mixture of the two was very evident, and indicated the existence here of both creeds as on a natural ground. The people are all alike called Bhot, though many amongst them are Musalmans of the despised heretic or Shia sect."[9]

Polo : A National Sport : People of Kargil are very fond of Polo game. In every village here has polo-ground. Bellew during his visit to Kargil explained that :

"The people of the place got up a game of polo for our amusement, and more for their own. It is the national sport of this country, and every village has its level strip of polo ground carefully kept for the practice of this exercise. The display, however, we witnessed in the native home of the game was a poor affair compared with what one sees in the countries of its adoption. The keen zest and enjoyment of both horse and rider, however, made amends for the want of speed and dexterity which one sees exhibited amongst ourselves, and the clumsy horsemanship was covered by the merry good-nature and docility of the rider and his little steed. On the conclusion of the game some of the men exhibited their equitation by picking a rupee off the ground whilst riding past without quitting the saddle. It was no great feet from the back of a pony no bigger than an English donkey, and whose pace was curbed to that of the proverbially obstinate creature to whose height I have compared this. The sport afforded a deal of merriment, however, amongst the crowd of spectators, owing to the laughable efforts made by some, and the awkward tumbles of others in their eager efforts to clutch the prize; and was followed by a general scramble for handsful of coppers thrown amongst the crowd, a struggle which called forth a boisterous activity, wonderful to say, unmarred by a single jar of ill-temper."[10]

Costume : Ladakhis wear *tipi* (cap), goatskin across the back, perag, goncha etc. Bellew beautifully explained about these in the following way :

"We first met the Tatar costume with which our subsequent journey made us more familiar. Most of the men wore the Bhot bonnet, or *tipi*, and carried a sheep or goatskin slung across the back. The bonnet is a mere bag of some strong woollen or goat's hair texture, and hangs jauntily on one side of the head which fills its opening, with the queue coiled in its interior or hanging down the back. For the Bhot wears his hair in the old style plaited into a tail, the length of which he is not too proud to increase by the artificial aid of braided wool. He is fond of ornament too, and decorates his bonnet with a bunch of flowers plucked from the weeds growing amongst his crops, or with the bright marigold which he patronises in the shelter of his homestead. He wears rings of gold or silver wire, strung with beads of red coral and green turquoise, in his ears and carries a big boss of amber or agate suspended as a necklet charm on his breast. The mantle of sheep or goatskin, called *hyugor*, is worn slung across the back by a cord which crosses the chest obliquely over one shoulder. It is cured with the hair or wool on, and is used as protection for the loins against the cold winds of the country. The people of Kafiristan which, from what I have heard of that country, is a somewhat similar mountain region of this, wear a mantle of the same kind which from its usual colour, is called *siyah post* or 'black skin', by their brethren converted to Islam; and they are by them, consequently, distinguished from other pagan tribes by the appellation *siyah post kafir*, or 'pagans of the back skin'. This term has been strangely misunderstood and rendered as *siyah posh*, or 'clothed in black', a term which is far more appropriately applicable to the indigo-dyed dress of the Afghans themselves, or to us, or any other people who wear clothes of a more or less dark colour, than to the mountaineer of Kafiristan, whose usual dress is a woollen home-made stuff of the natural hue, and not the grotesque costume I have seen represented in a photograph of a reputed kafir in his national dress. The dress of the Bhot peasant is very simple. A loose shirt of coarse cotton is covered by a long frock of thick and strong woollen material. They are bound round the waist by a leather belt, over which pass folds of a long scarf whose ends hang over the loose trousers, and these, like the scarf, are of the same texture as the frock. Coarse woollen socks over the feet, which are farther encased in clumsy shoes of felt and leather patch-work or in boots of sheepskin worn with the wool inside; whilst the legs are protected by the folds of a long woollen bandage, ornamented with an edging of varied colour. From his belt hang the several indispensable items of his travelling equipment, or indeed of his momentary requirements of ordinary life. His single-bladed knife, carried in a leather sheath, hangs on one side with a flint case which seems all brass binding; and a pouch bag for tea and tobacco, and odds and ends with this bright iron pipe, hangs on the other. Whilst in the capacious interior of his fob are stowed away his bag of parched barley-meal or as often a lump of its dough half-stewed by the heat of his body, and the wooden bowl from which he eats it. Suspended obliquely across his back is what looks like a quiver, but our peaceable Bhot carries neither bow nor arrow nor other weapon of war, and his suspicious looking cylinder of wood, fluted and chased with patterns of simple design, is only his tea-churn."[11]

First Buddhist monument appeared at Shargol : At Shargol, Bellew acknowledged Buddhist monuments for example he saw Mane wall about ninety-three places long, eight paces wide, and four feet high and its surface was covered by Mane mantra carved stone plates. As he remarks :

> "(Shargol), here we came upon the first monument of the Buddhist faith we had yet met in our march, and from this onwards until we passed on to the uninhabited wastes of the Tibet highlands, we saw no trace of any other creed. It was a *mane phane* on the bank overlooking our camp, and was nothing but a broad wall of loose-set stones; its measurements were ninety-three paces long, eight paces wide, and four feet high. On the north side of the wall, and exactly midway, was a square slab of stone set upright in a covered recess, and carved in very low relief with figures of Budh and his priests. On each side of it was a slab similarly set, and carved with writing chiselled on its surface. The broad top of the wall in all its surface was thickly strewed with a multitude of undressed stones, flat boulders, and slabs of slate, each of which was carefully inscribed with an unvarying formula of letters lightly chiselled on the surface. We subsequently saw several others of these *mane phane* and one at Leh nearly half a mile long. The inscribed stones on the top are deposited by the laity—for whom the priest or lamma does the writing—to propitiate the deity for the souls of defunct relatives, for protection against evil, for favour in some enterprise, or for the attainment of some desire or other—of which in their variety the Bhot mind is as susceptible as that of more tutored peoples. The mane is held in reverence by the people, and in passing is always kept on the right hand."[12]

Gigantic Chamba figure at Mulbe : The Chamba or Maitreya figure at Mulbe is carved on the north face rock below the main road. Bellew says :

> "On the north face of the rock is carved the gigantic figure called *Chamba*; and its base stands a little hut in which are kept the paraphernalia for his periodical service. On its summit are fixed two poles, each of which is topped by a bell-shaped mitre or copper cap; beneath the cap hangs a white calico petticoat of three flounces, trimmed with a deep border of red cloth. There is a similar figure also called *Chamba*, on an isolated rock near the village of Diggar, but the poles with the mitre and gown were absent."[13]

Lamayuru Monastery : After climbing 13,670 feet Photola (Po-to-la) pass Bellew descent down to Lamayuru monastery. Here he saw Buddhist idols, Thankas and wall paintings. He described about the Gonpa in the following way :

"I went up the steep in rear of the cliff to explore the Gonpa or Lammasary on its summit, and at the top of ascent were cordially welcomed by some very jovial looking priests, whose shaven crowns and rotund figures—barely concealed by their loose gowns and covering mantle—spoke of very comfortable fare; whilst the heavy sensual expression of their features, and merry mood of mind told that the life of the Buddhist monk is not one so entirely of privation and vigil as the solitude of his situation and poverty of his country, apart from the proper duties of his profession, would lead one to expect. ... introduced us to the mysteries of their 'sanctum sanatorium'. This was a succession of three low-roofed, dark chambers, the obscurity of which was dimly lighted by the flames of half-a-dozen cotton wicks, or spiles, stuck upright in as many pods of butter, set in little brass bowls which were ranged in front of the idols. These last were supported against the wall on a raised planking, and enshrouded by hanging curtains of embroidered wool and silk drapery, and were but indistinctly observable in the obscurity of their mysterious retreat. The idols bore very much the look of common Hindu deities, though they represented a different mythology, and on the shelf in front of them lay a number of the *lingam* and yuni emblems roughly modelled out of lumps of barley-meal paste. ... the walls of one of the chambers are painted with pictures representing episodes in the lives of particular deities whose morality is exhibited in a vicious form, whilst the shelves of another are piled with carefully folded manuscripts replete with Buddhist lore."[14]

Monastery has its own animals and Nuns, at the service of monks : In Lamayuru monastery lamas are engaged in ritual works whereas Nuns at the service of monks, they prepare meal for them. There were animal stock at the monastery, through which animal products were being used for the livelihood of monks at the monastery. Bellew remarks :

"We then entered some other low and narrow chambers which appeared to be the dormitories and refectories of the monks, and in one of them found two nuns engaged in working up some meal into dough for the evening repast. ... and led by a wood staircase down to some similar chambers full of stable litter, and evidently the stalls of the ponies, cows, and goats of the monastery. There are twenty monks (lamma) and eight nuns (kimi) attached to this monastery (gonpa). They appeared to

> be a happy community, and by no means discontented with their lot."[15]

Chang is used by monks : I have a doubt that chang drink was used by monks of Lamayuru monastery, however, chang often use during ritual performance. Bellew made the following remarks :

> "Our guides showed us some malt liquor prepared from the huskless barley of this country. It is called chhang, and is the daily drink of the monks who, under its influences, get comfortably fuddled and fat. A spirit is also distilled from the same malt, and is only used on special occasions when the community is permitted to revel in drunkenness."[16]

Head lama of the monastery is appointed from Lhasa and every Buddhist family donated one son to the monastery : In Ladakh, Buddhists have strong faith on monasteries. They offer one son to their respective monastery and thus strengthen the monastic tradition. Bellew says :

> "Their superior is always appointed from Hlassa, but the rest are recruited in the country, the second son of every family being dedicated to the priesthood. These lay priests, if I may so style the Bhots, who are thus dedicated to the church, wear the lamma dress, but pursue the ordinary avocations of life till called to the cloisters, according to the requirements of their church, when they must renounce the world, and assume the celibate life of the monk. With the nuns the monastic life is optional, and apparently is only adopted by the friendless and homeless. The monasteries are supported by the people, and governed by the Dalay Lamma (whose seat is Hlassa) as the head of the faith, through subordinate Lammas appointed by him. The priesthood thus provided for pass life with less of its cares and troubles than fall to the lot of most mortals, and by all evidence their service in the church is none of self-denial, nor of pious devotion to the pur doctrine enunciated by their great lawgiver."[17]

Discipline of mind or body helps to remove ignorance : In Buddhism, Buddhists through vinayic rule improve their conduct and behaviour. Thus by way of discipline mode of conduct they try to remove ignorance. Bellew explains :

> "It is a vain repetition of meaningless formula, and the degraded worship of images, without discipline of mind or body. And it flourishes here without a rival amongst a people stepped in the grossest ignorance and most timid superstition. A people who,

in every change in the elements, and every accident of daily life, see the intervention of an offended deity, or the malignity of an evil spirit; and whose anxiety is to appease the one, and avert the other through the mediation of their priests who are the only depositories of their mental culture. This institution of the priesthood, however, coupled with that of polyandry which obtains amongst this people, is not without its benefits, and perhaps under the existing conditions, owes its endurance to its adaptation to the requirements of the country. And the two together are probably the forms of polity best suited to the existence of the population as a peaceable, well ordered, and industrious community."[18]

Polyandry among Buddhist : In olden days Ladakh was dominated by Buddhists, but did not have sufficient economic resources, therefore, they offered polyandry system in order to control population growth and division of property. Bellew remarks :

"It is the custom for the brothers of one family to have a single wife in common, and for the children to take the name and obey, as head of the family, the eldest husband. By this means, and the transfer of so many to a life of celibacy in the monasteries, the population is kept down to a proportion which the country is capable of supporting."

Less Crime : Buddhists in Ladakh are non-violent, though their peaceful and harmless character Muslims got equal opportunity to flourish in Ladakh; however; they never mind for this slow and steadly propogation of Islam in Ladakh. Bellew says :

"As it is, under the existing institutions, the population is kept not only within the limit capable of supporting life in the country, but of living as a peaceful, happy, and well-ordered community amongst whom violent crime is a rare offence, and litigation happily at a minimum."[20]

Ruined Fort at Balu Khar : It is said that during 16th century Balu Khar was the sacred seat of Buddhist faith but was destructed by Yarkand army, later when Dogra army came into Ladakh, it further demolished. Bellew remarks :

"The Yarkand army on their return from the disastrous attempt to invade this sacred seat of the Buddhist faith in the sixteen century. The fort itself is now a barely—distinguishable ruin. Its remains are seen a mile or so further up the river, beyond a deep ravine which intervenes between it and the village,

> perched on an isolated rock which commands the passage at a narrow bend of the stream. It is called Balo Khasra (Balu Khar) by the Bhots, and is said to have been demolished some thirty years ago by the Zorawar Sing, the Sikh general who conquered this country for the Maharaja Gulab Sing. And the present little fort commanding the Khalsi bridge was built in its stead by Diwan Hira Sing, the Maharaja's first governor of the annexed province."[21]

Welcomed by Villagers and lamas with music : Bellew and his train was welcomed at each big village by villagers and concerned lamas. Ladies dressed up by their traditional style and saluted the pary with a low bow and by saying zu-zu. Lamas dressed in red robes and beg caps of their order and playing monastic musical instruments. Bellew express his views in this regards :

> "We were greeted by a full choir of the Lammas of the place. The stood in a row a little off the road, and gave us a performance of their instruments; whilst the women of the place, decked out in their best attire, and ranged in a line along the roadside, saluted us with a low bow and usual jo-jo (zu-zu). We received a similar marked of welcome at every place we came to on our onward journey through Ladakh, though the Lammas did not always appear in such grand as here. There were eight of them, all dressed alike in the red robes and high bonnets of their order, and playing upon the instruments peculiar to their craft. The character of the music was as strange and unique as the appearance of the performers and strikingly in accord with the surroundings of the scene. The beat of the drums and clang of the cymbals in no degree lessened the initial bray of the trumpets, nor marred the soft, sad airs of their final notes. The trumpets are awkward looking instruments from six to eight or nine feet long, and curved like a cow horn. The lower part rests on the ground, whilst the performer consists of a succession of jerky blasts which, in turn, lapse into plaintive strains of peculiar pathos, and again swell into sonorous and solemn sounds which are borne away on the air, and prolonged in its vibrations."[22]

Dress : Ladakhis are found of ornaments and dresses. They wear Goncha, head dress etc. Bellew explains :

> "Their dress is remarkable and like everything else in this strange country apparently well adapted to its requirements

and the habits of the people. The long frock and girdle sash, and the trousers differ little from those worn by the men. The material and the pattern are much the same, but the colour and finish are different; and in their choice the fair ones display their proverbial good taste. Dark colours or black relieved by an edging of red or blue are those usually seen, and they set off to the best advantage the ornaments the Bhot beauty is so found of; and not the least important of them the ample sheepskin mantle, which, next to her head dress, is her special pride and care. This is an oblong rug of sheepskin, loosely slung behind by a band of braid passing obliquely across the bosom and ornamented at the edges of the fleece by a broad border of particoloured patchwork. It serves as shawl, wrapper and bedding, as occasion requires; and it is always worn out of doors as a protection for the back against the cold winds of the country. But the head-dress is the most peculiar object of attraction amongst the strange fashions of the Bhotmo toilette. The hair, parted in the centre of the forehead, is plaited over the crown into two broad fillets, which are prolonged as lappets hanging down the back by means of braided wool adjuncts. The two fillets are united along the middle line by a mixed row of couries, bits of red coral, agate, turquoise, malachite, and gold coins, according to the means of the wearer. These ornaments are sometimes seen studding the filled so closely as to conceal the hair, and form a sort of plated shield to the head. Amongst the wealthy they are of finer quality, and look well, but as commonly seen they form a repulsive-looking medley suggestive of torment to the wearer; for, when once made up, they are seldom undone for months together, or may be years. The side tresses are arranged in puffs over each ear and kept in form by a patch of black fleece and braid, which covers the ears and temples, and looks somewhat like the blinkers of a coach horse; and hanging from the ears below their edges are strings of large beads of glass, or coral or turquoise, &c. Besides these the Bhot woman wears a necklace of similar ornaments, and large wristlets of a single bit of white couch, and in addition a chatelaine which hangs from her girdle and is loaded with white bosses of couch, or strung with couries, and beads of agate and turquoise; all conspicuous by their swinging against the dark ground of her frock. And yet, as if not already

> sufficiently decorated to the taste of their partner lords, the comely ones or those who consider themselves so, add to the charms of their personal adornment the improvement of the complexion by the process called *Shogholo*. This consists of smearing the cheeks and forehead with the juice and seeds of the ripe berry of the belladona plant which grows here as a weed amongst the cultivation."[23]

Ladakhis pronounced as Bhot : The majority of Ladakhi are belong to Mongolian type. Bellew has his opinion that Ladakhis have been pronounced as Bhot because of its climatic condition which is severe hot and cold, he explains :

> "It is to the effect probably of these combined causes—the clear rays of a powerful sun, and the bright glare from wide-spread snow, both acting in an unusually dry and rarefied atmosphere—that the Bhot, I mean the common Bhot who is exposed to the weather owes his peculiar complexion. It is not the clear dark colour of the people of India, however, varied its shades from the ruddy glow of the Afghan to the olive hue of the Hindu, or from the sallow tinge of the hill-tribes to the black skin of the outcast races of the peninsula. Nor is it the light colour of the people of Tartary, with its lesser range in variety from the dingy yellow of the Chinese settlers to the pink and pale of the Andijani conquerors."[24]

Leh, the capital of Ladakh : At the basin of Leh town Indus flows; along the course Spituk, Choglamsar, Chusood etc. villages are situated. Bellews describes :

> "As we rode past the Lammas appeared on the terraces of their elevated abode, and gave us their benediction in full band. From this we set our faces up the long gravelly slope at the top of which stands Leh piled up the hill sides in the fashion of the country. The valley is a deep circular basin crossed midway by the Indus, along whose course are several villages and much cultivation. For the rest the land slopes steeply from both sides to the river, and presents a wide surface of gravel and stone, for the most part waste. At the foot of the hills to the south are the villages of Stok and Matha (Matho) with their orchards and fields; and at the foot of those on the north are the town and fort and suburbs of Leh, the capital of the country."[25]

Excursion to the Hemis Gonpa : In Ladakh Hemis is one of the richest monastery situated at the south of Leh town. Bellew along with Colonel Gordon, Captain Chapman visited this monastery. He explains :

> "It is situated at the top of a singularly wild and solitary glen, frowned on at every turn in its winding course by some overhanging bluff of sombre conglomerate or gneiss. The silence here as we followed the steep path, looking for the first glimpses of the now familiar signs of the Lamma's retreat was oppressive; and it was not till we had come in full view of its white walls, shining against the dark ground of the towering masses of rock behind, that our ears were greeted by the melancholy music which floated on the air from their lofty terraces. The view of the monastery from below is wonderfully picturesque and altogether unique of its kind. The white walls with their dark squares of window and door and thick red lines of coping, from which project here and there poles topped with the bushy yak's tail, spread over the cliffs tier above tier and, with great masses of bare rock protruding amongst them appear isolated in the very crowd of their assemblage. The buildings of this monastery cover a considerable surface and form a small town. In many respects the architecture, even to that of the out-offices, resembles what is still traceable in the Buddhist ruins of Yusufzai, particularly in those known as Takhti Bahi. In these ruins, with the exception of those near Babozai. There are no traces to show how the houses were roofed; but from the resemblance of the structure of their walls, staircases, chambers & c., to what is now seen in the monasteries of this country, it is probable they too were of similar construction, particularly since the two localities are equally poor in timber trees. Here the roofs are flat, and supported on rafters laid with lath and brushwood and earth. And they have a parapet coping of one to two feet thick, formed of brush wood fascicles cut straight across, and laid with the ends thus trimmed projecting six or ten inches beyond the wall. These ends look much like those of a bundle of lead pencils in arrangements and are usually stained with red ochre or similar colour. The Hemis Gonpa is said to contain 800 monks and nuns. Through narrow passages and up flights of steps, with the prayer-wheel meeting us at every turn. Here we found it spinning on the

hand of a sedate Lamma, squatted solemn and silent in some solitary corner. Further on it was revolving under a thin jet of water, and elsewhere it was fixed in niches of the walls for the passer-by to turn us he went past, or it was stuck on some pinnacle for its wings to catch the moving breeze, and record so more prayers to praise to the Almighty. We were told, of Chinese devil dances. The designs on the rich silken robes of the monks were evidently from the Celestial Empire. Most of the masks represented the heads of wild animals, and these were some of ogres and demons. These last, however, were the devices most common on the embroidery of the robes worn by the actors. There were some twenty or thirty of them altogether, some of whom had been assembled here for the occasion from the monasteries of Tiksi (Thiksey), Matha (Matho), and Stok. Their performance consisted of a wild sort of dance round a flag staff in the centre of the court of the principal temple; and we witnessed it from the roof of a varandah facing a flight of steps at the entrance of the temple. The actors issued from the hall of the temple, headed by two portly Lammas in gorgeous silk robes (their appearance reminded one of the knave of cards), who took up a position opposite the musicians—beforehand seated in the varandah below us—whilst the rest, a troop of goblins, griffins, stags, boars, tigers, &c., running down the steps, ranged themselves in a circle round the flagstaff, from which floated streamers of different colours. The musicians now commenced some very lively and discordant music, and the dancers, at once set in motion, began to caper, and whirl, and fling their limbs about, the whole circle the while keeping its form and revolving round the centre pole. The bright colours of the loose mantles, covered with monstrons figures of flying dragons all eyes and teeth, of skulls and bones, of forked-tongue griffins, &c., with the huge masks of ogres and wild beasts all mixed together in a wild commotion, formed an absurd melange and with the noise of drums and trumpets, produced a perfect pandemonium, to the tumult of which the actors contributed by now and again joining in a chorus of unintelligible sounds. The performance concluded suddenly by the flight of the company up the steps down which they had come, back to the great hall of the temple from which they had emerged."[26]

Plantation of Islam in Ladakh : Kashgar army for the first time entered into Ladakh via Nubra under the command of Mirza Hydar during 1531 A.D. They forcefully converted Buddhists into Islam in Nubra, latter via Leh went to Kashmir. Bellew remarks :

> "He commenced his career as independent ruler of Kashgar by the conquest of Khutan and made some unsuccessful attempts to subjugate Tibat (Tibet), his incursions being always repelled at the Nubra frontier. His successor, however, in whom the government, in 1513 A.D., was restored to the line of the Mughal Khans, signalised the close of his reign by that invasion of Ladakh."[27]

Ali Mir destroyed monasteries of Ladakh : During 16th century Bastistan Chief Ali Mir invaded Ladakh and destroyed many monasteries. Bellew says :

> "Mir Ali (Ali Mir), The Mussalman Chief of Baltistan, took Leh, and destroyed the monasteries all over the country. He was obliged to retrace his steps to Skardo, his capital, and restore Jamya Namgyal (Jamyang Namgyal)[29], the native chief whom he had taken prisoner to the government of his own country."[30]

Soghpo army invasion on Ladakh : During 17th century Soghpo or Mongolian army invaded Ladakh. To expel Mongolians, Ladakh King sought help from Mughal army. Bellew made the following remarks :

> "In 1678, Khoja Afac usurped the government Kashmir from the descendants of Sultan Said Khan, in whom the rule of the Mughal Khans was restored, and sought the aid of the Calmac chief to support him against his opponents, the Ghaldan of Zunghar, coming in answer to this appeal with an army of his Buddhist Calmacs, seized the country for himself. And when some years later, in 1685, the member of the Khoja family rebelling were driven out of the country, and some of them fled to Kashmir through Tibat (Tibet), a force of Zunghar troops called Sarigh or Saigh (Yellow) Calmac of Tibat (Tibet)—was sent in pursuit of them to Leh, which they took possession of, the Gyalpo or chief of Ladakh tendering allegiance to the Mughal sovereign in India sought aid of Aurangzeb's governor of Kashmir to expel them."[31]

Ladakh was annexed with Skardo : In the beginning of 18th century Ladakh again annexed with Skardo by Mir Murad of Skardo. Bellew says:

"Ladakh remained in the hands of native rulers till 1720, when it was again invaded by Mir Murad of Skardo who annexed it to his principality of Baltistan and it so remained for thirty years."[32]

Khardong is the highest pass in Ladakh : Khardong la is the 18,380 feet high from the sea level, here Zangskar range separates from Ladakh. Bellew has the following opinion in this regards :

"We camped in this gully at the foot of the pass (Khardong pass). Its elevation is about 14,900 feet, or 3400 feet above Leh. The view across the valley at Kanari range, which separates Zanskar (Zangskar) from Ladakh. This pass, like that of Diggar on the same range farther round to the east of Leh, is very steep and difficult, and upward of 17,000 feet high. At the Khardong pass the barometer stood at 15.464, the aneroid at 15.58, and the hypsometer at 181°4F, with the temperature of the air at 28°F (recorded in 29th September 1873). The Khardong range runs from north-west to south-east, and separates the valley of Ladakh from that of the Shayok river."[33]

High altitude carrier : Yak : Yak is high altitude load carrier Ladakhis called him *dong*. Bellew says :

"The *dong* is a steady and sure animal at these great heights notwithstanding the pranks some of them are apt to play upon the stranger. He is led by a rope attached to a wood ring which passes through the division of the nostrils, and moves with a slow, easy, riggling sort of gait, rising or descending over obstructions with very little jar."[34]

Flood of the Shayok in 1859 : After crossing Shayok river one comes to Tagar village, it is a beautiful village has apricot, willow and poplar trees. It is said once the water-line area of this village being effected by Shayok river; Bellew writes :

"At half way we left the Shayok, and went up the course of the Nubra river to Tagar. The river runs in divided streams over a wide bed of shingle and sand, on which are island patches of buckthorn and myricaria brushwood. The aspect of the valley is much the same as that of the Shayok in this part of its course, but the opposite bank to that on which our route lies slopes steeply to the river, and is scored with a water-line which marks a flood of the Shayok in 1859."[35]

Residence of former chiefs of the Nubra : Opposite site of river in Tagar, had residence of former chiefs of Nubra district. Bellew says :

"From Tagar we marched to Panamik, twelve miles and halted there the 5th of October (1873). In about an hour we came abreast of Churasa on the opposite site of the river. It is the residence of the former chiefs of the Nubra district, and has a small palace, fort, and monastery; all very picturesquely perched on some rocks projecting towards the river from the range of hills behind, and conspicuous objects on the landscape—their white walls shining brightly above the green spread of vegetation below and against the bare rocks of the background."[36]

Panamik : A source of salt and copper : In olden days at the surroundings of Panamik salt and copper were collected by villagers and exported to Kashmir market. Bellew also agrees with this statement :

"On the road crosses a turfy hollow, white with soda efflorescence. We were informed that 3000 maunds of this salt had been collected here this season for the Kashmir market. It is used by the Tibetans to improve the colour and draw out the flavour of their tea. Copper is found in several spots of this and Shayok valleys. The ore is worked in the vicinity of Churasa, and there affords employment to a dozen families or so. I was shown some specimens of the ore found in the Shayok valley. It contained some nuggets of the kind called 'peacock ore' mixed up with crude sulphate of copper."[37]

Hot springs at Panamik village : In 1996 I visited Panamik and saw hot springs. Here boiling water comes out from the earth. Bellew also found the same and acknowledge a deposit of sulphur. He recorded the temperature, here follows the details :

"I took the temperature of the largest stream at different points, and found it 155.5°F at a little pool at the point of issue, 146°F, at 8 paces off, 124°F, at 20 paces, and 90°F, at 70 paces. Another stream close by was 167°F at the spring head. All the little streams of the group to the west are conducted by a single channel, 14 inches wide and 3 inches deep, into a couple of tanks which are enclosed by walls divided into two bathing compartments; whilst adjoining is a small hut used as a shelter by the bathers. There is a similar set of springs in the hill-side at Chang-lung, the next stage from this. I found the temperature of three of the upper springs to be respectively, 140°F, 172°F, and 174°F, at the point of issue and of three of the lower ones, 163°F, 169°F, and 170°F. One of the upper springs issued in a small pool under the ice of the great block of gneiss embedded in the surrounding grit and debris."[38]

In conclusion Bellew and his train after staying a few days in Leh marched towards Kashgar via Khardong la, Panamik, Saser la, Sakri la etc. The Kashmir authorities provided all kinds of necessary facilities at every important halts viz. to provide ponies, yaks and coolies for the transport.

Notes and References

1. Kút : It is a herb, generally used in making incense.
2. Ser : It is a measuring unit of weight, about four sers = One kilogram.
3. Bellew, H.W. : 'Kashmir and Kashgar : A narrative of journey of the Embassy to Kashgar in 1873-74', Trubner & Co., Ludgate Hill; London, 1875 and Reprint in India by Asian Educational Services, 1989 : 50.
4. *Ibid.*, 93.
5. *Ibid.*, 94.
6. *Ibid.*, 101.
7. *Ibid.*, 102.
8. *Ibid.*, 102-03.
9. *Ibid.*, 104-05.
10. *Ibid.*, 105-06.
11. *Ibid.*, 106-08.
12. *Ibid.*, 109-110.
13. *Ibid.*, 110-11.
14. *Ibid.*, 114-116.
15. *Ibid.*, 116-117.
16. *Ibid.*, 117.
17. *Ibid.*
18. *Ibid.*, 117-118.
19. *Ibid.*, 118.
20. *Ibid.*, 119.
21. *Ibid.*, 122.
22. *Ibid.*, 125-26.
23. *Ibid.*, 128-30.
24. *Ibid.*, 130-31.

25. *Ibid.*, 132.
26. *Ibid.*, 133-37.
27. *Ibid.*, 140.
28. Mir Ali : In fact he was a Duke of Skardu province in Baltistan.
29. Jamyang Namgyal (Jamyang Namgyal) : He was the king of Ladakh, and encouraged Islam religion in Ladakh.
30. Bellew, H.W. : *op. cit.* : 140.
31. *Ibid.*, 140-41.
32. *Ibid.*, 141.
33. *Ibid.*, 145-46.
34. *Ibid.*, 146.
35. *Ibid.*, 149.
36. *Ibid.*, 150-51.
37. *Ibid.*, 151.
38. *Ibid.*, 151-52.

15

Sir Francis Younghusband Journey to Ladakh, the Frontier Part of India

Early Life : Sir Francis Younghusband was born in a military family on 31 May 1863, at the hill station of Murree on the North-West Frontier. He was educated at Clifron and at Sandhurst, later commissioned in 1882 at the age of 19 into the 1st King's Dragron Guards, then serving in India.

In India : Probably in 1884 he arrived India, later walked upto Dharamsala in Himachal Pradesh where his uncle Robert Shaw once lived. He stayed a few hours there, later marched towards Shimla. Thereafter, made several expeditions in Central Asian countries.

Achievement : As a traveller Younghusband got distinguished place among the Gold Medalists of the Royal Geographical Society. In 1886 he visited Manchuria, thence to Peking. In 1890 he was sent to investigate the circumstances of the Kanjuri on the Kirghiz territory. In the same year he made famous expedition to the Pamirs. After two years went to Hunza, and established British representative office there. In early of the following year went to Chitral to control the disturbances after the death of the ruler, Aman-ul-Mulk. When peace restored, he stationed at the capital as a British representative for sometimes.

At the age of 47, Younghusband retired from Indian Government Service. In 1936 he founded the World Congress of Faiths, which aimed to bring together all important religious people. This great explorer died in 1942 at the age of 79.

I, now here to highlight some important movements of Younghusband who during the course of his expedition to Yarkand visited Ladakh.

At Zoji-la pass : In 1888 Younghusband after crossing Mustagh pass in Baltistan came to Skardu then returned to Kashmir. On the way came across Zoji-la pass. He had the following experiences about this pass :

> "The Zoji-la, eleven thousand four hundred feet high. It was perfectly easy, and then of descending the southern side we found all the mountain sides covered with forest. The change from the bare hillsides on the north was very striking and very pleasant. Hitherto, from far away at their rise from the Yarkand plains, the mountains had been barren and destitute of any trace of forest. Occasionally in some favoured sheltered spot a dwarfed tree or two might be seen, but as a whole it was only the valley bottoms and on cultivated lands that any trees were met with. Now of a sudden all was changed. We have reached the southern-facing slopes of the outward ridge of the Himalayas, and upon these slopes all the rains of the monsoon are expended, while none is left to reach the parched hill slopes beyond. Consequent upon this, the mountains of the one side of the water are densely packed with forest, and on the other are bare sun-baked rocks only."[1]

Entering in Ladakh : In the spring of 1889, Younghusband again thought to visit Central Asia. This time Mr. Ney Elias and Captain Bower advised to explore Tibet. But he got an assignment to stop the activities of Kanjuti raids. However, came in Ladakh via Zoji-la, and was guarded by six Gurkhas. Younghusband says :

> "Crossing the Zoji-la, the last of the passes on my way from Peking, we left behind us all the wooded beauties of Kashmir, its shady pine forest and bright flowery meadows, and entered that desolate region of barren mountains and unshaded valleys. Where the sun beat down upon the unprotected rocks and produced a degree of heat which would never have been expected at altitudes of nine thousand feet and over, and which made still more trying the cold blasts which, when the sun had set, came down from the snow above. We were entering Ladak, an offshoot of Tibet, and the only redeeming feature in the country was the picturesqueness of its monasteries, peached high upon every prominent rock. As regards its natural scenery, it would be difficult to find any more dreary-looking country than Ladak. Its mountains, though lofty, are not grand or rugged, but resemble a monotonous succession of gigantic cinder-heaps. But the Buddhist monasteries, the fluttering prayer-flags, the chortens, and the many other signs of a religion almost

totally unrepresented in India, gave the country a charm which just relieved it from utter condemnation. These signs of Buddhist life have many times before been described, so I need only refer here to the long rows of what appeared to be immense graves, overlaid with hundreds of slabs, each engraved with the formula, 'Om mane padme hum' ('Oh! the jewel of the lotus'), the talismanic prayer which the devotees of this religion believe will produce more and more beneficent results the oftener it is repeated; the many-coloured flags fluttering in the breeze inscribed with the same magic formula, and breathing with each new flutter one fresh prayer to heaven; the dirty, yellow-clad monks, with their shaven heads, their string of beads round their necks, and their prayer-wheel reeling off a prayer with each successive revolution. All these are well-known characteristics of Buddhist life, and require only a passing reference here. I admired their picturesqueness and wondered at the quaintness of such superstitions, but had no time to study in detail the particular phase the Buddhist religion has taken in this far-away corner of Tibet."[2]

At the Capital of Ladakh : On 31 July 1889 he reached Leh after travelling twenty days and crossed one eleven thousand and three thirteen thousand feet passes. On entering Leh, he met Shukar Ali, who was earlier in his caravan while crossing the Mustagh. Shukar Ali offered his services for further expedition. This time Younghusband accepted his services and promoted him to cook. He says :

"On July 31 reached its principal place, Leh. On entering Leh I was met by old Shukar Ali, the only Ladaki who had come across the Mustagh pass. Hearing of my return to these parts, he had come to offer his services, and I gladly accepted them, for a more willing, cheery servant I ever had. From pony-man he was now promoted to cook. He had no experience of cooking and these rough hill-men are not the persons one would ordinarily choose for cooks; but knowing the hardships my men would have to through, I was determined not to have a man from the plains of India, who might become ill or give in just when his services were most needed. Only men accustomed to 'roughing' it could come with me now, and no one could stand hard work better than Shukar Ali, with Shukar Ali as one of the party there would always be a volunteer for hard work when anything specially trying had to be done."[3]

Guest of Captain Ramsay at Leh : At Leh, Younghusband was the guest of Captain Ramsay, the British Joint Commissioner. Captain Ramsay made all necessary arrangements for his onward journey. Younghusband expressed his following views :

> "At Leh I was the guest of Captain Ramsay, the British Joint Commissioner. He had been asked to have ponies ready for me, and to have other necessary arrangements made for my onward journey, and he had done everything so thoroughly that I had little else to do but take over charge."[4]

Across the Khardung Pass : On August 8, 1889 Younghusband left Leh and via Khardong pass entered in Nubra valley. This pass is one of the high passes of Ladakh and was not easy to cross. Younghusband views about this as :

> "Directly behind Leh a high pass, the Khardung, seventeen thousand six hundred feet above the sea, has to be crossed, and as the ascent to it from Leh is very abrupt, I experienced a bout of mountain sickness, which depressed me greatly for the time. When the ascent to high altitudes is gradual, one becomes accustomed to the changed condition of the atmosphere; but when the ascent to such a height as seventeen thousand feet is abrupt most men seem to feel the change, and a racking headache and feeling of sickness and depression soon lets the traveller know that mountain sickness has come over him. Fortunately, however, mountain sickness wears off as one becomes accustomed to high altitudes, and I was never trouble with it again."[5]

Some more high passes in Nubra valley : In Nubra valley Younghusband came across beautiful orchards, Buddhist monuments and difficult Saser pass. Here he says :

> "We ascended the picturesque Nubra valley with its orchards of apricot trees and Buddhist monuments, and then crossed the Saser pass, seventeen thousand eight hundred feet—a pass which, no account of the glacier at its summit, is often very dangerous, but which at this season presented no difficulty whatever. The mountains about here and at the head of the Nubra are very grand and bold and rise to peaks of twenty-three thousand and twenty-four thousand feet in height, with fine glaciers rolling down their sides; but beyond the Saser pass we entered the most utterly desolate country that exists on the face of the globe."[6]

In conclusion I may say Younghusband like his uncle Robert Shaw was a great explores of Central Asian countries. He visited Manchuria, Peking, Gobi Desert, Chinese Turkestan to Kashgar, Yarkand and penetrated Chang-pai-shan summit. In 1889 on the eve to investigate the circumstances of the Kanjuti or Hunza raids on the Kirghiz territory, he visited Ladakh.

References

1. Younghusband, Francis : 'The Heart of a Continent', Hong Kong Oxford University Press, 1984 and First published by John Murray, 1896 : 210-11.
2. *Ibid.*, 218-19.
3. *Ibid.*, 219-20.
4. *Ibid.*, 220.
5. *Ibid.*, 224-25.
6. *Ibid.*, 225.

16

Captain Hamilton Bower Experiences in Ladakh

Captain Hamilton Bower started his journey to Tibet via Ladakh on 4th April 1891. He had a big caravan with him in which sufficient geographical instruments such as maximum and minimum thermometers, hypsometer, prismatic compasses, pocket chronometer, micrometer etc. To guard the caravan sufficient arms and ammunition also with them. On the 17th April 1891 Captain Bower accompanied with E.F. Knight left Srinagar. Zoji La pass was the first high mountain pass onwards to Leh. When the battery of Bower reached at Zoji La, snow started falling and caused some difficulty. He remarks :

> "From Gunderbal, which is reached by water, the road runs up the beautiful Sind valley to the Zoji La pass. Though this pass is very low, being only 11,300 feet high, yet, owing to the amount of the snow that falls early in the season, it is often difficult to cross, and this year it was unusually so. The only way to get our things over was to have them made into very light packages and carried by coolies, while to each pony a man was told off to help him through the deep snow; it was a long weary day."[1]

Thirteen days stay in Leh : Captain Bower reached Leh on 1st June 1891. Here he stayed for thirteen days in connection to arrange coolies for onward journey to Tibet. Finally with the help of Naib Wazir, Bower got six men who were willing to go to Tibet. He says :

> "Leh was reached on the 1st of June, and I halted there for thirteen days making final preparations. The difficulty about enlisting men was increased by my refusal to say what was the object of the expedition. However, six men willing to go and

to ask no questions were enlisted through the assistance kindly rendered by the Naib Wazir (assistant or lieutenant-governor). These men, with the exception of one, who however was far and away the most intelligent of the lot, bore excellent characters, and to prevent their deserting."[2]

Argoons the result of Nikka : On 14th June 1891 Captain Bower along with six Argoon caravan drivers marched towards Tibet. Argoons are a class of half-castes often resulted of the nikkha i.e. temporary marriages allowed by Mahomedan law. Under this act Mohamedan married with Ladakhi Buddhist woman and as the result concerned person is know by Argoon. Captain Bower had his following opinion :

"Argoons are a class of half-castes, mostly the result of the nikkha marriages made by Turki merchants with Tibetan women. Having no land, they eke out a subsistence by doing caravan work on the Yarkand road; they are hardy and patient, no one can honestly say they are cowards amidst the great physical difficulties encountered in these regions, and the way they work in the only line open to them is certainly in their favour. Personally, I should class them considerably higher than the pure bred Ladakhi, their manner of life tending to make them more self-reliant."[3]

Hemis Festival : In Ladakh Hemis monastery annually organise its annual festival during summer since early days. Therefore, visitors get chance to see this festival in which Lamas of the monastery wear masks of the different deities according to the Tantric practice and perform tantric dance at the chamra or courtyard before the main temple of the monastery. Captain Bower also visited to this monastery and saw the dance. He explains :

"The annual fair at Hemis monastery was on, so we paid a flying visit to it *en route*. The whole place was in gala costume, and as we approached, the band, consisting of six or seven men seated on the ground, some playing reed instruments resembling the chanter of big pipe and some beating tom-toms, struck up in our honour. Next day we saw a masked dance by the monks; the place was crowded and amongst the spectators were some unprepossessing-looking nuns with shaven heads and yellow caps, it evidently not being the fashion of doom the best looking ones to a convent life. The dance was one of the quaintest and weirdest sights I have ever seen; round and round went these hideously masked figures, adorned in gorgeous rament, while a solemn dirge was chanted in true cathedral style by a hidden choir. On my asking the meaning of the masks, I was informed that it was to accustom the people to fearful images, in order that after death, when their spirits were wandering in space, they might not be frightened by the demons they encountered."[4]

Hemis Monastery escaped in 1834 : Dogra Army Chief Zorawar Singh invaded Ladakh in 1834 and pluder many important monasteries like Lamayuru etc. Hemis monastery was being escaped as it is located far away from Leh in a narrow valley surrounded by high mountain rocks. Captain Bower also agreed with this statement and says :

"The monastery is situated in a narrow valley in which there is a little arable land cultivated by the peasantry, half the produce of which is given to the monks. We were given comfortable quarters in the monastery, which is very rich, having escaped plunder in 1834 by supplying provisions to Zorawar Singh's invading army."[5]

Game animals look as tame : In Ladakh and Leh district in particular is dominated by Buddhists, who are kind hearted and do not kill animals. The wild or game animals know this fact, hence graze nearby villages without any fear. Captain Bower has his following opinion :

"The game animals and birds in the valley are very tame, as they are never shot : some shapoo (Ovis vignei) were grazing close by, and a chukar (Caccabis chukar, a bird resembling a red-legged partridge) sat looking at us from about five yards off."[6]

Burhels found at Sakti : In olden days Sakti village on way to Tangtse was one of the mini Mandi of Central Asian trade. Captain Bower took rest here for some days and involved in shooting Burhels. He says :

"From Hemis we rejoined the caravan at Sakti crossing the Indus by a rather rickety bridge. During our halt I went out to look for burhel (Ovis nahura) and after a typical Himalayan 'stalk', succeeded in getting one. The heard was sighted soon after leaving camp, but while attempting to stalk them they moved on to ground where there was no cover at all, so there was nothing to do but sit down and await their moving. This they did about three o' clock, gradually grazing their way on to good stalking ground, where I got a very easy shot."[7]

Chang La Pass crossed before sunrise : In olden days all the high passes did not cross after sunrise, as pony and other loaded animals often slipped. Captain Bower also crossed Chang La pass before sunrise. He remarks :

> "Before five A.M. we were climbing the pass, having made an early start in order to get over before sun had melted the crust on the snow. One donkey knocked up, and one pony looked like following his example, but the caravan drives slit his nostrils—a remedy I have often seen tried on animals affected by altitude."[8]

Tibetan wall near Chang La pass : After occupied Leh and its adjoining areas General Zorawar Singh marched towards Tibet. He got first obstruction by Tibetans near Chang La pass where they built safety wall. Captain Bower remarks :

> "On the eastern side of the pass there is a wall built by the Tibetans to keep Zorawar Singh's army out; but since, in order to make the obstruction effective, it was necessary to defend the wall a part of the programme the Tibetans omitted to carry out, the Dogra General did not find it an insurmountable obstracle."[9]

Tankse is the last place of trading for Chang Chenmo : In olden days Tankse was also one of the important trading mandi for Central Asian trade. Traders after crossing Samarkand came upto Tankse for trade. Captain Bower knowing this facts hired sheep, yak and ponies for further journey. He writes :

> "Tankse, though a small place, is very well known, as it is the last place at which sportsmen bound to Chang Chenmo can lay in supplies. Flour is of inferior quality and dear, 18 lbs. for the rupee being about the normal rate. Sheep-fine, large and much superior to the Indian—are sheep enough, costing two rupees each. Out of one hundred and fifty paraded for my inspection, I chose the ten fattest at that rate. From Tankse I hired some yaks and ponies, and having halted for one day we continued our route towards Chang Chenmo."[10]

Panggong : A deep blue colour : I visited Panggong lake in 1992 it was looking like a beautiful deep blue colour and varies as clouds cover the sun. Captain also acknowledged the same, he says :

> "Pobrang, which consists of a few huts with grass close by, surrounded by barren hills. On the road, the west end of the Pangong lake is passed; they are slat, contain no fish, though plenty are found in the rivers flowing in and are of a beautiful deep blue colour. We bought a Tibetan sheep-dog[11] here, to guard the camp."[12]

Captain Bower saw many wild animals during his journey to Tibet. In his book "Diary of a journey across Tibet", he gave the following information :

The Yak (Paephagus grunniens) : In Ladakh Yak is a very popular animal. He is a slow but very suitable transport animal for high altitude regions. In olden days travellers used to prefer to hair yak from Ladakh for the journey to Tibet or Yarkand. Captain Bower says :

> "The Yak is the typical animal of Tibet, herds and occasionally solitary old bulls, are to be seen all over the Chang. Sometimes as many as a hundred were seen in a day, and for days together some were always in sight. Tame yaks are largely used as beasts of burden. They are very sure-footed, and carry loads over places where ponies could never go; and their habitat being at great elevations, they are not oppressed by mountain sickness; but they travel very slowly, and soon get footsore. Thus the progeny of yak bulls and common domestic cows is also largely used."[14]

Tibetan antelope (Panthalops hodgsonii) : In Ladakh it is popularly known as 'tros', its wool in market famous by 'shatoosh', Ladakhis called 'tsoskul'. In Ladakh one can see these along the high passes. However, in Tibet they can be seen often along the mountain passes. Captain Bower says :

> "Tibetan antelope are very widely distributed over the Chang. Their habitat may be said to commence in the west at the Karakarum Pass, and extends to the Lhasa-Sining road on the east, and probably they are found in occasional patches of suitable country still farther east. On the south they are found on the plateaux north of Sikkim and Kumaun, and towards the north as far as the Tibetan plateau extends. They are most plentiful between 16,000 feet and 18,500 feet and are very rarely found below 15,000 feet. A peculiarity about them is that in summer the sexes inhabit quite different stretches of country. On the Karakorum, for instance nothing but does are found on the southern slope, and nothing but males on the northern. They make a form like a hare in the open valleys, and their presence is only detected by the graceful lyre-shaped horns showing above the bare plain. Their flesh is excellent eating, and during our long tramp across the Chang we lived almost entirely on it. Had they not been plentiful and widely distributed, our commissariat would have been a source of much greater anxiety than it was."[15]

The Tibetan gazelle (Gazella picticaudata) : It is restricted to the south of the Indus river and today extremely rare. Bower also saw this animal, while visiting to Tibet via Ladakh. Let's know what he says :

> "The Tibetan gagelle is even more widely distribution than the antelope, but is nowhere so numerous an antelope are in certain places. They are handsome little animals, very much resembling the Chinkara of India and Jeran of Turkistan. Shooting them is not nearly such easy work as shooting antelope, in addition to being a much smaller mark to aim at, they are much more wary, and in the most out-of-the way places fled incontinently directly the caravan was viewed, whereas the antelope continually trotted past, very little, if at all out of express rifle range. In British territory they are found in the neighbourhood of Hanli[16] and the Tso Morari lake in Ladakh; and we found them in Tibet as far east as Asi, on the road between Chiamdo and Garthok. It is probable that they are found as far north as the suitable country exists, that is, plateaux at an elevation of 13,000 to 18,000 feet. In the Gobi desert their place is taken by Gazella Subgutturosa."[17]

The Kiang (Equus hemionus) : In Ladakh Kiangs are scattered throughout in Chang-Thang. In 1992 I visited Chusul and other parts of Chang-Thang sub-division of Leh district, and saw Kiangs thousand in number. Captain Bower says :

> "The Kiang belongs to the same class as the ghorkhar of Western India and the zebra of Africa. They are widely distributed over Tibet, where they are very common. In colour they are a sort of chestnut on the upper part of the body, fading into fawn colour and white on the abdomen, and with a dark brown stripe down the back. The mane is thin and erect, and the grace of their appearance in much spoilt by the enormous head and large ears. They are by no means shy, being, on the contrary very inquisitive, and their ill-timed curiosity often spoils a stalk after nobler game. Sometimes they may be seen wheeling and turning on the Tibetan plains like a troop of cavalry."[18]

The Tibetan Argali (Ovis ammon hodgsoni) or Nyan : In Ladakh Nyans are also found in Chang-Thang region. In 1988, Leh-Manali road was just opened I went to Manali by truck, on the way beyond Taglungla pass 17,500 feet high from the sea level, saw a beautiful brown colour with massive horns Nyan. Today they are small in number. Captain Bower describes about this animal in the following way :

"The Ovis ammon is the noblest of all Tibetan game, and with the Ovis poli of the Pamirs, claims kingship over all the sheep tribe. A full-grown ram stands about 12 hands at the shoulder and its horns measure 40 inches with a girth at the base of 16 to 17, and the horns have been obtained 40 inches in length and 20 in girth. It is not found below 15,000 feet and as it prefers the slopes of hills to the open valleys, and in its pursuit it would have been necessary to go out of our way and climb the hills, we never attempted to shoot them. It is found in Ladakh, where it has been known to cross with *Ovis Vignei*, and we saw its horns lying about as far east as the 88th degree of longitude. The probabilities are that it is to be found still farther east. Shady stony slopes where it is impossible to approach silently, are its favourite resting-places, and this considerably militates against the sportsman's chance of success. The fact that sportsmen every year shoot some in Ladakh, where they have never been otherwise than scarce, points to their numbers being augmented by immigrants from across the frontier."[19]

Ladakh Urial (Ovis orientalis Vignei) or Shapoo : In 1988 I saw shapoo in good number along the Gya-Miru mountain slope. Later when I visited Lamayuru in 1997, they were found quite in good number in the mountain slopes other side of Lamayuru monastery or at the surrounding to Atiche. Let's see what Bower says about this animal :

"The *Ovis Vignei* or Shapoo is found in Ladakh and Astor, and according to Mr. Dalgleish, in Northern Tibet, but in our route across the Chang, after leaving British territory, we never saw any nor even their horns lying about. The general elevation of the country is higher than that of the places they are found in Ladakh, which probably accounts for their absence. They are only a climatic variety of the Oorial or Salt Range sheep, though their horns run probably a shader larger. The maximum recorded is length 37.75, girth 11.5. This species breeds freely with tame sheep, and as has been mentioned, has been known to do so with Ovis ammon."[20]

Blue sheep (Pseudois nayaur), the Burhel or Napo : It is found in large number in Ladakh, and very much looks like sheep. According to Bower :

"The Burhel or Napoo is link between the sheep and the goat tribe. It is widely distributed, and in places exceedingly common, but does not descend below 10,000 feet. It is found in Ladakh, Baltistan, and the northern slopes of the Himalayas, west of the Yarkand road, and we saw some in the country between Chiando and Garthok, and occasionally during our march across the Chang. It affects only broken ground it is a very conspicuous animal owing to the black marking on the face, chest, and legs that the males possess, amongst the strong lights and shades that are so characteristic of Tibet it is extremely heard to distinguish on the ground it prefers to rest on. Its flesh is excellent, particularly towards the end of the summer, when it is in good condition. The largest horns recorded are length 32.1, girth 13 inches."[21]

Polyandry in Ladakh : Population growth in Ladakh is being controlled by the traditional system under which Buddhists in Ladakh followed Polyandry system of marriage. In my opinion polyandry system was practiced by Buddhists on economic ground as they have limited land for cultivation and migration means they would die by heat. Bower also agrees with this opinion, he remarks :

"Polyandry, we may safely assume was originally introduced on economic grounds by some far-seeing statesman, who realised that in a country where so little land was capable of being brought under cultivation, a large increase in population must either lead to great poverty or emigration, and emigration is rendered out of question by the fact that Tibetans[22] are quite incapable of living out of their country—moved to a more genial climate they quickly sicken. The practical value of polyandry is plainly demonstrated when we regarded Ladakh and Baltistan."[23]

In conclusion Captain Hamilton Bower made an extensive journey across Tibet, and during the course of his journey he stayed in Ladakh quite a long time. He made a valuable discussion about Ladakhi culture, custom, festival and wild animals.

Notes and References

1. Captain Hamilton Bower : 'Diary of a Journey across Tibet', Rivington, Percival and Co., London, 1894 : 7-8.
2. *Ibid.*, 10-11.
3. *Ibid.*, 11.

4. *Ibid.*, 11-12.
5. *Ibid.*, 12.
6. *Ibid.*, 8.
7. *Ibid.*, 13.
8. *Ibid.*, 14.
9. *Ibid.*
10. *Ibid.*, 14-15.
11. Tibetan sheep-dog : In Chang-Thang sub-division of Ladakh people rare sheep and goat in large number. To guard herd they take the help of big dogs who guard these animals. These dogs are the excellent watchers and powerful built.
12. Captain Bower : *op. cit.* : 16.
13.
14. *Ibid.*, 286.
15. *Ibid.*, 286-87.
16. Hanli : Hanley is a village located in Chang-Thang sub-division of Leh district.
17. Captain Bower : *op. cit.* : 287-88.
18. *Ibid.*, 288.
19. *Ibid.*, 288-89.
20. *Ibid.*, 289.
21. *Ibid.*, 289-90.
22. Tibetan : Like Tibetans, Ladakhis also belong to the same race as Mongolian. Therefore, Ladakhis also do not prefer to go out as they quickly sicken by hot climate.
23. Bower : *op. cit.* : 277.

17

K.F. Knight Journey to Ladakh and Its Neighbouring Countries

On February 26, 1891 K.F. Knight left London, on 4th May arrived at Srinagar. Later with Captain Bower he promised to visit Ladakh. On 21 May reached at Zoji la, which was then known horrible pass and had been noticed that sometimes destroy whole caravans of travellers with their deadly cold. Therefore, had a bad reputation among travellers. The height of this pass is only 11,500 feet, but wind velocity in this gap is so high, that snow at top of mountain peaks suddenly falls and caused snow avalanches. So on crossing this pass one suddenly enters in a rainless zone where snow fall occurs during winter on the mountain-tops, but often finds no snow left lying in summer.

Knight remarks : "One never hears of any other pass than the Zoji La on the Leh road—and it is, indeed, the only difficulty one encounters, for it is here that the southerly wind deposits its heavy burden of snow, but as a matter of fact, a great portion of the road beyond, though left bare of snow in early spring, is at a considerably higher elevation than the summit of the Zoji La."[1]

Marmots are more clever than dogs : After crossing Zoji-la, when knight came across in Dras valley, he saw hide and seek game of marmots and dogs, in which marmots driven dogs fantastically. He described this moment in the following words :

> "As we toiled across the weary fields of snow that only living things we saw were certain queer little beasts that are very familiar to travellers on these highlands. Every now and again we would hear an uncanny shrill whistling and on looking in the direction whence it came would observe a little marmot

sitting up on it shind legs on the top of some rock and gazing impertinently at us. These marmots drive dogs frantic with their exceedingly irritating ways. A dog seldom succeeds in catching a marmot. The marmot stands still lures him on with jeering whistles and then but not until the infuriated dog is just on him, drops into his hole between the rocks; when the disappointed dog has retired to a safe distance, he pops out again like a jack-in-the box and resumes his tantalising jibes."[2]

Once Dras was influenced by Buddhism : Knight arrived at Dras on 23 May 1891 and acknowledged various races who spoke four languages. Besides, he saw Buddhist idols along road side, which indicate that in olden days Buddhism had its roots right upto Dras valley. Knight writes :

> "The inhabitants of Dras are of various races and limited as is the population, no less than four languages are in constant use here—Kashmiri, Tibetan, Balti and Brokpa, the last being the tongue of a shepherd-race inhabiting the high valleys. The Dras people are Mussalmans, we saw here large stones on which idols were carved, showing that the Buddhist creed had once prevailed in this district."[3]

Burtsa is the only fuel save cattle-dung : Burtsa, though was invaluable for travellers, it was widely used by the Ladakhis as fuel and collected on the roofs. Knight says :

> "Boortsa, or Eurotia, a most invaluable plant to travellers on the high desert-valleys and plateaus of Tibet, and without which vast regions would be quite impassable for man and beast. It is full of an aromatic oil that smells something like camphor. It burns the better the greener it is. On the wind-swept, bitterly cold wastes, where there is no wood or grass the burtsa is the only fuel save cattle-dung, and is often the only fodder procurable for one's animals. It flourishes best, it seems, in extremely arid regions, and at a much higher elevation."[4]

Wide variation in day and night temperature : Ladakh has cold arid and dry atmosphere, as a result of thin dry medium during sun shine you will feel extremely hot and when sun sets suddenly temperature drops to 10-15°C. Knight explains this incident beautifully in the following way:

> "We were certainly marching through a very changeable climate, for summer and winter alternated several times this day. At one moment the heat would be tropical, the next moment a bitter. When sitting down this day to tiffin, with the sun blazing on one cheek and the other cheek in the freezing shade, one

almost felt, as was remarked at the time, that it was a question by which one would be attacked first-sun-stroke on one side of one one's head, or frostbite on the other."[5]

Mahomedans[6] at Tashgam[7] were converted from Buddhists : It is said that in olden days Ladakh was a land of Buddhists. However, after 14th century A.D. many of them converted to Muslims. Tashgam village is one of the example where inhabitants converted from Buddhists. Knight says :

"At Tashgam we were still among Mahomedans, but these were converted, or perverted, Ladaki[8] Buddhists, and spoke the Tibetan tongue[9]. Instead of the greeting of 'salaam', the word with which we were welcomed here, and on all the road beyond, was the Tibetan equivalent jooly[10]."[11]

Chortens and Honeycliff monastery in Shargol : In Buddhist dominated area one may often see chortens and monasteries. Chortens usually constructed near monasteries or at the entering point of village. Monasteries always have a isolated place and situated at high location than the village level. Knight writes :

"*Chortens*, or sarcophagi, of dried mud, gaily painted, containing the ashes of pious lamas. On the mountain-side, near the village, is a *gompa*, or monastery of lama, carved out of a honeycombed cliff, forming with some other cliffs of the same description of giant flight of stairs on the slope of a bleak mountain of loose stones. The gompa itself is painted white, with bands of bright colour on the projecting wooden gallery, so that it stands out distinctly against the darker rocks."[12]

Ladakhis are ready to fight in defence of their Lamas : Red Lamas use little red cap whereas yellow cap by others. Yellow lamas are in many respects more ascetic and strict than Red. They are recognised as spiritual, and in some respects temporal ruler. Therefore, people of Ladakh always ready to fight if anybody harm them. Knight remarks :

"No less than one-sixth of the population of Ladak[13] are in the Church[14], either as monks or nuns; and as almost each family, wealthy or poor, contributes one or more of its members to the priesthood, the church is a popular institution, and any interference with its privileges is bitterly resented. Unwar like and timid as the Ladakis are, they are ready to fight in defence of their lamas, and a few years since, when it was proposed to increase the revenue paid by the monasteries, the country was on the brink of revolution, and artillery had to be brought out to overawe the rioters in the bazaar at Leh. The Kashmir Government now forbids any communication by letter on secular business the lamas of Ladak and those of Chinese Tibet; but a good deal of correspondence is smuggled across the frontier. The church of Ladak is very well endowed. Its extensive estates comprise much of the most fertile land in the country, and on this the state exacts as revenue only one-sixth of the amount per acre that has to be paid in the case of private land. It is also said that the monasteries own pastures and cultivated land in remote valleys, the existence of which is unknown to, or ignored by the authorities, so that no revenue at all is levied on them. A rich monastery, too, has no difficulty in obtaining leniency of assessment by the bribery of the tax-collectors. These lamaseries appear to be organised in a very business-like way. There are two classes of monks in each. There are, in the first place, the working monks, who attend to the temporal interests of the community. They cultivate the land, collect the rents of the monastery tenants, travel through the villages to beg alms for the brotherhood, and advance coin and grain to farmers at a usurious rate of interest. Among this class is steward, who keeps the monastery accounts. The second class is composed of the spiritual monks, who have nothing to do with worldly matters, but devote their time to dreaming and religious exercises, and to whom, to judge from their abstracted expression and general appearance, the bladder-flappers of the Laputan sages would be useful attendants, to wake them up when it was time to wash. Their sole duties are to mumble and intone words they do not understand, and to dance the complicated figures of the sacred dances. From this class the abbot is chosen and in a few cases a monastery has its spiritual head a very holy person indeed, no less than a skooshok, or incarnation."[16]

Ladakhis have a magnificent capacity to belief in incarnation : In Ladakh all rinpoches or kushoks are incarnated lama. After the perinirvana rinpoche takes birth again in human life and work for the human being. Knight explains how rinpoche is selected for the concern monastery :

"When (Kushok) is about to die, he calls around him his disciples, and tell them where he will be re-born and all the circumstances of the re-birth. As soon as he is dead the disciples repair to the place he has indicated and search for a newly-born child which bears the sacred marks, and is for other reasons the most probable incarnation of the departed saint. Having found the child, they leave him with his mother till he is four years old, when they return, bringing with them a quantity of praying-books, rosaries, praying-wheels, bells and other priestly articles among which are those that belonged to the late incarnation. Then the child has to prove that he is the new incarnation by recognising the property that was his in his previous existence, and by relating reminiscences of his past. If he is successful in this, as is nearly always the case, he is acknowledged as the skooshok and is carried off for ever from his home and family, to be educated in the sacred mysteries first in the gompa[17] of which he is to be the head, and afterwards, for some years, in the sacred city of Lassa[18]. He then returns to his own gompa, therein to take up his residence in separate building, not busying himself with the worldly affairs of the brotherhood, but dreaming away the long, quiet years until the time comes for him again to die."[19]

Praying by Machinery : In olden day water-power praying wheels were very popular. Ladakhis then believed that the continuous turning of prayer wheel by water-power helps to get peace and harmony in the society. Normally Buddhists in Ladakh do not bother to understand the philosophy of religion. They consider that its the duty of every lama to pray for their welfare. Knight writes :

> "The bulk of the praying is, as everyone knows, carried on by machinery in Ladak. For instance, wheels containing rolls of prayers are turned by water-power; and every time a wheel revolved it is working out the salvation of the man who put it up: every turn exempts him from some infinitesimal portion of time which would otherwise be passed in one of the six inferior spheres—hla, or gods[20]; demigods; man; animals; eedak[21], temporary hell. In order to escape these existences it is only necessary to twist round a wheel so many million of times."[22]

Head Ornament Perag : Perag is a famous head ornament of Ladakhi Buddhist lady. It sometimes shows the status of her family. Knight writes :

> "The ornament known as the peyrak[23], covers the top of the head and falls some way down the back. The peyrak is a piece of leather studded with flat turquioses; it is about two feet in length and about eight inches broad. The turquoises vary in

size from that of a two-shilling piece downwards; they are found in Chinese Tibet, are of a greenish colour, and of inferior quality. However, a good peyrak may be worth as much as twenty-five pounds. All the personal property of Ladaki woman is invested in the turquoises of her peyrak."[24]

Custom of Polyandry keep Ladakhis Happy : In olden days Ladakhi Buddhists had a custom of polyandry, which helped to control population growth, on the other side in Baltistan where Balti Muslims had a plurality tradition on large families, thus dragged them to a pitiable condition. Knight remarks :

"Ladakis are a very dirty people indeed; but this is from choice, and not from poverty. It is easy to see that the cultivators are fairly prosperous, and exempt from the hard hand-to-mouth struggle for bare subsistence which is the lot of their Mahomedan neighbour. This happy condition of the Ladakhis is due to the curious, and to our ideas, unpleasant custom of polyandry, to which the merit must be allowed of keeping the population within reasonable limits in a unfertile region. Polyandry appears to be singularly well suited to the country and to the character of this people."[25]

In the Polyandry system eldest married son is the head of the family: According to Ladakhi Polyandry system, when the eldest son married he got better position than his father in the joint family. The other two unmarried brothers shared sex with eldest brother's wife. Knight explains this tradition briefly as :

"The first curious point to notice in (polyandry) system is that the eldest married son of a family is placed in a better position that his own father, and is practically the head of the family. For as soon as the eldest son marries he enters into possession of the family estate, a small portion only being retained by his parents for the support of themselves and their unmarried daughters; and that portion also becomes the property of the eldest son on the death of the parents and marriage of the daughters. But the eldest son, when thus marrying and taking possession of the family estate, is oblige to support the two sons next to himself in age, and these two are not allowed to contract independent marriages, but share the wife of their eldest brother, becoming the minor husbands of that lady. The children of this strange union recognise all three husbands as father, but pay more respect to the eldest, as the head of the family. If there are more brothers than two, the others do not share the family wife, but have to leave the estate and seek their fortunes outside, becoming lamas; if they be fortunate as magpas. (In case of the death of eldest brother), the wife, provided she has no children, can rid herself of his brothers, who are her minor husbands, by a simple ceremony. One of her fingers is attached with a thread to a finger of her dead husband. The thread is then broken, and by this action she is divorced from the corpse, and consequently from the two surviving brothers at the same time."

Magpa Marriage System : If man lives with her wife at her house after marriage is called Magpa. Knight explains :

"If there be no son, the eldest daughter inherits the land, the lady (then) selects some well-favoured younger brother of a large family, who has no interest in the lands of his family or share in his eldest brother's wife, and makes this person her magpa. He is the property of his wife, and cannot leave her, except in the case of gross misconduct on her part. But if she is displeased with him, she can turn him out of doors, and be rid of him without any excuse or form of divorce."[27]

Mani and Chorten in Shargol : One can often see little images in the cavities of ancient chortens; Knight says :

"Outside Shergol we saw the first mani or wall of praying-stones. This is a massive stone wall or embankment about eight feet in height, its top sloping from the centre to either side, like the roof of a house. Every one of the large flat stones that form this roof is elaborately carved in the pictorial characters of Tibet with prayers, generally with the inscription. 'Om mani patmi Om'[28]. The stones forming a mani vary in size from a few inches to four or five feet in diameter. The carvings are often artistic and beautiful. Images of Buddha and designs of mystic figures are represented upon them, as well as prayers. At either end of the mani in the illustration is a large chorten, of the shape most frequently met with in Ladak. After the corpse of a Buddhist has been burnt by the lamas, some of the ashes of the dead man are mixed with clay and moulded into a little idol, which, if the deceased was a man of wealth, is placed by itself in the middle of a chorten built expressly for it; if he was a poor man, his idol is placed in some old chorten, with other idols of the poor."[29]

Old Kharbu Destroyed by Dogras : Dogra force under the command of General Zorawar Singh attacked Ladakh on 1834. When Dogras came at Kharbu, Ladakhi troops tried to resist them, as a result Dogras destroyed the Kharbu. Knight during his interview with local inhabitant got the following information :

> "(The) old Kharbu was a well-fortified castle before the Dogras came. (The white ruined) building was one of the palaces of the Rajah of Ladak; villagers (then) lived in the castle up there; but when the Maharajah's troops came here and deposed our Rajah, they burnt the old town and no one has dwelt there since."[30]

How a Lady Satisfied all his husbands : Under the polyandry system, Ladakhi lady very cleverly satisfy her husbands putting something outside the house door. Knight says :

> "When her eldest, or principal husband was at home the other two had to keep out of the way. Thus, if he happened to return, he would place his stick or winter boots outside the house-door, to intimate to his juniors that he had taken up his residence in the family mansion, and that their presence there was undesirable until he should go away again."[31]

Inside Ladakh some passes are higher than Zoji-la but do not have snow : Namika-la and Fotu-la (Potu-la) are such higher passes in between Leh-Srinagar road, but don't get high snow precipitation. Knight says :

> "Namika-la, 13,000 feet above the sea. But there was no snow, and here we found the easiest bit of road we have experienced. The Fotu-la, the highest point of the Leh road, being 13,400 feet above. We (also) found no snow lying."[32]

Hinniscoot had ruined castle : In olden days at Hinniscoot ruined castle, one could see Dogra sepoys, Knight remarks :

> "When we reached the village of Hinniscoot, which is built on the steep slope of a hill, with a ruined castle above it, we found some sepoys on the Maharajah's army awaiting us."[33]

Violation of Lord Elgin's Tientsin Treaty : In olden days traders from Kashmir smuggled brick tea, which had high value in Kashmir market. Knight reports :

> "We met a caravan of Tibetans who were on their way from Lassa to Kashmir with a number of horses laden with brick tea. This brick tea is not very palatable to Europeans, but is held in high estimation by the Kashmiris, for it fetches two

rupees or so a pound in the bazar at Srinagur[34]. It is often smuggled across the frontier. Our commercial arrangements with China in this part of the world are, by the way, in a somewhat unsatisfactory condition. The Russians, who maintain a consulate at Yarkand, have thing their own way there, and the trade between India and Turkestan is crippled, as far as possible, to the advantage of the Russian traders. For instance, merchants who are Indian subjects of ours pay dues on entering and on leaving any city in Chinese Turkestan; while in the other hand, the Russian merchants pass free of toll. This partiality is a direct violation of Lord Elgin's Tientsin Treaty, by which it was stipulated that England should not be debarred from any other nation. It is high time that there should be someone at Yarkand to guard the interests of our subjects who trade there. Every English traveller in Turkestan is met by the resident Indian merchants with bitter complaints of the treatment they receive."[35]

Commercial treaty between the Governments of India and Kashmir in 1870 : Under the 1870 Commercial Treaty British Joint Commissioner, at Leh had duty to settle all disputes of traders. Knight reports :

"Since the commercial treaty that was entered into between the Governments of India and Kashmir in 1870 we have a representative, known as the British Joint Commissioner, at Leh, which town is the centre of the trade with eastern Turkestan, as well as with Tibet. His duty it is to settle all disputes between our subjects and natives of Kashmir on the one hand, and the Central Asian merchants who are subjects of Russia and China on the other hand. The duties that were once levied on caravans passing through Leh were abolished some years ago by the Maharajah's Council; but it is said that the officials of that city quietly ignored the order."[36]

Donkeys laden with wool : Tibetan caravan carried wool from Tibet, which later taken up to Darjeeling by Englishmen. Knight reports :

"Tibetan caravan of donkeys laden with wool come from the Chung Tung[37], or Northern Plateau, by way of Rupshu. The wool trade between Tibet and India is now considerable, and Englishman who have taken up this enterprise at Darjeeling are making large profits. The Chinese Tibetans who travel with these caravan on this road, often impress the Ladaki coolies to carry their goods through the country for nothing."[38]

Dogra fort near Khalatse : In olden days at the bank of Indus near Khalatse, Dogra army had a fort, who inspected the traders and travellers passed through the bridge. Knight says :

> "We crossed the river by a long cantilever bridge, rode through a Dogra fort which defended the passage. Soon rows of manis and chortens indicated the approach to a village Khalsi, where we had our tiffin by an artificial pond of clear water under the shade of walnut trees."[39]

Basgo had two large lamaseries and fortress : In olden days Basgo had two big monasteries and fortress, which are now ruined. Knight reports :

> "(Basgo) covers the side of a rocky hill. High above it, on the crages, are the ruins of the ancient fortress, which once resisted a very long siege, and two large lamaseries. I ascended the cliffs and explored the strange wilderness of great rocks, riven as by earthquakes, on which these buildings stand. The gompas, surrounded by precipices and pinnacles, command extensive views, but over stony desolation only."[40]

Dad Mahomed murdered Dalgleish : Dalgleish was a English traveller, when he was on to Karakoram pass, murdered by Dad Mahomed, later captured. Knight said this interesting story in this way :

> "Dad Mahomed, a Pathan from Quetta, a notorious suffian and assassin, who had established himself as a merchant at Leh, murdered the English traveller, Dalgleish, on the Karakoram pass, where the caravans of both happened to be encamped on the same night. Dalgleish's followers were cowardly Ladakis and Russian Turkis, who made no attempt to defend him. (Later) made the Mussulman Turkis take an oath on the Koran not to reveal what he had done. He then escaped into Turkestan with his Pathan followers."[41]

Epidemic in Ladakh : When Knight reached at Leh, he was informed that Ladakh was under a grip of epidemic. He described this incident in the following way :

> "There was an epidemic of Russian influenza in Ladak, to which Dr. Marx, the Moravian missionary, had fallen a victim. This disease had been raging for some time in Central Asia. The epidemic in Leh, however, turned out to be, not influenza, but a fever peculiar to this province, somewhat resembling typhus, but of a milder nature; its symptoms are fever and very high temperature lasting for twelve days intense headache, a slight

rash, and disordered mental faculties, followed by extreme prostration for several weeks. It breaks out regularly in Ladak every spring, and is probably due to the filthy habits of the people when confined within their dark, unwholesome huts, during the intense cold of the winter, through which they practically hybernate, so that in early spring, when they come forth debilitated by the poisonous air they have been breathing for months the fierce sun has plenty of material out of which to engender a pestilence."[42]

Ancient gompa and fort at Spituk : It is said in olden days near Spituk monastery, one fort was also built. Today this monastery has been renovated and fort hardly be seen. Knight says :

"We came to the isolated rock of Pitak[43], rising from the river-bank, with an ancient gompa and fort at its summit. Here two spurs of mountain-range to the north of the Indus open out, leaving a great sand plain between them. At the head of this plain, stands the city of Leh, surrounded by cultivated fields, groves of lofty poplars and other trees. The Indus at Pitak is 10,500 feet above the sea, Leh is 11,500 feet, so that one gradually ascends 1,000 feet in the course of the five miles' journey."[44]

Massive palace of Ladakh King in the City : Leh town, then popular for trade was the capital of Ladakh. Ladakh King palace here was the massive multistoreys building. Today one can still see this palace. Knight remarks :

"As one approaches this important city, the capital of western Tibet, towering above all the groves and houses stands the massive palace of the deposed *Gialpos*, or Rajahs of Ladak, with many irregular storeys and lofty, inleaving walls, and with giant chortens containing the ashes of kings surrounding it. Higher up, on the crags behind, is the gompa."[45]

Leh was one of busiest city in September : In those days Leh city was covered by boundary wall, every trader or traveller had to come and go by a small wicket gate. However, during summer Leh bazar was busy by trading activities. Knight here follows described :

"We rode upto the city, passed through the walls by a small wicket-gate, and found ourselves at the head of the bazar, which has been built since the Dogra conquest—a long, broad street, bordered by the shops of the merchants and with the great white palace rising conspicuously at the farther end. Leh, conveniently situated as it is about half-way between the markets of India and those of Central Asia, has become the terminus for the caravans from both regions. In the summer, traders arrive at Leh from every part of India, and from Turkestan, Tibet, Siberia, and the remotest districts of Central Asia. Here the goods and produce of the south are exchanged for those of the north. It is seldom that a caravan from India goes north of Leh, or that one from Central Asia proceeds south of it. The merchants, who have been travelling for months along the difficult roads from either direction, meet here and dispose of their loads, to a great extent by barter; but before the commence the long, weary homeward journey, they rest here for a month or two, so that the bazaar and the environs of the city are thronged with the camels, yaks, and other beasts of burden, as well as with men from all corners of Asia. At this time there is such a motley collection of types and various costumes, and such a label of different languages as it would not be easy to find elsewhere. Leh in September is, indeed one of the busiest and most crowded of cities. (It) is therefore a very cosmopolitan city, even in the dead season; for there are resident merchants and others of various races and creeds. Small as is the permanent population at least four languages are in common use here—Hindostani, Tibetan, Turki, and Kashmiri—while several others are spoken. Six religions have their followers in Leh—Sunis, Shiahs, and Maulais; Hindoos, and Sikhs. The people are fairly tolerant to each other's beliefs, and intermarriages in families of rival creeds are not infrequent. There is a mongrel race here of Arghons[46], as they are called—the half-caste offspring of Mussulman Turki caravan-drivers, who enter into temporary (Nikah) marriages with Ladak Buddhist women. The polyandry is loathsome to a Mohamedan, while a Ladakh lady is averse to sharing her husband with other wives; so one finds here that a Mussulman has seldom more than one wife, and that a Buddhist woman has generally but one husband, the contact of two extremes, polygamy and polyandry having developed the intermediate custom of monogamy."[47]

Leh had Moravian and Roman Catholic Missions : On June, 1891 Leh town had the establishments of two missionaries—the Moravian and Catholic. The latter had been recently established. Knight writes :

"The only European residents in Leh were the members of the two missions, the Moravian and the Roman Catholic. The latter mission had but recently been established, and consisted of only two fathers, an Englishman and a Dutchman, who had just arrived in the country, and had not yet acquired the vernacular or commenced their labours. The Moravian mission is an old institution."[48]

Some great scholars belong to Moravian institution : When E.F. Knight arrived at Leh in 1891, he came across with some scholars—Dr. Marx, Mr. Shaw etc. Dr. Redslop died while he was in Leh. The perpetual dustiness of the air, and the manner of their life in winter, makes the natives of Ladak particularly subject to ophthalmia and other diseases of the eye, for the treatment of which they flock to the hospital in great numbers. In one year Dr. Marx performed thirty operations for cataract alone. Dr. Redslop was a man who had acquired a complete mastery of the Tibetan dialects. He had many friends at Lassa, and his intention was to visit that great centre of Buddhism."[49]

Passport was required to visit Gilgit : In olden days no foreigner was allowed to visit Gilgit with the permission of Kashmir Government. Knight explains :

"No Europeans, sane officers of Her Majesty's Service, are allowed to travel in Kashmir territory without a passport from the Residency. But this passport does not extend to the road between Gilgit and Kashmir, which is closed to private travellers. So great is the difficulty of sending up a sufficiency of necessaries to the Gilgit garrison during the four months that the passes are open, so limited are the supplies procurable on that barran route, and so great is the drain on the scanty population for coolie labour."[50]

Polo game was the main amusements : In Ladakh Polo is a very popular game. It was played on the street of Leh bazar. Knight explains :

"The Naib Wazir also got up some amusements for us, notably polo, the indigenous game of all the highland country between Tibet and Chitral, as well as of Manipur. At Leh it is the custom to play in the bazaar, all business being suspended for the purpose. The Naib Wazir issued the order, all the shops were closed, and the strains of native band in which kettle-drums, trumpets, and *surnais*—the sound of which last is like that of bagpipes without the drone—were the principal instruments, gave notice to the citizens that the play was about to commence.

The players were all Ladakis mounted on capital little ponies. There can be no doubt that, though this game is native to the country, we have much improved upon it and polo as played by British officers in India is a far superior sport. We sat on the flat roof of the Court House, with the Naib Wazir and other notables, to view the curious spectacle, while the populace crowded all the other roofs on either side of the ground. The band played without pause. The air always becoming more rapid and noisy when either side was approaching a goal, and subsiding to low and querulous notes if the chance were lost, when a goal was won there would be a triumphant and discordant outburst of music."[51]

Chung[52] : A Ladakhi Beer : In Ladakh, Buddhists are very fond of Chang (local beer), and is served in every important occasion. Knight writes :

"I tasted the Ladaki beer[53] or chung, which is made from *grim*[54], a species of barley that ripens at high altitudes. This beer has the muddy appearance of thames water below bridge, and tastes rather like inferior cider; it not unpalatable, however, and is refreshing on a hot day."[55]

Hunting of Ibex-stalking : In Ladakh, Ibex are found in high mountain ridges. When Knight came in Ladakh, Jammu Kashmir *Riashad* had banned in killing Ibex. However, Knight shot a male Ibex. Here follows his report :

"We only saw female ibex and these according to the Maharajah's game laws, must not be shot. Each day we toiled along the high ridges. (At last) we clambered over the crags and slopes of loose debris to see plenty of female ibex, but the few males we stalked down were small. I only shot one, whose horns proved to be of inconsiderable size, not the sort of trophy to exhibit to Himalayan sportsmen."[56]

Hemis monastery of Ladakh : Hemis monastery belongs to Drugpa Ka-gyud order and the richest one in Ladakh. Knight writes : "Hemis Gompa is the most important and wealthy monastery in Ladak, and, according to Duke's guide, contains accommodation for 800 monks and nuns. The annual festival that is held here commences at a fixed date according to the Tibetan calendar, but on a variable date according to ours. The proceedings continue for two days, and attract great numbers of Buddhists from Chinese Tibet as well as from Ladak, the Yellow lamas and nuns from Lassa mingling with their Red brethren of Western Tibet.

This fair is naturally a great centre of intrigue between the Buddhist subjects of the Maharajah and the priests of Lassa, and is therefore not looked upon with great favour by the Kashmir authorities."[57]

Devil Dance : This is not a devil dance, in fact properly spell as 'cham' or Tseh-lu (Tse-cu). It is said that human 'chitta' is very sensitive after his death. His 'chitta' comes in contact with different faces of helpful (gods) and harmful (evil spirits), then through the cham it can recognise good spirits which show the right path, to take birth in good sphere. Knight explains :

> "The Devil dance, which is the most important feature in the function, has at least one definite object. It seems that after a man has died his soul, on its way to its next sphere, is waylaid by demons with horrible faces and forms, who endeavour to terrify the soul out of its proper road. Should the demons succeed in this, that belated soul will wander about space for an indefinite period, in vain seeking its proper sphere. In order to lessen the risk of such mischance the lamas during this festival put on masks resembling the faces of these demons, and initiate their awful antics; in this way the spectators are familiarised with these sights and sounds of horror, and when they die their souls will not be so readily dismayed by the apparitions."[58]

Naib Wazir of Ladakh was the custodian of Hemis monastery : During 1834-41, Dogras destroyed many monasteries in Ladakh. As Hemis monastery is located far away from the trade route, was escaped. Later it was in the rumour that lamas of the monastery decided to supply some offering to the invading army. Knight explains :

> "When Ladak was conquered by the Dogras, some fifty years ago, Hemis was the one important monastery which escaped pilage. It is rumoured that the lamas purchased this exemption by proffering supplies to the invading army. However, this may be, the fact remains that Hemis Gompa is still in possession of great treasurers, which however, the Kashmir Durbar does not permit the lamas to dispose of as they please. Were it not for this control the Buddhists would naturally feel dispose to carry this wealth across the frontier into Chinese Tibet, and found another monastery under happier auspices in that sacred and inviolate land. The Naib Wazir, as representative of the Durbar, is in custody of one of the keys, without which the principal treasure-room cannot be entered, and the lamas are not permitted to visit it unless he be present."[59]

Stok : The estate of Rajah of Ladakh : In 1834, Dogras occupied Ladakh, King dethorned and given him Stok estate near Leh. Knight writes :

"Stok, the estate of the Gialpo[60], or Rajah of Ladak, the grandson of the ruler who was overthrown by the Dogras. Here the deposed monarch sulks in state, and looks across the Indus at the grand old palace of his ancestors dominating the city of Leh. The Gyalpo is treated with the greatest respect by the Ladakis, who still look upto him as their prince."[61]

Polo match for amusement : In olden days villagers often arranged polo match in honour of their guests. Knight, when arrived Shushot[62] with Naib Wazir, villagers of Shushot (or chu-shod) showed polo-match. Knight says :

"As we neared Shushot, where we were to encamp for the night, we found that the authorities had got up a polo-match for our amusement. The men of Shushot are famed for their skill in the game, and have an excellent polo-ground in the village. The polo was followed by a *nach* of Ladaki women. The ladies, who were not possessed of any charms, wore the usual clumsy, and very large boots of felt or raw hide, which would have done well for some gouty rajah, but were not what one expects to see on the dainty feet of a *coryphee*. There was no dancing in the strict sense of the word, nor were there any of the graceful undulations of the body which distinguish some eastern *naches*. These well-wrapped-up creatures stepped in solemn figures to the strains of the band, gesticulating queerly with their hands, turning the palms, now up, now down, opening and shutting their hands, and extending or closing their fingers, in concert. They waddled about thus for some time, looking inexpressibly miserable, until the music suddenly stopped, when they formed themselves into a row, *salaamed* us by bowing their heads to the ground, and took themselves off."[63]

Tenants of Hemis monastery were exempted from tax : Hemis monastery since early days got good reputation among Ladakhis as well as got favoured by the Kashmir Darbar; as a result tenants of this monastery got full exemption from taxation. Knight describes :

"At the entrance of the Hemis nullah we passed through some good land. I made inquiry of my companions, and learnt that this was church property, being held by zemindars of the monastery on the Metayer system, the tenants handing over one-half of the produce to the lamas, and being practically exempt from taxation and begar."[64]

Hemis festival crowded with various categories of spectators : On the eve of Hemis festival spectators came not only from Ladakh, Tibetans also attended the function. Knight describes :

"As an undress rehearsal of the Devil dance was taking place in the quadrangle when we arrived, all the gallaries, windows, and roof-tops round it were crowded with spectators. The Ladaki women were conspicuous in their bright holiday dress: each had her dowry of turquoises on her head and shoulders, and her cloak of scarlet and sage-green cloth lined with snowy fleece. Many visitors from Chinese Tibet were present, lamas and nuns of the Yellow order, their robes and caps of dingy yellow contrasting with the dark red of the Ladak priesthood. Nearly all the spectators were twisting their praying-wheels as they chatted to each other and contemplated the rehearsal. When the barbaric music arose, and the Devil dance commenced, it was not only a very weired, but a really very impressive experience. Among these surroundings, one felt very far from the western world and its nineteen-century civilisation and beliefs."[65]

The mystery play at Hemis : It is said that after death, human soul does not able to understand evil and good spirits. 'Tse-cu' helps human being to recognise good spirits, who latter shows the right path of nirvana. Knight describes in details :

"The principal motive of this mystery play appeared to be the lesson that the helpless naked soul of man has its being in the midst of a vast and obscure space full of malignant demons—the earth, the air, the water crowded with them—perpetually seeking to destroy him with tortures and terrors; and that against this infinite oppression of the powers of evil he can of himself do nothing, but that occasionally the exorcisms or prayers of some good lama or incarnation may come to his assistance and shield him, and even then only after a fierce and doubtful contest between the saint and the devils. And only for a time too, can this relief from persecution endure, for all the exorcisms of all the saints are of little avail to keep back the advancing hordes. The shrieking demons must soon close in upon the soul-again. Such is the gloomy prospect of human existence. The lamas, who represented the saints in this mummery, had the appearance of early; they wore mitres and copes, and carried pastoral crooks; they swung censers of incense as they walked in procession, slowly chanting. Little bells were rung at intervals during the ceremony. There was a dipping of fingers in bowls of holy water; the shaven monks, who were looking on, occasionally bowed their heads and laid their hands across their breasts. (On the occasion of ceremony) the musical instruments employed by the lama orchestra (are) shawms and other huge brazen wind instruments, surnair, cymbals, gongs, tambourines, and rattles made of human bones. The many coloured and grostesquely-designed robes worn by the numerous were of beautiful chine silk, while the masks exhibited great powers of horrible invention on the part of their makers. The gongs and shawns sounded, and mummery commenced. First came some priests with mitres on their heads, clad in rich robes, who swung censers, filling the courtyard with the odour of incense. After a stately dance to slow music these went out; and then entered, with wild antics, figures in yellow ropes and peaked hoods, looking something like victims destined for *an auto da fe*; flames and effigies of human skulls were on their breasts and other portions of their raiment. As their hoods fell back hideous features, as of leering satyrs, were disclosed. Then the music became fast and furious, and troop after troop of different masks rushed on, some beating wooden tambourines, others swelling the din with rattles and bells. All of these masks were horrible, and malice of infernal beings was well expressed on some of them. As they danced to the wild music with strange steps and gestures, they howled in savage chorus. These, I believe, were intended to represent some of the ugly forms that meet the dead man's soul in space while it is winging its way from one sphere to the next. The loud music suddenly ceased, and all the demons scampered off, shrieking as if in fear, for a holy thing was approaching. To solemn chanting, low music, and swinging of censers, a stately procession came through the porch of the temple and slowly descended the steps. Under a canopy borne by attendants walked a tall form in beautiful silk robes, wearing a large mask representing a benign and peaceful face. He was followed by six other masks, who were treated with similar respect. (Some say these) seven masks were representations of the Dalai lama[66] and his previous incarnations; (the other say) there were the incarnation of Buddha. Again there came a change, and then rushed on the scene a crowd of wan shapes, almost naked, these represented the unfortunate souls of dead men which had been lost in space, and were vainly seeking their proper sphere through the darkness. One never knew when some peaceful anthem and stately dance of holy figures would be suddenly interrupted by the clashing discord of cymbals, and trumpets and the whirling torrent of shrieking fiends. For a time the spirits of evil ruled supreme in the arena. The variously masked to represent skeletons; dragon-faced fiends, naked save for tiger-skins about their loins; and many others. Sometimes they appeared to be taunting and terrifying the stray souls of men-grim shapes who fled hither and thither among their tormentors waving their arms and wailing miserably, souls who had not obtained Nirvana, and yet who had no incarnation. The demons went through complicated evolutions—accompanied by mystical rhythmical motions of hands and fingers. There were solo dances, too, while the other demons stood round beating gongs, clashing cymbals and clapping hands. Then the demons were repelled again by holy men; but no sooner did these last exercise one hideous band than other crowds came shrieking on. At one period of the ceremony a holy man with an archbishop's mitre on his head advanced to the beautiful chanting of men and boys, the basses, trebles, and tenors taking successive parts in solo and chorus. This holy man blessed a goblet of water by lying his hands on it and intoning some prayer. Then he sprinked the water in all directions, and the defeated demons stayed their shrieking, dancing and infernal music, and gradually crept out the arena. But the power of the exorcism was evanescent, for the routed soon returned in howling shoals, and then lamas and spirit appeared to be contending with rival magic, strange signs were made and rites performed on either side, all no doubt symbolical, only the outward forms remaining to them of their ancient creed, the inward signification lost centuries on centuries ago. A small black image representing a human corpse was placed within a magic triangle designed upon the pavement of the quadrangle. Figures painted black and white to stimulate skeletons, some in chains, other bearing sickles or swords, engaged in a frantic dance around the corpse. They were apparently attempting to snatch it away or inflict some injury on it, but were deterred by the magic of the surrounding triangle, and by the chanting and censer-swinging of several holy men in mitres and purple copes, who stood beneath the temple porch. A more potent and very ugly fiend, with great horns on his head and huge, lolling tongue, rain in, hovered threatingly over the corpse, and with a great sword slashed furiously about it, just failing by little more than a hair's breadth to touch it with each sweep of the blade. He seemed as if he were about to overcome the opposing enchantment, when a saint of still greater power than he now came to the rescue. The saint approached the corpse and threw a handful of flour on it, making mystic signs and muttering incantations. This appeared from, the mask to be one of the incarnations of Buddha. He had more control over the evil spirits than any other who had yet contended with them. The skeletons, and also he that bore the great sword, grovelled before him, and with inarticulate and beast-like cries implored mercy. He yielded to their supplication, gave each one a little of the flour he carried with him, which the fiends ate gratefully, kneeling before him; and he also gave them to drink out of a vessel of holy water. And so on, hour after hour, the ever-changing mumming proceeded."[67]

The next day cham : In olden days spectators remain in their respective tents at nearby monastery. During night for the amusement of the visitors Ladakhi women offer Chang. Next day's ceremony started by dragging six creatures painted by red paint, later exempted from any work called Tsethar (Tib. Tse 'thar) in Ladakhi language. Knight explains :

"At one stage three richly-caparisoned horses were brought into the quadrangle by some masked lamas, robed and hatted like Chinese mandarins. The fine clothes were taken off the horses, and the unfortunate beasts were then dragged hither and thither by the men, who also shouted and gesticulated before them, as if to scare and enrage them, while the whole crowd of spectators joined in with discordant howls and cheers. The lamas now poured buckets of red paint upon the horses and smeared their bodies over with it. Three large Tibetan dogs were also led in, and painted and worried in a similar fashion, until all six creatures were frantic with terror. (It is said) that the red paint symbolised the sin of the people, that was being transferred to the animals. (Later) these creatures were dedicated to the gompa, and would henceforth be exempt from any work and be considered as holy. Ceremonies of unknown meaning succeeded each other. There was a blessing of little pan of corn; a lighting of fires with mystic rites; there were dances of warriors, of savages in skins, of wild beasts of fabulous monsters. At one time four masks came forward and placed a black cloth on the ground, danced round it with intricate steps, then raising it, disclosed a prone black image of a man. But now, after a protracted conflict between rival spirits, the devils broke through the lama's magic and rent the image to pieces with their claws; and being filled with some red paste, it bled most realistically during the operation. A comic school was one of the chief features of this part of the performance. The school master was a famous old pantaloon. The bare-armed and bare-legged boys who represented the scholars wore large masks of moon shaped, grinning faces. They fought among each other; they chaffed their old pedagogue, pinched him from behind and ran away, throw things at him, stole his hat and writing materials, and played all manner of other tricks on him; while he tottered after them with his stick, trembling with rage, and unable to catch them. Last of all, the school master portrated himself with comical action before the bowls of consecrated corn and the images of the Gods, and proceeded to ape the worship of the lamas. His scholars imitating him, prostrated themselves in a row beside him, and engaged in mock prayer and ridiculous gestures and antics at the expense of their own religion. Thus, with an orgie of indecency and blasphemons caricature of all that these people are supposed to hold sacred the festival ended at dusk."[68]

Trade activities during Hemis Fair : On June 18, 1891; E.F. Knight acknowledged Tibetan caravans during Hemis Fair, engaged in small scale bartered activities. He remarks :

"(During) The Hemis Fair, a very limited amount of trade was carried on, for few Tibetan caravans had crossed the passes at so early a season. On a small scale, however, the produce of the two countries was being bartered—the dried apricots of Baltistan, the saffron and sugar of India, being exchanged for the brick tea, the incense-sticks, the medicinal herbs, and the turquoises of China."[69]

Conclusion : E.F. Knight visited Ladakh with Captain Bower in 1891. Later Bower went towards Tibet, whereas Knight stayed at Leh and waited for the permission to visit Baltistan. On June 22, 1891 he was allowed. In those days the distance from Leh to Gilgit by road was roughly, 370 miles, or thirty two marches. On July 3 he along his party travelling via Hanu Gongma reached at the foot of the Chorbat La, then entered into Baltistan, or Little Tibet. During his stay in Leh, Knight visited Hemis festival and nearby monasteries like : Thiksey, Lamayuru etc. At Leh Moravian Missionery had learned scholars—Dr. Marx, Dr. Redslop and Mr. Shaw, but all were suffered by fever. Dr. Redslop later died. As a result of this setback, Moravians decided to postponed their mission to convert natives to Christianity.

Knight during his one year journey in the middle of 1891-92 covered many countries of high altitude regions of Trans-Himalayas. Popular among them were Ladakh, Baltistan, Gilgit, Hunza, Kanjut etc. In Ladakh he entered from Zoji la and followed the old trade route in which, Dras, Kargil, Bodhkharbu, Mulbek, Lamayuru, Khalatse, Saspol, Nimo etc. were the popular villages. Dras to Kargil villages were Muslim and rest of the villages were Buddhist dominated. Finally in 1905 he published his book entitle 'Where Three Empires Meet' in which he narrated in details about his journey.

Notes and References

1. Knight, E.F. : 'Where Three Empires Meet', Longmans, Green and Co., London; 1905 & Reprinted by Asian Educational Services, New Delhi, 1993 : 107.
2. *Ibid.*, 108-09.
3. *Ibid.*, 111.
4. *Ibid.*, 112-13.
5. *Ibid.*, 113.
6. Mahomedans = Mohamedans = Muslims.
7. Tashgam = Tib. stas-dgam
8. Ladaki = Ladakhi.
9. Tibetan tongue = Bodhi.
10. Jooly = Juley.
11. Knight, E.F. : 'Where Three Empires Meet', *op. cit.* : p. 114.
12. *Ibid.*, 124-25.
13. Ladak = Ladakh.
14. Church = Monastery = Gonpa.

15. Skooshok = Kushok = Head Lama = Incarnated lama.
16. Knight, E.F. : *op. cit.* : 128-29.
17. Gompa = Gonpa = monastery.
18. Lassa = Lahasa = The rinpoches here got higher education in their respective monasteries.
19. Knight, E.F. : *op. cit.* : 130-31.
20. hla = lha = gods.
21. eedak : A fabulous animal always suffering hunger or thirst, having a large belly and a long, thin neck, through which enough food can never pass.
22. Knight, E.F. : *op. cit.* : 132.
23. Peyrak = Perak.
24. Knight, E.F. : *op. cit.* : 135-36.
25. *Ibid.*, 137.
26. *Ibid.*, 138-39.
27. *Ibid.*, 139-40.
28. 'Om mani patmi Om' = 'Om Mane Padme Hum' translated as 'O! thou jewel in the Lotus, O!'. This mantra consists six syllables of the prayer represents one of the six spheres in which human being can take birth according to Karma. It is said that if one chant this mantra several times in his life, he may get nirvana : Om : represents Fairy sphere, ma : Demigod sphere and so on, Knight, E.F. : *op. cit.* : 141-42.
29. Knight, E.F. : *op. cit.* : 141-43.
30. *Ibid.*, 149-50.
31. *Ibid.*, 150.
32. *Ibid.*, 148-51.
33. *Ibid.*, 151.
34. Srinagur = Srinagar.
35. Knight ; *op. cit.* : 157-59.
36. *Ibid.*, 159.
37. Chung-Tung = Chang-Thang.
38. Knight ; *op. cit.* : 159-60.
39. *Ibid.*, 160.
40. *Ibid.*, 163-64.
41. *Ibid.*, 167-68.

42. *Ibid.*, 172-73.
43. Pitak = Spituk.
44. Knight; *op. cit.* : 173.
45. *Ibid.*,
46. Arghons = Argons.
47. Knight ; *op. cit.* : 174-79.
48. *Ibid.*, 180.
49. *Ibid.*, 181.
50. *Ibid.*, 184.
51. *Ibid.*, 185.
52. Chung : Chang = Ladakhi beer.
53. Ladadi beer = Ladakhi beer.
54. Grim = Barley.
55. Knight ; *op. cit.* : 189.
56. *Ibid.*, 190-91.
57. *Ibid.*, 193.
58. *Ibid.*, 193-94.
59. *Ibid.*, 194.
60. Gialpo = Gyalpo = King of Ladakh.
61. Knight; *op. cit.* : 197-98.
62. Shushot = Chushot (Tib Chu-shod).
63. Knight ; *op. cit.* 198-99.
64. *Ibid.*, 200.
65. *Ibid.*, 204.
66. Delai lama = Dalai Lama.
67. Knight; *op. cit.* : 207-19.
68. *Ibid.*, 221-23.
69. *Ibid.*, 223-24.

18

A Reeve Heber and Kathleen M. Heber in Ladakh

Ladakh was attracted by many visitors in past like botanists, geologists ornithologists, archeologists, topographers, sportsmen, trekkers, mountaineers and hunters. Every year British Commissioner had a long list of such travellers. Among them sportsmen entered in Ladakh when they got shooting license. However, they enjoyed in Ladakh. In fact, Ladakh for them a place of lure. Heber and Heber say :

> "Indeed they are part of that lure of Ladak which every year provides the British Joint Commissioner with a waiting list for travellers desiring passes for longer than that of the successful applicants. Falling into a different category from the ordinary visitor is the sportsman, whose pass is included in his shooting license, men and even women to whose primeval hunting instincts the great hills call, the mere traveller may be lured by the everlasting hills also, or the peculiar bare country, or its strange inhabitants and their quaint customs. The mere joy of the road calls some, while few can on arrival resist being curio hunters."[1]

Land and People of Ladakh : The English traveller A. Reeve Heber and his wife Kathleen visited Leh in 1902, and impressed very much among the families who had Mongolian faces weared varieties of dress and ornaments such as 'Perag', red and yellow hats by lamas lived in small mud and stones constructed houses. Heber and Heber remark :

> "Sometimes flat and Mongolian in type, but often with large lustrous brown eyes, probably from a Kashmiri admixture. See these elf-like little faces framed in the astrakhan edging of their

> high fur-lined caps with turned-up corners, a fashion worn by all ages and sexes, including the pig-tailed men, these very corners being so typical of the whole goblin land. So, too, are the still taller peaked mitre-shaped hats of the lamas, red or yellow, while the national head-dress or 'Perag' of the women, is the most extraordinary thing of all. Their dwellings, strange habitations of mud and stones, crudely put together with crooked lines and strange little tiny windows, with or without a rough wooden framework. The larger of these may have a wooden partition down the centre of the framework and the upper edge of the latter is curved upwards in each partition, adding the expression of an eyebrow to the aperture."[2]

Houses : In Ladakh people generally have two storeyed houses, that is ground and first floor. Poors have only ground floor. Those who have two storeyed houses, in summer they go to upper storey and during winter to ground floor. Moreover, they keep their animals in ground floor only Heber and Heber came to understand that the first floor in Ladakh treated as good accommodation. They explain :

> "In Ladak, the higher you go the better the rooms, and the flat roof is the most used place of all, especially in the sunny hours of winter, when many domestic activities can be carried out in the warm sunshine there. Often there is a small porch on one side, a shelter from the keen spring winds or a shade from the heat of summer. The fact that horse-manure or cows' dung is spread out in patches on the floor to dry. Descending, we come to a large room with an open varandah, which can be closed in by short planks, and whose wooden framework may be crudely carved; this will be the summer kitchen-living room. Its winter counterpart, a smaller, darker room. The ground floor serves to stable the cattles."[3]

Civilization in Ladakh is reversed to West : When Heber and Heber visited to the countryside of Ladakh they acknowledged everything reversed, what they had practised usually in England. They write :

> "Our idea of the place for a flower garden is just outside the front door and around the house, but these people cannot spare land there for, if the house is built on land, which can be irrigated, every bit must be used for agriculture and any spare little plot for a few vegetables. But their appreciation of flowers is seen by the boxes full of gay blossom on the roof or balcony, and the place for a 'buttonhole', is behind the ears. In our

civilization the poorest will aim at being tidy outside. Not so the Ladaki. He wears his oldest dress outside, and his best one underneath, reversing the order for special occasions. Roughly sewn patches are applied at any angle; there is no need to attempt invisible patches as we do, for the more patches with the edges overlapping, the warmer the dress. Our chief meals are completed with a hot beverage, such as coffee, but they begin as well as end theirs with their butter-tea. Even the teeth of the carpenter's saw are sloped in the wrong direction compared with ours. If we listen to the cow, we note that she descends the scale as she moos, whereas our western cows moo from below upwards."

Past Story of Ladakh : Heroetotus was the first historian who described that Ladakh was a land where ants burrowing out their homes in the earth threw up gold. Tibetan nomades, who in search of pasture lands first came and settled down on the upper Ladakh. These nomads were the follower of 'Bon Chos', Mons, about the same period or earlier settled down in Zangskar. They were professionally skilled in crafts and well known musician. The next people to arrive in the land were Dards, who emigrated from Gilgit and settled down in Lower Ladakh. About 9-10th century A.D. Tibetan dynasty descended first became the king of Upper Ladakh. Dard King ruled Lower Ladakh. It seems that the presence of two king in Ladakh caused continual strife, but at last the Leh ruler won the mastery in matters temporal and increasingly in matters spiritual. One king introduced Buddhist literature from Central Tibet, another made it obligatory on all candidates for the priesthood to go to Lhasa for their training. By about fourteen century Buddhism had quite prevailed and subdued the indigenous faith, it incorporated Bon-chos in its own tenants. In the same period Tsongkhapa propagated yellow cap Buddhism. In this way red and yellow cap Buddhism flourished side by side in Ladakh. Towards the end of the fifteen century, Lodos Chogdan was ruling in Leh, his cousin Bagan lived and ruled Tingmogang. He with the help of third ruler defeated the king of Leh. Bagan then ascended the throne. However, there was no peace in Ladakh. Conflicts were often occurred within the boundaries of Ladakh. King Jamyang Namgyal, the grandson of Bagan with the interest to enlarge his kingdom attacked Purig, of which Kargil was the capital, but lost the battle and later helped in the propogation Islam in Ladakh. During the middle of seventeenth century quarrel between red and yellow lamas had now became acute in Tibet, and the yellow sect called in the king of Mongolia as their ally. He overran the whole country of Central Tibet, and then turned his eyes further afield, first letting them rest on Bhutan, with the result that, without waste of time, the king of Mongolia immediately attacked Ladakh, king took the help of Mogul, as a result they were driving back to the fortress of Basgo finally joint army of Ladakh and Mogul slowly drove the Mongolian invader back over the border. The final fall of the Buddhist Empire occured about the year 1840, when General Zorawar of Rajah of Jammu conquered Ladakh. After Indian independence, Ladakh became the integral part of India.[5]

Joint Commissioner of Kashmir and British in Ladakh : During the middle of nineteen century Ladakh was looked after by the Wazir of Ladakh, however, at the same time British Joint Commissioner also had his banglow in Leh, he looked foreigners activities. Heber and Heber say in this connection in the following manner :

> "Wazir of Ladak, who spends the summer in Leh and the winter in Skardu, the capital of Baltistan, and may be regarded as the Kashmir Joint Commissioner, whereas his Majesty, the Emperor of India is represented by the British Joint Commissioner who spends about three months here in the summer, and the rest of the year resides in Srinagar as one of the assistants to the British Resident there. The chief duties of the latter are to look after things pertaining to the 'Treaty Road' and to watch over the interests of foreigners in Ladak, whether they be Europeans, Yarkandis or Central Tibetans. During the absence of both these officials in winter, the highest authority in Leh is vested in the Chief Magistrate or Tehsildar, whose Tehsil or area of jurisdiction extends as far as Botkharbu, where exists at Skardu. These Tehsildars are of course, servants of the state of Kashmir, so also is the Naib Tehsildar. The State Dispensary with its Sub-Assistant Surgeon, the Telegraph Office with its 'Babu' in charge, are also State Services, but the Post Office is Imperial, and the Aksakal, who represents the British Government in assisting Yarkandi traders, and the 'charas officer' in charge of the Indian hemp trade from Yarkand, both of the latter connected with the 'Treaty Road', are also Imperial Government servants. These officials are prominent in the public life of Leh, and are all down country men."[6]

Nature's Setting : Ladakh has multi-faces character, after each high pass you can see a changed kind of nature, Heber and Heber explained this strange mixture of nature in the following way :

"On the road between Bot Kharbu and Lamayuru one of the most quaint little clusters of transitional rock-dwellings suddenly comes into view up a narrow ravine on one's left. The Photu La (Po-tu-la), a 13,400 feet pass, at the top of which one seems to have had a bird's eye view of a world of far reaching mountain tops, so deserted of any sign of humanity that on looking upon this sea mountains. 'Lhato' erected to mark the top of the pass. This structure is a collection of rocks and stones supporting a crooked staff bearing some tags and rags with prayers inscribed on them, and with sundry marks of gratitude in the shape of old sheep and goats' horns, or best of all, a bit of yak's tail, thrown on to the pile. The men express to the presiding genius of the pass their own relief and gratitude at once more having achieved the ascent, and then cheerfully start in the steep downward track."[7]

Mani walls and chortens : In the entrance of every Buddhist village you can see Mani walls and chortens. Heber and Heber also saw these near the Lamayuru monastery :

"Running down towards the village, interspersed with 'chorten' flat round structures, rather like gigantic pepperpots are long 'mani walls' built of stones and surmounted by two flattened sides, gently sloping upto meet each, these tops being formed of flat stones covered with prayers. Nearer the village they end in arches, often with chortens on the top, under which the road may run."[8]

Prayer-walls : In Ladakh one can often see prayer walls or Mani walls before entering to Buddhist villages and monasteries in Ladakh. The long prayer-walls mostly have chortens both ends and in between wall piles of stones consisting Avalokitesvara Mantra and other mantras. Heber and Heber say :

"Prayer-walls, the longest of which just outside Leh, stretches for half a mile across the desert, looking for all the world as though some giant children had been playing trains in the sand, the chortens at both ends resembling clumsy engines, the lower one to give an extra push up the hill. Then there are the little piles of stones so often put up by lonely shepherds, or tired wayfarers, who have made their resting-places wherever a big rock will give them shade, these themselves in their sauciness looking more likely to attract evil spirits then repel them."[9]

Lhatos in Ladakh : One can see Lhatos at every top of passes, at the end of village boundaries and on the tops of hills. Heber and Heber say :

> "Lhato, erected to mark the top of the pass. This structure is a collection of rocks and stones supporting a crooked staff bearing some tags and rags with prayers inscribed on them, and with sundry marks of gratitude in the shape of old sheep and goat horns, or best of all, a bit of yak's tail thrown on to the pile. In the words Sola, sola, sola the men express to the presiding genius of the pass their own relief and gratitude."[10]

Changing nature and landscape : In Ladakh valleys in different altitudes, varing landscapes have black, brown, gray and purple colour. Similarly lakes which look purple in the morning, become black when cloudy and again to raddish at sun sets. Heber and Heber explain :

> "Yet the strangeness of the land is after all but a minor aspect of these mountain uplands. The majesty of range after range of glistening peaks and shining glaciers in the regions of everlasting snow, their everchanging colour from morning to night and from winter to summer, always new, always different, who shall tell of their never failing inspiration or of their picturesque parables? While every possible shade of blue and purple and crimson and gold steal across the great ranges flanking each side of the long valley, and when to go out and wander along the green-turfed flats by the river is to go out to worship. Living year in and year out in these valleys, bounded by their mighty ranges with their sense of mysteries guarded but capable of interpretation in some beautiful way infinitely beyond our limited human ken. Then, too, there is such a joyousness in the land, between the long stretches of bare desert of rock and barren hill, which have their own beauty, especially when in an autumn setting of a blue-green river and an azure sky. Whenever a green village snuggles into the brown-red hillside, a rippling stream is heard and a cooling breeze felt in the little plantations of trees, whilst the soft evening light makes the green corn look like plush or contrasts its autumn gold with the yellow glory of the poplars all set against a background of white snow peaks and blue sky. Nor must we omit the fairy touch of spring, which turns each nestling hamlet into a fairy-land of apricot blossom, exquisite prelude to the return of the green after the long bare winter. Surely this joyousness gives

our people their merry look, their cheerful willingness and the happiness that bursts into song over every kind of work."[11]

Flora in Ladakh : In Ladakh has various colour of wild roses like pink, light pink to the deepest crimson. Heber and Heber found bushes of yellow roses, between Kharbu and Kargil during summer. At the neighbourhood of Khalatse you can see flowers of cyclamen-like caper and near Dras river bank beautiful bushes of tamarisk. In the summer time along the village walls all sorts of little feathery plants, one resembling a wild maidenhair with wee brown flowers, one species of ferns can be acknowledged on those parts of wall over which the water flows. Ice plants, such as we conserve in pots and rockeries at home, with their pinky white flowers abound, and the walls are often overgrown with a wild clematis which has the quaintest little brown flowers surely turning into little elves and gnomes when no human is at hand. The edges of the fields and watercourses are adorned with yellow members of the ranunculaceae, vetches, purple representatives of the scrophulariaceae, species of milkwort, wild parsley and mint, and even dandelions. Beladonna is plentiful to the verge of nuisance in gardens, and lucerne popularly called Yarkandi oal crops up everywhere. Besides I saw violet colour flowers, members of the ranunculaceae at the edges of watercourses. Heber and Heber found Edelweiss in broad patches over the lawns of the Leh Residency and yellow Iceland poppies, Michaelmas daisies, small deep-blue gentians, forgent-me-nots, forming a carpet of blue on the Zogi stretches at an elevation between 15,000 to 16,000 feet. The deep-blue of the borade below the Kardong, deep purple archids, primulas in all shardes of magenta and purple, cow parsley, a kind of stinging nettle, asters, saxifrage, vetches, cantenbury bell, and on the zogi the single anemone and the tall bunched Japanese variety, even the green foxglove and the coarse edelweiss.[12]

Though Ladakh would hardly credit green cover, you may see here all sorts of little herbs and flowering thistles grow, each showing marked adaptation to its very dry habitat. Most important of these is the pungent-smelling, low-growing, bushy herb called *Burtsa*. Sometimes, little stunted blue and white iris that springs up all along the water courses. I have seen these dwarfed mountain habitat along the stream at Choglamsar, 8 km. far away from Leh.[13]

In this high altitude region I have seen high density of poplars along the river bed or watercourses. Heber and Heber found pencil cedars at lower regions, as at Hemis Shukpachan, called 'Shukpa', trees, branches of these are used in religious rites. The other trees belong to horticulture viz. walnut, apple, and apricot trees. All these are found in Lower Ladakh. According to Heber and Heber these do not survive above the Basgo-Nyemo Valley.[14]

Fauna of Ladakh : In 1923, B.B. Osmaston visited Ladakh, he made a list of sixty-seven bird species. Heber and Heber saw some of them in their studies, such as : ravens, magpies, pigeons (Rock and Blue Hill), chough with its red or yellow bill, who in the early spring build their nests in the sandy cliff near Leh. The sparrow, Mountain Finches manage to stay throughout the year. However, Eagle and the Vulture, come down. The little Robin Accentor, with his dull red breast finds in mountains. During autumn, common Redstart & Desert Larks leave lower part of Ladakh. Seventzov's Rose Finch, Guldenstadt's Redstart and Elwes' Horned Larks are belong to their families.[15]

Besides, Heber and Heber found ducks, Mallard, Tufted Pochard, Ruddy Shelldrake, and common Tea and Snipe in all the swampy little rivulets. Chikor and Himalayan Snow Cock also attract people by their peculiar and shrill whistle. During summer some migrants have been noticed along the rivulets, wagtails (Hodgson's pied; grey and yellow headed) first come. Soon to be followed by the Siberian Chiffchaff, Redstrart, Hoopoo, Cuckoo. Besides, Heber and Heber noticed Western Blue Rock Thrush, coat of slaty blue, above the river, Gulls and Ternwheel and sweep, kept companied by Swift and Martin. Ibisbill on the stones, whilst the royal Heron by the water's edge with his neck well trucked in.[16]

Climate of Ladakh : Ladakh, because of its cold, dry and arid climatic condition has changing behaviour, as sun shines, the temperature rises rapidly and after sun sets drops very fast, suppose, you sit in the shade of the rock, the part of your body within the shadow freezes, while that in the sun-shine boils! The short summer from June to mid-September sees the ripening of the wheat, barley and lucerne crops. Rainfall is less, the snowfall is also not severe in the Indus valley. Sunny winter is quite pleasant owing to the dryness of the cold. According to Heber and Heber winters are quite enjoyable as one sits out of door in the sunshine during the day time. Though the temperature may go down to minus ten degrees F in mid-winter. The spring, however, is heralded by bitter piercing winds, and often they raise little spiral hurricanes of dust seen chasing across the valley from afar, but woe if one of these 'sand devils' blows across sandy portion.[17]

Zogi La, the dread pass : Zogi-La (or Zoji) means the dread pass, closes the road in winter. In past was the meeting place for the roads from Tibet, Yarkand, Baltistan and Kashmir. Tibetan called this pass as 'the place of four demons'. In the centre of the pass was a rest-house called 'Machoi', situated on the top of a small sharp hill, one side of which was sheltered from the prevailing winds, and had two or three small buildings, a serai and a telegraph office nestling under it. The telegraph master must had a dreary time in winter, and in the middle of May was moved to another post higher up on the road to Leh.[18]

Zogi-La is a flower garden : Though Zogi- (or zoji)-La is a place of snow avalanches, yet during summer you can see various species of flowers such as the carpet of edelweiss and blue gentian, mauve daisies, yellow ragwort pink 'coral flower' and rich purple pelargonium. The whole hillside in one part would be sky blue with a sheet of forget-me-nots, further beyond the rich verdure of the grass there would be a mass of pink or mauve where the flower grew in rich profusion.[19]

Respas (or Sub-res) : Res = Turn & Pa = men, during olden days when Sahib or any official from Jammu & Kashmir Riyashad visited Ladakh, at every halt or at the Banglows Ladakhis according their turn waited in service of these officials. These Banglaws were at Matayan, Dras, Shimsha Kharbu, Kargil, Mulbek, Khalatse, Leh etc. These respas normally transport Sahib goods to the next halting place. When Heber and Heber visited Ladakh, respas were as usual waiting them at Mulbek to secure the job of their goods transport for the next day. Here respas came forwarded with their traditional dress and things; for example. They wore long woollen coats, tied up by a belt and fitted it with an array of instruments, such as flint and finder, knife, long spoon, spectacles in case, sewing purse and pen-case. These were all depending from the waist and often a large brass soup or tea ladle was stuck in the folds of their ample sash behind. In front, hanging by a small chain, one man had a little pair of broad-ended forceps for extracting thorns or obstructive whiskers, the nasal vibrissae being special objects of dislike. Some wore necklaces of turquoise and coral or red beads, others had ear-rings and many had bracelets, often in the form of a clasp not quite meeting round the wrist, whose two ends represented the heads of snakes.[20]

Namika La Pass : After Mulbek, the next halting place was at Stagtse, here one could see noticeable cluster of houses, rest-house and dak banglow on high rock with ruined castle or forts. In between Namika La, literally means the sky-high pass of 13,000 feet and a few ruined forts and castles on the hill tops. These were the scenes of fighting in the seventeenth century.[21]

Rong : The march ascends called 'rong' which may be defined as a pass 'which goes up, but not down', a narrow defile which opens out eventually on to a broad plain. For example, when we climb from Nyemo towards Leh, we have to pass through 'rong' that is to ascend, then we soon come out on to a long terraced plain with a glorious view of Leh valley.

Horse-gate : In olden days Leh town was covered by boundary wall and at the entrance there was a gate called horse-gate (Tib. Sta-rgo). The Leh bazar was broad enough in which traders after exchanging their goods, played polo game. There were row of poplar trees on one side, castle high on a hill to the right and behind it the mountains, over which the Kardong Pass leads to the Karakoram and distant Yarkand.[22]

Indus River : Indus is the main river of Ladakh, in Ladakhi language called 'Senge Kabab', means the one which 'descends from the mouth of the lion'. This river flowing from the region of the holy lake Mansarowar, also indicate the true sources of their mighty waters, for does not the Sutlej or 'Langchen Kabab' descend from the mouth of the elephand, the Ganga is the 'Mamzhi Kabab' descending from the mouth of the peacock, while the Brahmaputra or 'Damchog Kabab' descends from the ear of horse.[23]

Ri-gyal : Lamayuru just near the Khalatse village has many turns and thus called 'Ri-gyal' or mountain King range. In fact from here one can trek towards Zangskar then Lahul. Therefore, after covering a pass, one could reach at Wanla village. Crowing the hill by a fine old ruin, and behind it a most peculiar built monastery has a huge maitreya statue.

Shugpa : At the top of every pass you can see lhato or a place of good spirit, covered it by Shugpa stems. The Shugpa or pencil cedar, in Ladakh regarded as a holy tree, and of certain Shugpa it is said that to break off a twig or branch will cause the death of the offender within a year. Thus, among the oldest trees in the land, where wood is in such demand for fuel, is the Shugpa, owing its existence to the protection of its gods.[24]

Dough (Tib. Dok-sa) : High mountain pastures where nomads graze their animals and in night stay in Dough or Dok-sa. Heber and Heber while travelling towards Zangskar via Sengela or lion pass acknowledged Dough. The wall of it was made of large dry plaques of cow manure, and the roof of a big slab of the same material. Asking about how nomads made of this. He was informed that nomads throughout the whole winter the stables are not cleared out, but the continual stamping of animals and men makes quite a hard floor of manure, which is cut out in large chunks in the spring.[25]

Rope bridge : In Ladakh, particularly Zangskar region had many rope bridges. Heber and Heber also crossed such bridges. Describing about this they say :

"We have another type of bridge to cross, this time made of rope. A prominent rock from which to sling the ropes, is selected on either side of the river. These ropes are made of the twigs of birch or poplar, plaited together. Four such ropes tied together constitute the actual pathway, just broad enough to accommodate a boot. On either side is a rail of the same material connected by similar strands to the footway, and at each end the latter and the rails are wound and tied round beams, kept in position by large pieces of rock. To cross this bridge we first mount the cliff over which its end is swung, then lean well forward to catch hold of one rail with each hand and place the foot gingerly on the footway. It is impossible to grasp the whole handrail, for it is far too thick, and so rough that it may tear the hands. The bridge sags in the centre, so the first half descends at rather a steep angle, which does not make matters easier. Towards the middle the bridge begins to sway, as a slight wind is blowing, but there can be no turning back now; moreover the worst half is over, far from the centre the ascent to the further side begins."[26]

Shingkung La : In olden days Zangla was the capital of Zangskar. It is said that in 1834, King of Zangskar who stayed at Zangla, rendered aid to Zorawar Singh, the Dogra General, on his way through to the conquest of Ladakh. Heber and Heber who also stayed at Zangla palace, then marched towards Lahul via Shingkiang La, which divides Zangskar from Lahul, and takes four day to cross from Zangla. Heber and Heber when reached at the foot of the Shingkung La, noticed some peculiar huts on the opposite side of the river, built of yak's dung. During the summer, when the yaks were allowed to graze the hillsides, their shepherds first built low walls of stone, then brought the plaques of dung, which they collected each day, to build a slanting roof, of which each superimposed layer overlaps slightly inwards. When winter came, the yaks were driven back into the village, and the collections of dung taken home for the winter fuel.[27]

Baralacha is the source of two rivers : Baralacha is only dangerous pass in between Leh and Keylong, the source of two rivers. Chandra and Bhaga. Bhaga which comes from this pass, joins the Chandra little further, later form the Chenab.[28]

Brogpas, or Brok-pas originated from Gilgit : In Ladakh Brogpas are settled down in Dras and beyond Hanu valleys. However, Dras and its adjoining converted into Muslims, whilst other into Buddhist. It is explained they were migrated from Gilgit, where they played polo game, thus introduced this in Ladakh. As a result in olden days every village in Ladakh had polo ground.[29]

Brogpas (Brok-pas) refused to work as forced labour : Brogpas belong to a brave race. It is said once enemy siege the castle of Brogpas, they remained in the castle, when food ran out, all of them then decided to die instead of surrendering. Thus they all gathered in the large hall, and the oldest man was given the privi!ege of pushing away the stone on which stood the main pillar which supported the roof. Thus these courageous men passed away. Similarly when King of Ladakh wished to do their share of forced labour, to which they objected.[30]

Hat is of great diagnostic value : Brogpas wear different hat than Ladakhis. It is turned up not lined with lamskin, and is continuous all the way round. Those worn by the ladies are different again, the upper half being turned over somewhat like a billycock hat; the side turned over and uppermost is usually a veritable needle case with rows of needless stuck into it. Each needle which stuck represented a symbol of friendship.[31]

Brogpas (Brok-pas) do not eat eggs : Brogpas who converted Buddhist do not kill animals, therefore, encourage one member of his family to become Muslim, so that family may have meat. However, Brogpas by and large do not raise fowl, nor they eat their eggs. The cow may be employed for the ploughing of their fields, but the gods would most certainly be displeased were they to drink their milk or even use the butter which is made from the same.[32]

Khampas : They are originally migrated from Kham of Tibet, and are well organised Buddhist creed like Gipsies involved themselves in business. Heber and Heber didn't find them much number in Leh bazaar. However, they were involved in Zangskari pony business, as they buy them for about Rs. 60/- and sold them at three or four times that amount down-country.[33]

Boundary dispute : Heber and Heber reported that on the occasion to settled down boundary dispute between Ladakh and Tibet he went to Changthan, a closed land where the Changpa, who wanders over the high plateaus of Ladakh. British Joint Commissioner, Major Robson, who attended the meeting from Government of India side, Wazir Sahib, who represented His Highness, the Maharaja of Kashmir and Gaspon, who acted on behalf of His Holiness, the Dalai Lama. The cause of the dispute was a Ladakhi who had settled down in Tibet proper, where he had taken unto himself a lady of the country as wife, and had grown rich. As a result liable for the heavy Tibetan taxation, and wishing to escape this, returned to Ladakh. But Tibetans calmly entered Ladakh, seized the man and took him back again. His brother then appealed to Kashmir and Indian authorities to settled down his case as he was illegally taken to Tibet from his homeland. Tibet tried to contest the matter by saying the place from which they had removed the Ladakhi was in Tibetan territory, but from the discussion, had no grounds at all for their contentions.[34]

Greeting by Ladakhis : The officials when passed through the villages, villagers then came to the roadside to pay their greeting. According to Heber and Heber on this occasion group of four women, gay in their bright red and green, ceremonial or dancing cloaks, lined with long sheep-skins; one holds a pot of local beer, the next a plate of flour, the third a vessel of water, and the last presented glowing embers. This tradition still prevalent in Ladakh.[35]

Changpas of Ladakh : The inhabitants of the Northern Plain are known as Changpas. Their eyes are typically Mongolian, noses large and firmly flattened long hair, and which ends in a pigtail, surmounts faces. Their long coats reach just below the knees, and are cut without shape or form of any kind. The fronts of these over-lap, and in lieu of buttons they wear a long, broad Kammerband round their waists to keep their coats closed. They wear long boots reaching up to the knees, red in colour and with very thick soles.[36]

In Chang-Thang wind is the worse evil. To protect them from this they pitch their tents in such a manner that the wind finds difficult to get in, while the smoke of the fire inside shall have an easy egress. To do this he leaves the top of his canvas home absolutely open to the sky. His shelter consists merely of two sides of black woollen cover made from yak's hair, of which the upper two corners only are fastened together and fixed on the top of upright poles whilst the lower corners are fastened to the ground. These tents are so low that, if the Changpa wants to see sheep or other animals, he can see easily only to stand up and put his head and shoulders out of his 'chimney'. Inside their tents they sleep, cook meals, and keep their goods. In meals they use meat maximum."[37]

Sheep : A load carrier : Changpas used their sheep as load carrier. When they move from one pasture to another, sheep carry their bedding and food. They do not seem in trouble to carry light load. They give them two fold benefits, as they carried salt to Leh for selling and there they themself turned into mutton.[38]

Gaspon : A Representative of H.H. Dalai Lama : Heber and Heber when arrived at Drogpa Karpo for the conference. Gaspon from Tibet also arrived there. His dress consisted of a lovely blue skirt, and a Chinese coat of the same colour which was buttoned up to his neck. His ear-ring made of turquoises. The Tehsildar on this occasion weared a chorten on his head.[39]

Chorten gate : In Ladakh chortens are found in every Buddhist village, and mostly constructed at the entrance of the villages. They are various shapes, but one can see eight kinds. Besides, there are chortens, particularly in Lower Ladakh, where you can enter and leave the village through a chorten gate. Heber and Heber explain as suppose a child sets up two plain bricks with a third across the top, and on this placed a fat chess pawn, he would have quite a good model of these chorten-crowned archways.[40]

Yarsa and Doks : Every village in Ladakh, one can finds Yarsa, the summer place usually consists of a small hut with a stable below, and a kitchen-room above, leading on to a balcony or flat roof. Yarsas, may be on the outskirts of the village, or a mile up the valley behind. Anywhere on the hillsides, where a spring or brook is available to water a small patch of cultivated land. Whereas as brogs or Dok are the pasture grounds where a considerable proportion of the population move in the summer along with their animals for grazing.[41]

Apricot oil : In olden days Ladakhis used apricot oil for cooking, dressing the hair and for burning lamp before the altar. This oil taken out from apricot-kernels.[42]

Best room alloted to religious purpose : In Ladakh mostly Buddhist alloted his best room to religious purpose called Chot Khang. Whereas according to Heber and Heber among Muslim homes, the best room was always used by the head of the house.[43]

Fire blower : In Ladakh, if I am not wrong, Ladakhis usually had Fire blower in their kitchen, called Thap. Heber and Heber explained this Fire blower in the following way :

> "In front of the stove on the right hand side is a projection of the same hardened mud, which is to accommodate the right-hand of the 'Fire blower', as he operates on the Bellews. These are very effective instruments with a large nozzle pushed well under the glowing fuel, and an elongated bag of goat skin at the outer end of which two small bars of wood are attached, with small loops of strongly-twisted thread with middle. Through these the thumb and fingers are placed to open and close the mouth, and though it sounds and looks a simple process a certain knack must be acquired to get a good fire. The stove has a large central tunnel with branches radiating

out to the corner holes, and in the middle is a depression for the biggest hole of all."[44]

Gurgur : In Ladakh, Ladakhis drink salt tea prepared by Gurgur, with butter, soda, salt and milk. It stimulates body, butter helps to supply the carbohydrates. The fat also warms and sustains him in bitter winter.[45]

Ladakhi dishes : In Ladakh various dishes are made in the kitchen by meat, bread and vegetable. Popular among them are : Chu tagi, tagi khambir, gyatug, tukpa, etc. Heber and Heber say gyatug, a dish of long vermicelli like strips of flour-paste over which mincemeat in a nicely flavoured sauce is poured and small breads, raised with leaven called Kambir (Khambir), *Darra* or buttermilk. This is used as a sauce with *zan* or *baba*, which is made by boiling the milled flour of roast wheat, barley and peas into a mash.[46]

Lena : The fine wool : The best wool called *lena*, is of soft, silky texture, and is the short downy growth near the skin of the goat, which grows in winter under the long shaggy hairs. Heber and Heber who visited Ladakh during 1924-25 said that one *batti* of lena or pashmina equal to four pounds, cost Rs. 20/- in the raw state. The ordinary soft *lena* wool was then sent in large quantity to Kashmir, were Kashmiri craftmen prepared Cashmere shawls. History tells that at the time of the great Mugal Emperors, Mirza Hedar, grandfather of the celebrated Akbar, came to Ladakh from Yarkand with five hundred men, and paid a long visit to the King of Ladakh. At the latter's request, he conquered the country of Purig, and presented it to his host, then went on down to Kashmir and subdued it for himself. The Ladakhi King then presented him *Snambu* woven of *lena*. Mirza admired it so much that he introduced the import of the wool into Kashmir, where woven into two shawls, or *shal*, the word meaning 'a board', a name which he seems to have given them *faut de mieux*, for it hardly suits such essentially fine soft cloth. Two Persians then came to Kashmir to buy saffron and cummin, and brought these shawls to take back to present to their King. Next year they tried to obtain more; later the cloth was taken also to Alexandria, and so its fame slowly became world-wide.[47]

Snambu, Kalches, malches and p'ang process : Wool has played an important role in Ladakhi life, as they make woollen clothes from it. Here follows the details how they prepare the same. Ladakhi lady first wash the raw wool and dry up. The next pulling out of the wool, and teasing out all little bits of tangled, extraneous matter, so that it is quite soft and ready to spin called this process *malches*. Then comes the actual *Kalches* or spinning, which is carried out on a slender cone of wood, elongated at both ends, called a *p'ang*. Then resulting cloth or snambu.[48]

Skerag or Kammarband : In Ladakh, Ladakhi wears long coat called Kos or Goncha to tied up, skerag, a long woollen sash about six inches wide and six feet long is needed, bound in many turns round the waist with the ends tucked in, is wound over it, so as to keep it in place.[49]

Perag : A head dress of Ladakhi woman : Ladakhi Buddhist woman wears Perag at every auspicious occasions and festivals. In olden days head dress wore by the Purig and Central Tibetan ladies. Later during sixteen century this tradition brought into Ladakh by new queen probably Gyal Khatun. Heber and Heber explained :

> In olden times the women of this country wore a round head-dress like that which adorns the lady of Purig or of Central Tibet, until a Ladakhi King brought his royal consort from a small state in the closed land where the perage was the national head-dress, and the ladies of his realm at once copied their new queen. The perage consists of a central elongated piece of leather, covered with red cloth, converging slowly to a long narrow point below the waist behind, and a shorter blunt one in front. The whole thing is supposed to represent a snake, and the front part appearing over the forehead certainly, resembles the head of the cobra. On this bright red background rows of turquoise matrix are sewn, often ending in front with a chased gold and silver ornament, studded with small turquoises. Sometimes a large red cornelian also varies the apex. This would seem startling enough, but unfortunately a later queen had an attack of earache, so attached a large piece of black lambskin each side to protect her ears. The court ladies then accordingly accompanied by these large ear-flaps, and the *coiffure* was most wonderfully adapted to them by plaiting the hair into a number of small plaits, which were sewn into the ear-pieces at each side, and continued with wool down the back on both sides of the perag to unite below in a large tassel, which reaches to the bottom of the skirt. To one side of the perag a projection of silver from which rows of coral-beads depend was also fastened. This is said to represent the serpent's tail.[50]

Pha-spun : Ladhaki Buddhist has an especial linked with others as brotherhood, the members of which are called Pha-spun. These are originally relations, though outsiders may be sworn in at a special feast and all worship at a common altar, presided over by their special deity.

After death only a Pha-spun may touch the corpse, and in marriages he carries all the bride's belongings and dowry to her new home.[51]

Professions : In Ladakh you can see Amchi, Onpo, Zomo, Lamas and Spons. They are considered as professionals. Amchi, the Tibetan doctor give treatment to his patient by herbs. Onpo or Horologist, will tell you when you should plaugh your field, the best day on which to marry, in fact for the decision of all the important affairs of life, you must get him to settle the auspicious day. Como and Lamas perform religious works for Buddhist whereas Spons involve in paintings clay statue and wood craft making. Musicians and minstrels do not have good status in the Buddhist society.[52]

Merchants meet at Leh : In olden days Leh was one of the important trading centre, where Yarkandi, Khotani, Lahuli, Kashmiri, Baltis, Tibetans and Hoshiyarpuri gathered and sold their products. Heber and Heber say:

> "From the North comes the Yarkandi with carpets of garish colours, furs of snow-leopard, fox and wolf, stone martin and beaver, Khotan silks and thick felt mats. It has taken him a full month of most difficult travelling over vast mountain ranges to get here, before he can sell his wares, he will have to travel another month to reach the Plains of India. Here he purchases cloth which he takes back to his home and sells there at a good price. The Yarkandi has either to buy horses or sell them. The Tibetan brought salt, borax and Lhasa tea to barter with the Balti for his dried apricots and cooking butter. Changpa brings the long soft wool from his long-haired sheep, which the Kashmiri trader carries down to be transformed into pashmina, the basis of the far-famed delicate Cashmere shawls. The man from Kulu has carried kerosine up here, and perhaps also China caps, whilst the merchant from India supplies German cloth or rich stuffs for Ladakhi dresses, Chemises and pantaloons, Indian tea, spices, cigarattes and many things which are needed by Ladakhi's.[53]

Notables of Ladakh : Heber and Heber were at Leh town when First World War was over and acknowledge peace ceremony on the eve of this, a large bonfire was made. All notables on this occasion were present there, consisting Tehsildar, Naib Tehsildar, Darogas, Naib Darogas, Policemen, Naib Policemen, Telegraph Master, Post Master, Charas Officer, Aksakal.[54]

Human Sacrifice : It seems that before Buddhism, cannibalism was prevalent in Ladakh. Heber and Heber say :

"A relic of the old cannibalism and human sacrifice which preceded the arrival of Buddhism, and is till reflected in a common oath constantly heard in the roads—*Amai sha*, which means 'by my mother's flesh'. Our friend had to obtain these occult powers without our help!"[55]

Polo-game in Ladakh : Polo is the favourite game of Ladakh. It arose in Persia, soon migrated to Gilgit, Dards brought it to Ladakh. In olden days every big village in Ladakh had own polo ground. Leh bazar was then a polo ground. Heber and Heber explained in details how the polo game was played in Leh bazar :

"This consists of a level space about two hundred yards long, which cannot boast of a blade of grass, but is covered by a layer of dust so thick that before play begins, it has to be laid with water. On one side it is bounded by the high wall of the Wazir's on the other by a low wall about one foot high built of large stone, piled one on top of the other without mortar or cement or even mud. Halfway along this, a platform of mud and stones has been erected, from the top of which 'the notables' watch the game. Two large stones at either end are sufficient as goal-posts. On the ground itself to one side sits the band of four; two flageolets and two kettle-drums. These at one moment are announcing another goal obtained and at another are defending themselves from the polo sticks, for the game is raging right in their midst. Here it is not the rich man's game, a stud of horses is quite unnecessary. Even a poor farmer possesses one pony, and if he makes himself a stick, he, too, can join in. The stick is quite easily manufactured, its shape being that of hockey stick, but with a longer handle. Rules seems to be none. If your opponent gets in your way, ride him down. If only six players have come, three a side will do, if ten players turn up, two fives make an equally good game. Play can last as long as you like."[56]

Horse Race : In Ladakh horse race is a popular game. Today in Chang-Thang, Chang-pas play this game with full joy. Heber and Heber explain :

"This peculiar species of horse-racing is quite in keeping with this quaint country. At the further end of the bazar about thirty ponies and their jockeys are gathered. First along the course comes a rider decked out in the most wonderful garments. His dress is a beautifully embroided Chinese mandarin's robe and

> the insignia of his office is a tiger skin tunic. On his head he wears a large round hat covered with gilt tinsel, the crown rising to a dome, surmounted by a knob to which streamers of gilt tinsel passing from the brim are attached. This is quite a personage who assumes the title of *glabdog*, which means one to whom the gods are subject. The office boasts a long lineage and is traceable to pre-Buddhist times. Its representative is always chosen from one of the three families and his duty is to serve the king personally, one especial task being to change the pencil cedar on His Majesty's altar on New Year's he is acting as his King's Viceroy. Having led the way, the race can begin, but a starter is quite unnecessary. Each man starts off just when he likes and simply tears down the bazar a hard as his pony will carry him; though they often elect to start in a bunch, there seems to be no behind carry on with equal zest. Needless to say bookies are unnecessary. Sometimes a wag will add to the delight of the spectators by performing gymnastic feats as he rides, possibly having dressed up to enhance the exhibition, which is loudly applauded. When all have ridden the course, they canter back and repeat from the beginning. This goes on for two or three days, and Ladakhis find it interesting to the end."[57]

Games on Horseback : In olden days this game was popular among Ladakhis and Yarkandis. On this occasion a dead sheep thrown on to the ground. Among the players one catches up the sheep as best as he can, then rides with it for the goal. If he accomplishes this, he may look forward to many a big supper of mutton, but all the other horsemen try to make this impossible. The falls, pullings, and pushings this piece of mutton gets, should go for to make it tender, whatever its age may be.[58]

Arrow Shooting : This is a popular game in Ladakh, known as 'Dar-ches', and always takes place in spring, just before the fields are sown. Heber and Heber say :

> "A garden or an enclosure with trees round an open space is chosen, at one end of which a heap of earth is piled up about four feet high. Into the centre of this is stuck a bull's eye, about the size of a china plate and made of white clay. At the opposite end, about twenty yards from the target, are several tents, nicely decorated, in which sit those members of their respective community, who, by subscribing towards the shoot, have bought themselves the right to be present and take part. Others may

join in, but there on sufferance, and if they have not paid, even superb shooting will not obtain the applause of either the band or the onlookers. The shooting begins. An archer takes up his position, draws his bown, his friends encouraging him by calling: 'Shok (Tib. So lo)... shok... shok...' and continuing to do so until the shaft has flown. Should it break the clay, the band strikes up and is rewarded with a backsheesh, whilst the archer has a salutation scarf thrown round his neck. If an enemy should be shooting, he can be discouraged by shouting : 'kyor (Tib.' 'khyor)... kyor... kyor...', which means 'miss'. Each man shoots three, they retire for refreshments and conversation, whilst the arrows are fetched back. This competition lasts three days."[59]

Wild Life : In olden days shooting licences were given from Kashmir forest department. Every year 40 such licences were given, out of that first 20 for the first half of the year and 20 for the second for hunting in Ladakh. Here Shapo, wolf, snow leopard, Ibex, Ovis Ammon etc. are some popular wild animals. Heber and Heber have gathered following views about them :

"The Ladakhis hate snow-leopards for they do much harm to their flocks. In order to catch them, they dig deep holes in the ground and build over hanging walls round. They then put the sheep, whose bleating attracts the leopard. Having jumped in, he cannot negotiate the overhanging wall and meets an ignoble death from stoning. The people also make a very useful wolf-trap. One end of a large rock is balanced on a stick, to which they tie a piece of meat. A pull on this brings the stone down on the animal's head. On the higher hills the burhel can be found grazing sometimes in herds of fifty to a hundred. Much higher up one finds that Ovis Ammon, a magnificent animal, whose horns at the base measure about eighteen inches in girth, and whose length is about fifty inches when full grown. The Ladakhi Ibex is not as fine as that from Baltistan, yet even he can boast of horns some forty inches long. Right on the uplands towards Tibet, one can also get antelope, with beautifully slender, graceful horns, which at their ends cure forwards, not backwards. At one time it was possible to shoot the wild yak, but, even were he not almost extinct now, it would not be permissible to shoot him."[60]

Ladakhi Buddhists Belief : One can see skull of goat, Tarchok etc.

traditional practice they may bar the entry of evil spirits, on the contrary get peace and prosperity. Heber and Heber made the following explanation :

> "On an outside wall we notice the skull of a goat, framed in small sticks tied together by twins, which is the *storma* obtained at the New Year's festival, and keeps those in the house insured against sickness. The corners of the house have been painted a red colour, which effectually bars the entry of evil spirits. In the court-yard is a high pole, to which is attached a strip of thin muslin about twelve inches broad and running the length of the flagstaff, which surmounted by the black bushy tail of the holy yak. On the flag are painted a great number of prayers, which crude drawings of Tiger, Lion, Garuda and Dragon all being mystical signs ensuring safety against enemies, earthly and celestical, increasing the number of children and wealth, in short achieving the entire health and happiness of the household."[61]

Chorten and its Meaning : Though chortens are of eight different shapes, but in Ladakh we can see such which are made on the ashes of deceased monks and high ranked personalities. Heber and Heber explained about them how these structures are made, and what does the different portion of it signifies :

> "From below upwards there is first a large square base, which is called the throne, on whole sides are painted figures of animals or holy eyes from which the throne derives its name, such as a Peacock or a Lion Throne. From this there rise five square steps, the lowest of which represent the holy carpet, for each lama sits on holy carpet. Above this, two steps represent legs and two more arms. Then comes a large pudding-shaped arrangement to represent the head. The body seems to have been omitted. From this there rises a high cone made of red tiles and divided into thirteen rings, these are said to represent the thirteen ages (Skalpas, each of 100,000 years) of the Buddhist. Others have a different interpretation. From the axis of the earth there towers up Mount Meru, which supports the heaven. This is said to have twenty-five steps, which halved gives approximately enough thirteen, and the thirteen consecutive rings of the *chorten* cone represent those steps belonging to the earth. Surmounting this cone there is a large gilt ornament made of tin or some such metal which denotes

the *zarazak*, or the Umbrella of office. Above this comes a globe for the sun, a crescent for the moon and a smaller globe for the stars, from which there rises up into 'nothingness' a fine piece of wire. Yet a totally different explanation is given according to which, reading from below upwards, the *chorten* represents the five elements, earth, water, fire, air and ether."[62]

Buddhist Calendar : It is derived from the Chinese and consists of sixty-year cycles, which are sub-divided into five periods of twelve years each. Heber and Heber say :

"The periods are named after the Buddhist element of wood, fire, earth, iron and water, whilst the single years are called after various animals, such as mouse, ox, tiger or hare."[63]

Seven Days of the Week : Like English explanation, Buddhists belief their days of the week denoted to deities. Heber and Heber explain as :

"Seven days, which are devoted to deities similar to our own, such as Sunday and Monday to Sun and Moon. They have noticed that Mercury looks like a red eye, so Tuesday is called the day of the red eye. Wednesday is the day of Venus, whilst Thursday, the day of the dagger, must belong to the god of war. Jupiter and Saturn, even in Ladakh, claim Friday and Saturday."[64]

Dosmoche : In olden day the official New Year celebration was known Dosmoche, later becomes tradition. Heber and Heber write in details as :

"The firing of a gun announces that procession has left the castle and is descending the hill, and soon it turning into the further end of the main street, near the mosque. Heading the procession come four lamas in their clerical red garments, and with their funny yellow peaked hats. These are blowing their flageolets; after an interval they are followed by two or three laymen, who have the supposed honour of being allowed to carry the *storma*, but one cannot help noticing that the e'lite do not trouble to obtain this distinction for themselves. *Storma* means a thing which is lost, and consists of effigies made in various sizes to represent men and demons. A group of lamas, dressed up in their fantastic devil-masks, and dancing as they move along. More laymen follow, bearing religious flags, and then there come four priests, blowing shawons so long that two small acolytes precede them, holding up the ends. Thus group after passes through the gate till the celebrating abbot appears, to be followed by further priests and laymen carrying *storma*. Bringing up the rear are a number of Buddhist horsemen, prominent among them the king. The procession has passed through the bazar. There the fires have been lit, illuminating the weird devil-dancing lamas as they gyrate and jump round them. At a given moment all the *storma* are thrown into the flames, and with their burning the sin and disease of the town are consumed. Now the erection of twigs is knocked over, and every man makes a mad rush to obtain even a small piece if he can, which is carried home in triumph and placed on one of the outer walls of the house, thus protecting its inmates from disease and death, or if it put into their store-room, much blessing will accrue to their gain."[65]

Ceremony performed for the benefit of Maharaja : In Ladakh when Ladakhi disease has not be cured by the MBBS Doctor or by Amchi, he approach to Lama, who perform a certain ceremony, under which an effigy is made and after reading certain books throw away outside a lonely place. Similar ceremony was performed for the benefit of Maharaja. Heber and Heber saw this ceremony and described this in the following way :

"Holy books having been read for seven days, a scapegoat, consisting of an effigy the size of man is prepared. Placed in the region of its heart is a bottle of red fluid, and it is then set up in the wilderness. A company of sepoys in smart khaki uniforms marches out behind lamas dressed in fantastic clothes and devil-masks. They take careful aim, even lying down to do so, but in spite of many rounds being fired, the effigy is never hit, and eventually cruder methods have to be adopted for its destruction."[66]

Chos-spun : In Ladakh during annual festival of at the monastery, young boys and girls make chos-spun means making of the brethren of the religion. Therefore, those who wish to have *chos-spun* take fast one whole day, during which he is not allowed to swallow even his own scliva. Then each man throws into a receptacle some personal belonging. The officiating priest takes these out in twos, thus making their owners spiritual brethren, after ceremony, he/she invite his or her cos-spun.[67]

Birth Ceremony : After birth of a child, mother is not allowed to touch any cooking utensils. On this occasion phaspun is called who filled pot with barley and implant an arrow. Later father and Phaspun do kitchen works. At the end of a month the burning of incense purifies the mother. Then she is allowed to do kitchen work later birth feast is celebrated. Heber and Heber say :

"Every guest brings with him to the pot of barley-meal called *Marzan*. All the contributions are now mixed together, and each lady present partakes of joint dish. This is called the Dargang. The *Ming tagches*, which means the 'tying on' of a name, is postponed till a convenient season, this being the coming of a skushog, who is requested to select a suitable designation. Until then a boy is called *Brogpa* (Brok-pa), or his little sister *Brogmo*. To cheat foolish spirits a dirty black mark across the forehead over the bridge to the tip of the nose on child is made. At the end of two years the lad's head is shaved, all except a piece of hair, which is the rudiment of his pigtail, and which is now carefully preserved, dressed and well-greased with butter; this being an occasion, it is celebrated gastronomically and no doubt alcoholically."[68]

Marriage Ceremony : When husband brought to lady's house called a *magpa*, but if lady is taken as a bride to husband's house, is called *gnama* or *pagma*. Heber and Heber said in details about marriage ceremony in Ladakh in the following way :

"Three methods of getting married are sanctioned by custom. The first to grant him the power of choosing any girl he like in the country as his bride. The second method to steal the chosen partner. The selection having been made, only relatives are admitted into the secret. No big wedding-feast is prepared, just a small one is made with the native beer or *chang* alone is unlimited. Bride and bridegroom each donning a very small white head-dress, called *mgo-ras*. The *gnama* or *magpa* has to say *'zhu-le'* to everybody. Lastly the orthodox wedding. For this neither parents nor child must decide on their choice before they have consulted the *Onpo*. The first overtures are made by a third party, who must never go to the house of the bride-elect empty-handed, and the fateful day on which he sets out must be decided by the *Onpo*. If the young lady's presents received him favourably more beer must be sent on several occasions. The first of these, called *holchang*, is only a small affair, but marks a definite betrothal. The *nyenchang* (relation beer), it is decided what presents in kind and in cash these must be given. The next feast is called the *trabschang* (conference beer), to decide upon the responsibilities of giving the various articles needed for the actual wedding feast. *Nyobjhol* is the procedure of fetching the bride (or bridegroom).

Those who carry this out are called nyopas (Tib. nyo-pa), and their official costume consists of beautiful silk dresses, and high-crowned, gilt hats. Their number varies from five to eleven. When nyopas enter the house. Lamas arrived to perform the *yangkuk* ceremonies (*yang* means blessing, *kuk* calling forth). The nyopas present each lama with a piece of cloth, which the latter place on their heads. The leader of the nyopas now takes her into the small temple of the house to say a last good-bye, for after this day she may never again enter this temple. She is then taken on a pony to her new home by the *nyopas*. Before arriving at her future home, the bride and her escort are met by lamas who perform the service of *Gyagsrod* that is, the driving away of any evil spirits which may have chosen to accompany the bride. Lamas, after preliminary incantation break, and with it throw away a *storma*. The lamas now enter the bridegroom's house, and the leader of the *nyopas* follows with the bride. Here new mother-in-law comes to meet her and leads her into the living room, where if she is only to marry one boy, she finds him sitting on a carpet, bearing the mystic sign and wearing the white head-dress; but if the brothers also included, they all set similarly side by side, while near them is an empty carpet for her, upon which is the sign *'nor bu gyas a kil'*, meaning 'jewel'. The next day there is dancing again in front of a crowd. The following day is called *nyendron* (relative feast). The next day is called the *dronchung* to which only the nearest relatives come. If the divorce, she is not allowed to enter her parents 'temple'. A man or woman may marry a second time, but there are no wedding festivities, and called *'chanchung'*."[69]

In conclusion since early days Ladakh was a part of lure when every year tourists were in the waiting list. Then British Joint Commissioner was the only important authority who allowed the visitors after carefully studying their application. Among them sportsmen visited Ladakh as shooters, they were given shooting licences. Then there were visitors who were specialists in some particular line of research. Among them were botanists, geologists, ornithologists, archaeologists and topographers. Besides some expeditions were also taken place such as 1913-14, Anglo-Italian was led by Sir Filippo De Filippi, which passed on into the Karakoram and the Depsang Plateau. It comprised many experts in different sciences, those who were engaged in gravimetric observations in the course of their investigations sent up several air balloons in Leh. These eventually descended in the surrounding villages. Then the Dutch expedition of 1922, and again in 1925, at work on the glaciers of the Karakoram, led by Mr. and Mrs. Visser with their Swiss guides. Then there was political visitors in the consular service, who occasionally came here through Central Asia, and even China. Thus during British India period visitors from America, Norway, Sweden, Germany, Holland, Switzerland, France, Austria, Italy, Russia, Persia, China and Japan visited Ladakh. Today similarly, visitors from European countries came here in large number that is about sixteen thousand. Among them American, Britishers, German, French, Israelis, Japanese and Italians visited Ladakh this year, i.e., in 2004 in good number.[70]

Notes and References

1. Heber, A. Reeve & Heber, Kathleen, M. : 'Himalayan Tibet & Ladakh', Ess Ess Pub. Delhi; 1976 (First Print 1903) : 273.
2. *Ibid.*, 17-18.
3. *Ibid.*, 18-19.
4. *Ibid.*, 19-20.
5. *Ibid.*, 23-29.
6. *Ibid.*, 29-30.
7. *Ibid.*, 33-34.
8. *Ibid.*, 34.
9. *Ibid.*, 36.
10. *Ibid.*, 34.
11. *Ibid.*, 36-37.
12. *Ibid.*, 38-39.
13. *Ibid.*, 40.
14. *Ibid.*, 39.
15. *Ibid.*, 41.
16. *Ibid.*, 42.
17. *Ibid.*, 43.
18. *Ibid.*, 46.
19. *Ibid.*, 57 & quoted from Mrs. Lilian Starr : 'Tales of Tirah and Lesser Tibet'.
20. Heber and Heber; *op. cit.* : 68-69.
21. *Ibid.*, 69-70.

22. *Ibid.*, 73-74.
23. *Ibid.*, 76.
24. *Ibid.*, 78.
25. *Ibid.*, 83.
26. *Ibid.*, 87-88.
27. *Ibid.*, 88.
28. *Ibid.*, 89.
29. *Ibid.*, 93
30. *Ibid.*, 94.
31. *Ibid.*
32. *Ibid.*, 96.
33. *Ibid.*, 97.
34. *Ibid.*, 100-01.
35. *Ibid.*, 102.
36. *Ibid.*, 104.
37. *Ibid.*
38. *Ibid.*, 105.
39. *Ibid.*, 107-08.
40. *Ibid.*, 110.
41. *Ibid.*, 111.
42. *Ibid.*
43. *Ibid.*, 112.
44. *Ibid.*, 113.
45. *Ibid.*, 113-14.
46. *Ibid.*, 118-19.
47. *Ibid.*, 121-22.
48. *Ibid.*, 122.
49. *Ibid.*, 125.
50. *Ibid.*, 127-28.
51. *Ibid.*, 132-33.
52. *Ibid.*, 135.
53. *Ibid.*, 140-41.
54. *Ibid.*, 144.
55. *Ibid.*, 146.
56. *Ibid.*, 154.

57. *Ibid.*, 157.
58. *Ibid.*
59. *Ibid.*, 158.
60. *Ibid.*, 159-60.
61. *Ibid.*, 167.
62. *Ibid.*, 168-69.
63. *Ibid.*, 171.
64. *Ibid.*, 171-72.
65. *Ibid.*, 174.
66. *Ibid.*
67. *Ibid.*, 177.
68. *bid.*
69. *Ibid.*, 179-90.
70. *Ibid.*, 276-77.

19

Seven Hedin and Ladakh

In the spring 1905 Seven Hedin visited Tibet via Srinagar and Ladakh. In this paper I have taken those portion of his journey to Trans-Himalaya which deal with Ladakh. Here follows the details :

On May 20, 1906 Seven Hedin started his journey for Tibet from Simla. Later from Kashmir he purchased all the necessary goods and made all possible transport arrangements. For his onward journey he loaded money bags of 22,000 silver and 9000 gold rupees. On 15th July 1906 he took leave from his old friend Younghusband and bade farewell to the Maharaja Amar Singh, Daya Krishan Kaul and Mrs. Annie Besant.

Zoji-la pass the first pass on the road to Leh : The Zoji-la when covered with snow, it would be difficult to cross. Seven Hedin further says :

> "The state of the road from Baltal over the Zoji-la pass was very difficult now from what it was in the year 1902. Then the whole country was covered with snow, and we slid almost the whole way down over glaciated slopes. Now some five hundred workmen were engaged in mending the road up to the pass. Their industry was indicated by thundering blasts, and now and then great blocks of stone fell down uncomfortably near to us. Now our heavily laden caravan had to cross the pass. Slowly and carefully we march up over hard and dirty but smooth avalanche cones, in which a small winding path has been worn out by the traffic. Water trickles and drops in the porous mass, and here and there small rivulets issue from openings in the snow. After a stretch of good road comes a steep slope along a wall of rock—a regular staircase, with steps of timber laid across the way. It was a hard task for laden

animals to struggle up. Now and then one of them slipped, and a mule narrowly escaped falling over—a fall from the steep acclivity into the deep trough of the roaring Sind would have been almost certain destruction, not a trace of the unfortunate beast would have been found again. From our lofty station the river looked like a thread. After some sacks of maize had fallen overboard, each of the animals was led by two men. The train advanced slowly up. Piercing cries were constantly heard when one of the animals was almost lost. But at last we got over the difficulties, and travelled over firm snow and level ground."[1]

Buddhists figures above Dras : There are some famous Buddhist figures near Dras and onwards to Karbu, he acknowledge many pleasant rocks like silver ribands. He says :

"On the heights above the Dras we pass the famous stone figures of Buddha, and then we descend a narrow picturesque valley to Karbu. The river constantly increase in volume, and presents a grand spectacle; small effluents fall between the rocks like silver ribands and spread out over the dejection fans. The pink blossoms of the hawthorn wave gracefully in the wind, which cools us during the hot hours of the day. Fine dark juniper bushes, tall as cypresses, adorn the right bank."[2]

Meeting with Abdullah in front of the Karbu station house : Seven Hedin in front of the Karbu station met Abdullah, who helped him over the snow fields of the Zoji-la on earlier occasion. He wished to go on a long journey with Seven Hedin, but asked him 60 rupees monthly.[3]

Where Dras Valley joins to Wakkha : Seven Hedin before reaching Kargil came across the valley where Dras joins the Wakkha, he remarks :

"We approached the striking spot where two valleys coverage and the Dras joins the Wakkha, passed the sharp rocky angle; and rode up close by the bank of the Wakkha. The valley has a very great fall, and the powerful stream rushes down in wild commotion, swells up and leaps over the blocks in its way, or breaks into foaming tumultuous surge."[4]

At Kargil : When Seven Hedin reached at Kargil, he was surrounded by the authorities of Kargil with the Pandit Lashman Dás and the Vazir Vezarat at their head. Here he got some relief over the embarrassment made in the first week journey from Zoji-la to Kargil. For instance all the Kashmiris, with their leader Aziza, were dismissed. Then came the turn of their fellow-countrymen and lastly to the Poonch men, as regards the sheep-stealing."[5]

First Lama Temple : Seven Hedin caravan left Kargil on 26th July with 77 hired horses with their leaders. At Shargul (Shargol) he came across Buddhist monastery which later became more numerous. He says :

> "At Shargul (Shargol) we passed the first lama temple on this route; beyond Mulbe they gradually became more numerous. At every step one finds evidence that one is in the country of the lamas; the small white temples in Tibetan style crown the rocky points and projections like storks' nests and dominate the valley and villages below them. But a monk in his red toga is seldom seen; the temples seem silent and abandoned among the picturesque chhorten monuments and manis. The whole relief of the country is now much more prominent than in winter, when the universal snow-mantle makes all alike and obliterates all the forms. The fantastic contours of the mountains stand out sharply with their wild pinnacles of rock and embattled crests, which above Bod-Karbu mingle with the old walls and towers, of which only ruins are now left."[6]

Lamayuru Monastery : On July 28, after crossing Potu-la Seven Hedin came to Lamayuru monastery, where lamas welcomed him with their traditional dress and custom. He expressed his views in this regards as :

> "Continued to ascend the valley which leads to the Potu-la. Just beyond the pass the authorities of Lamayuru came to meet us with flowers and fruits, and each one, according to the custom to the country, offered a rupee which, however, we needed only to touch with the hand. A little father the first chhorten appeared, followed by a long row of others, the stone heaps pointed towards the famous monastery of Lamayuru. Passing round a projecting corner a little farther on, we had a clear view of a small valley between lofty mountains, and here rose a precipitous terrace of detritus, on which the monastery is built. Some white buildings up there stood out sharply against a grey background, and is the depths of the valley cultivated fields spread out among a few groups of trees. As soon as our party was visible from the valley, music was heard, and long brass drums boomed from the temple roofs with a deep, solemn organ tone, which was joyously echoed among the mountains. Would the lama monasteries of Tibet give us such a friendly welcome? As we entered the village, about thirty women were standing in their best clothes, in fur-trimmed coloured mantles,

with blinkers firmly plaited to the hair, and with turquoises on the top. All the inhabitants had turned out, and formed a picturesque group round the band, which started a deafening tune with its flutes and drums. In the afternoon we went up to the monastery, where the prior and the monks received us at the main entrance. They led us into the open court of the monastery, surrounded by old buildings, chhortens, and flagstaffs. From here one has a grand view of the valley which slopes down to the Indus. Under dark masses of cloud, and in fine rain, seven monks executed an incarnation dance; they had tied on masks of wild animals, evil spirits, and monsters with laughing mouths, tusks for teeth, and uncanny staring eyes. Their motley coats stood out like bells as they danced, and all the time weird music was played. How the monks must be wearied in their voluntary imprisonment! Evidently their only relaxation is to display their religious fanaticism before the inquisitive eyes of passing stangers."[7]

Swinging wooden bridge near Nurla station house : After Lamayuru village Seven Hedin descended to a wild ravine which leads to the Indus. Hedin here says :

"Immediately beyond the village we descend a dangerously steep road in the small, narrow and wild ravine which leads to the Indus. The deep trough of the Dras is crossed by small, neat wooden bridges, and after a couple of hours' journey one rides as through a portal into the great, bright valley of the Indus, and has the famous river before one. It is a grand sight, and I halt for some time on a swinging wooden bridge to gaze at the vast volume of water which, with its great load and its rapid current, must excavate its channel ever deeper and deeper. The station-house Nurla stands just above the river, which tosses and roars its windows."[8]

Dangerous rock cut near Alchi bridge : Seven Hedin when reached near Alchi bridge, he saw two dangerous things together—one the rock cut route another Alchi bridge. He remarks :

"As far as Saspul we rode along the right bank close to the river. Here the road is often dangerous, for it is cut like a shelf in the steep wall of rock, and one feels at ease only when the valuable baggage has passed safely. The danger is that a pack-horse on the mountain side may thrust itself past another, and force this one over the edge of the rock, so that one may in a moment lose one's instruments, photographic apparatus, or

> sacks of rupees—the clear green water is swallowed up instantaneously by the muddy water of the Indus which comes from the forbidden land, from Gartok, from the regions north of the Kailas mountain."[9]

Basgo monastery : The Basgo monastery, situated at the side valley of Indus surrounded by chhortens and mains. Seven Hedin says :

> "Basgho-gompa[10] has a fine situation in a side valley of the Indus. The monastery is built on the left side of the valley, the white walls of three storeys, with balconies, effective cornices and pendants, standing on a long cliff. A number of chhortens and manis surround Basgho. The sacred formula 'Om mani padme hum' is carved on a slab of green slate and lizards, as green as the stone, dart about over the words of eternal truth."[11]

1st August 1906, the last journey to Leh : On first August 1906, Seven Hedin caravan near Spittol (Spituk) monastery[12] turned towards Leh where he was welcomed by a Leh merchant Mohanlal. He further says :

The 1st of August was the last day of our journey to Leh. A bright, peaceful morning, the rays of the sun crept warm and agreeably through the foliage of the apricot trees, and threw green reflections into the station-room. We rode near the Indus as far as where the monastery Spittol stands on its hills, beyond which the road turns aside from the river and runs straight up to Leh, which is visible from a distance, surrounded by verdant gardens. Mohanlal, a merchant of Leh, who had undertaken a large part of the final equipment of the expedition, came to meet us. We dismounted at the gate of a large garden, and went in. In the midst of the garden stands a stone house among poplars and willows. It is usually the residence of the Vazir Vezarat, the representative of Kashmir in Ladak, but now it was to be my headquarter for twelve days. Here I had a roof over my head for the last time for two long years, I found myself very comfortable in my study up one flight of stairs. Robert[13] occupied another room, and an open, shady balcony was fitted up as a meteorological observatory.[14] Manuel and the two Rajputs had the control of the ground-floor; in the courtyard purveyors and new servants were continually coming and going, and adjoining the garden was our stable, where the newly obtained horses were posted in the open air."[15]

Captain Patterson, Joint Commissioner of Ladakh; a true friend : In Leh, Seven Hedin met Captain Patterson, was then the Joint Commissioner of Ladakh, later after long discussion about the future of Asia he became his true friend. He remarks :

"Captain Patterson was now Joint Commissioner of the province of Ladak. He received me from the first with the greatest hospitality and kindness, and was one of the finest men I have ever come in contact with. Having a thorough knowledge of India, Ladak, and Tibet, he was able to give me valuable hints and advice, and was untiring in assisting to equip the great caravan, the object of which was still, officially, Eastern Turkestan, without overstepping his instructions by a hair's breadth. I found in him a true friend, and after dinner, which I always took at eight o'clock in the evening, we often sat together till long after midnight, talking of the future of Asia and the doings of the world."[16]

Muhamed Isa name recommended by Younghusband for caravan leader : In Srinagar, Younghusband recommended Muhamed Isa name for caravan leader. He belonged to Leh to whom Seven Hedin earlier saw him in his Kashgar expedition. He made the following statement in this regards :

"Sir Francis Younghusband had recommended to me a well known caravan leader, Muhamed Isa. During about thirty years he had travelled in most parts of Central Asia, and was also acquainted with many parts of Tibet. Besides a number of shorter journeys which he had accomplished in the service of various sahibs, he had also been Carey and Dalgleish's caravan leader on their great march through Central Asia, and had served a couple of years under Dutreuil de Rhins. He accompanied Younghusband on his famous march over the Mustagh Pass (1887), and had been his caravan leader in the campaign to Lhasa (1903-04). During all these journeys he had acquired experience which might be very useful to me, and I gratefully accepted Younghusband's proposal. Besides, Muhamed Isa spoke fluently Turki, Tibetan and Hindostani. His father was a man of Yarkand, his mother a Lamaist of Leh. The mixed race of such unions is called Argon, and is generally distinguished by physical power and extraordinary well developed muscular structure. Muhamed Isa also was a fine man, tall and strong as a bear, with great power of endurance, reliable and honest. He kept splendid discipline among the men, and if he were sometimes strict, it was for the good of the caravan, and he permitted no neglect of duty. The remembrance of Dutreuil de Rhins (the French explorer, murdered by him on June 5, 1894) especially seemed to affect him; he frequently returned to his account of the attack made on the unfortunate Frenchman. He was also a good boaster, and declared that once in mid winter he had carried a letter in ten days from Yarkand to Leh, with all his provisions on his back—a journey that an ordinary moral takes a month to accomplish. But there was no harm in his exaggerations; he was always witty and amusing, always cheerful and ready for a joke, and kept up the spirits of the rest in depressing circumstances. (Under the terms of Mohammed Isa asked for forty rupees a month, and an advance of two hundred rupees to leave with his wife)."[17]

Seven Hedin caravan had 31 people of different religion : Finally Seven Hedin, for his mission to Tibet appointed Mohammed Isa as a leader of caravan and rest from the different parts of Ladakh. All together in his caravan had nine sons of Islam, seventeen were Buddhists, two Hindus, one Catholic and two Protestants including Seven Hedin. Introducing about his famous people from Ladakh he says :

"I have abundant opportunities of introducing these men—Sonam Tsering, whom Captain Rawling had strongly recommended, was chosen as leader of this caravan. He received 100 rupees for the expenses of the caravan. Mohammed Isa accompanied it part of the way to see that everything went on smoothly. Besides Sonam Tsering, who had served under Deasy and Rawling, I will name old Guffaru, a grey-headed man with a long white beard, who thirty-three years ago accompanied Forsyth's embassy to Jakub Bek of Kashgar. He had seen the great Bedaulet ('the fortunate one') in all his pomp and state, and had many tales of his experiences on Forsyth's famous journey, a man of sixty two. Another was Shukkur Ali. I had known him in 1890 in Kashgar, where he was in Younghusband's service, he had taken part in Wellby's journey. A year later he shared in my boating trips on the holy lake Mansarowar, was an honest soul, and a stout fellow."[18]

Mohanlal : A supplier of food products : At Leh Mohanlal was a wholesale merchant, who supplied food stuffs to explorers. Seven Hedin also purchased 1700 rupees products from him, he says :

"For the men rice, flour, talkan or roasted meal, which is eaten mixed with water, and brick tea in bulk were taken. For myself several hundred tins of preserved meat, tea, sugar, tobacco etc., all provided by the merchant Mohanlal, whose bill came to 1700 rupees. New pack-saddles, ropes, frieze rugs, horsehoes, spades, axes, and crowbars, Bellews, cooking-pots, copper cans, and other cooking utensils of the men with other articles cost nearly a thousand rupees."[19]

Hospitality by Moravian missionaries in Leh : Seven Hedin got home atmosphere at Mission hospital in Leh. He remarks :

"The Moravian missionaries in Leh rendered me invaluable service. Pastor Peter had endless worriers over my affairs; he managed both now and afterwards all the business with the new retainers. Dr. Shawe, the physician of the mission, was an old friend I had known on my former journey, when he treated my sick cossack, Shagdur, in the excellent Mission Hospital. Now, too, he helped me by both word and deed. He died in Leh a year, after a life devoted to suffering humanity. All the Moravians I met in the Western Himalayas are educated to a very high standard and come out exceptionally well prepared for the work before them. I need only mention Dr. Karl Marx and Pastor A.H. Francke as two men who are thoroughly at home in strictly scientific archaeological investigation."[20]

Missionaries have got confidence over Ladakhis : In Leh the missionaries did community welfare work among Ladakhi Buddhist community. He remarks :

"In Leh the missionaries have a community which they treat with great gentleness and piety, for they know well that the religion inherited from their fathers has sunk deep into the bone and marrow of the natives, and can only be overcome by cautious patient labour. Even the Ladakhis who never visit the mission stations always speak well of the missionaries, and have a blind confidence an effect by their good example. The hospital is made great use of, and medical science is a sure way of access to the hearts of the natives. During the last days of my stay in Leh I saw Mr. and Mrs. Ribbach, in whose hospitable house I had spent many pleasant winter evenings four years ago."[21]

Meeting with the wealthy merchant Haiji Nazer Shah : Seven Hedin on the request of Captain Patterson met Haiji Nazer Shah, who had big family and had various branches of the houses in Lhasa, Shigatse, Gartok, Yarkand and Srinagar. He migrated from Srinagar and later settled down in Leh. Now let us see what Seven Hedin speaks ?

> "One day Captain Patterson proposed that I should go with him to call on the wealthy merchant Hajji Nazer Shah. In a large room on the first floor, with a large window looking over the Indus valley, the old man sat by the wall, on soft cushions, with his sons and grandsons around him. All about stood chests full of silver and gold dust, turquoise and coral, materials and goods which would be sold in Tibet. Hajji Nazer Shah's commercial house is managed entirely by himself and his large family. This consists of about in Lhasa, Shigatse, Gartok, Yarkand, and Srinagar are all under the control of his sons. Three hundred years ago the family migrated from Kashmir to Ladak. The real source of their wealth is the so-called Lopchak mission, of which they posses a monopoly."[22]

Lopchak Mission : According to the treaty between Kings of Ladakh and Tibet, every third year Ladakh sent a special mission to the Dalai Lama, to convey presents. Seven Hedin gave the following information in this regards :

> "Lopchak mission, in accordance with a treat nearly 200 years old the kinds of Ladak sent every third year a special mission to the Dalai Lama, to convey presents which were a token of subjection to the supremacy of Tibet, at any rate in spiritual matters. However, after Soravar Sing (Zorawar Singh), Gulab Sing's general, conquered Ladak in 1841 and annexed the greater part of this country to Kashmir, the Maharaja of Kashmir took over the duty of carrying out the Lopchak mission, and always entrusted it to one of the noblest, most prominent families of Ladak. For some fifty years this confidential post has been in the family of Nazer Shah, and has been a source of great profit to them, especially as several hundred baggage animals are provided for the mission gratis, for the journey from Leh to Lhasa. A commercial agent is also sent yearly from Lhasa to Leh, and he enjoys the same transport privileges. The old Hajji (who attached with Lopchak, yearly earn) a net profit of 25,000 rupees, and his name was known and respected throughout the interior Asia."[23]

Leh Town : Leh is a small town, which, was busy with Central Asian trader during summer. Seven Hedin has his following impression :

> "The small town itself is full of the most attractive and fascinating examples of Tibetan architecture. On all sides are seen quiet nooks with motley figures, temple portals, mosques,

houses rising one above another, and open shops, whither customers flock; and the traffic became brisker everyday after the summer caravans from Yarkand over the Kardang pass[24] began to arrive at Leh. Round the town stands a crescent of bare, lumpy, sun-lighted hills; to the south and south-east the dry gravelly plain slopes down to the Indus, where a series of villages among green fields and woods impart some life to the picture. On the farther side is seen Stokpa peeps[25] out of a valley mouth. Here resides an ex-king of the third generation, the Raja of Stok, whose grandfather ruled as king of Ladak but was deprived by Soravar Sing[26] of his dignity and state."[27]

Raja of Stok : Raja of Stok, though, did not have any administrative role over Ladakh, yet Seven Hedin took a recommendation letter from him for his onward journey to Tibet. According to him :

"The Raja of Stok, or to give him his full name and title, Yigmet Kungak Singhei Lundup Thinlis Zangpo Sodnam Nampar Gelvela[28], Yagirdar of the state of Stok, awakes one's sympathy in his somewhat sad position; he was a visit to Leh, for the owns an unpretending but pretty house in the main street. The Tibetans[29] still look upon him as the true and rightful king, while the ruler of the country, the Maharaja of Kashmir, we therefore concluded that a letter of recommendation from this Raja of Stok might be very useful some day or other. He was evidently flattered by my request and quite ready to grant it. In his open letter he ordered, (all men in Tibet of whatever rank, from Rudok, Gartok and Rundor to Shigatse and Gyantse to allow Sahib Hedin to pass freely and unmolested, and to render him all necessary assistance.) This highly important document, with the date and the red square seal of the Raja affixed, was afterwards read by many Tibetan Chieftains, on whom it made not the slightest impression. They quietly answered, we have only to obey the orders of the Devashung in Lhasa."[30]

Leh palace : an old monument : In Leh, on the rock an old Leh palace is constructed from the roof of this one can see all activities of Leh bazar as well a grand view of mountains and Indus valley. Seven Hedin says :

"The old palace of Leh stands on its rock like a gigantic monument of vanished greatness. From its roof one has a grand view of the town, the Indus valley, and the great mountains beyond the river. In the foreground stretch fields of wheat and barley, still staringly green amidst and general grey, small groups of garden trees, groves of poplar, far-houses, and small knobby ridges, while dreary Mohammedan graveyard stands out sharply and obtrusively in the evening sunshine. Immediately below us lies a chaos of quadrangular houses of stone or mud, with wooden balconies and verandahs, interrupted only by the main street and the lanes branching out of it. On the point of a rock to the east is seen a monastery, for which a lama gave the name of Semo-gungma[31]. Semo-yogma stands in the palace itself. The temple hall here is called Diva[32], and the two principal images Guru and Sakya-tubpa[33], that is Buddha. The portal of the palace with its pillars has a very picturesque effect. Through this portal you enter a long, dark, paved entrance and then pass up a stone staircase and through gloomy passages and corridors, with small offshoots running up to balcony windows; in the interior, however, you roam about through halls all equally dark."[34]

Graves of some popular Europeans : At Leh near Captain Patterson's bungalow lied a burial ground in which some European graves were found. Seven Hedin has given the following details in this regard :

"Over Stoliczka's grave a grand monument has been erected. The inscription on a tablet in front informs us that he was born in June 1838 and died in June 1874 at Murgoo, near the Karakoram Pass. The Indian Government erected the memorial in 1876 as a mark of respect and gratitude for the service which Stoliczka had rendered during the journey of Forsyth's embassy. The same inscription is repeated on the other side in Latin. Dalgeish's tombstone is simpler, but is also adorned with a tablet of cast-iron. He was born in 1853 and was murdered on the Karakorum Pass in 1888."[35]

Marched for Tibet : On August 13, 1906 caravan of Seven Hedin started early in the morning for Tibet from Leh. On this occasion many reknowned personalities—Hajji Nazer Shah, his sons, pundits, officers had assembled to see off the caravan. Later Seven Hedin's caravan passed through mani ringmos[36], Shey, Thiksey, Rambirpur, Stagna, Chemre, Changla pass, etc. reached Tankse. Here follows the details :

"We went down from Leh past innumerable mani ringmos and through narrow gullies between small rocky ridges, and so drew near to the Indus again, and then Shey came in sight with its small monastery on a point of rock. The road runs through the village, over canals by miniature stone bridges. After we had lost sight of the river and ridden through the village, we found ourselves in front of the monastery Tikze (Thiksey) on a commanding rock, with the village Tikze and its fields and gardens at the foot. At Tikze we are much lower than at, and then we begin to mount up again. After a short march we came to the village Rambirpur, reconstructed thirty years ago, and to the road the small monastery Stagna-gompa[37] stands on a pinnacle of rock. On the left bank is seen the village Changra, and a little higher up the well-hidden, small, and narrow valley where the famous temple of Hemis[38] lies concealed. Now we leave the Indus for good and all, turned the rocky corner into the side valley through which the road runs up past the monasteries Karu and Chimre to Chang-la pass. At Chimre we are at a height of 11,978 feet, and we all the day's journey to Singrul, where we find ourselves 16,070 feet above sea-level. The road keeps for the most part to the stony barren slopes on the left side of the valley, while the brook flows nearer to the right side, where bright green fields appropriate so much of its water that little is left to flow out of the path. A path to Nubra follows a side valley on the right. In Sakti we wander in a labyrinth of narrow passages and alleys between huts and chhortens, boulders and walls, mani ringmos and terraces which support cultivated patches laid out in horizontal steps. Above us is seen the Chang-la, Tagar is the last village before the pass; I had halted twice before. After four and a half hours we are up on the small terrace shaped halting-place, Singrul[39], and the bluish-grey smoke of the fires of yak-dung floats over the soil, scantily carpeted with grass and traversed by a rivulet of crystal-clear water. Fifty mules from Rudok laden with salt threaten to block our way, but are driven to one side by our men. At last we were at the top, 17,585 feet above sea-level. Certainly the thermometer marked 41.4°, but the wind was in the north, thick clouds obscured the sky, sweeping over the crest of the mountains and soon hail came down, slashing us like a whip. On the summit of the Chang-la pass stands a stone heap with sacrificial poles, which are decked with ragged streamers torn by the wind. All these streamers bear in Tibetan characters the prayer of six sacred letters; coloured or faded, they flap and rustle in the wind as if they would drive the prayers up higher and higher by unknown paths to the ears of the gods. Horns and skulls adorn this elevated altar. Here all our Ladakis in turn come to a halt, raise a cheer, dance, swing their caps, and rejoice at having reached this critical point without mishap. At the foot of the descent (is) Drugub[40] (and) lies at a height of 12,795 feet, and on the short way to Tankse[41] we ascended only 299 feet. Beyond Tankse a massive, finely sculptured mountain rises in the background; deep valleys open on either side; through the southern runs a road to Gartok, which I was to follow later; through the northern, the road to Muglib, by which I had travelled before; thus I was to take now. The Tankse river has a fair volume of water; we crossed it at a broad."[42]

Panggong-Tso : Panggong is a big lake at the height of 14,196 feet. Seven Hedin says :

"A heap of stones be decked with flags and a mani mark the point of hydrographical importance which is the watershed between the Panggong-tso and the Indian ocean; here the height is 14,196 feet. From this point the valley descends slowly to the lake, and we ride in the channel through which at one time it discharged itself into the Shyok and Indus. Now, the Panggong-tso is cut off from the Indus and consequently contains salt water. Behind a spur on the right side of the lake peeped out, and a few minutes later a grand panorma unfolded itself before us; the great bluish-green lake between its colossal cliffs."[43]

Conclusion : Seven Hedin with his caravan of about 58 horses and 31 people of various discipline and religions marched for Tibet on August 13, 1906. He stayed almost 12 days at Leh and made all preparation from here for his destination. He earlier visited Ladakh in 1901 and probably 1904. All together by 1906 he spent 21 years of his life in expedition of various parts of Central Asia. In those days some famous adventurers like Tsering Sonam, Mohammad Isa, Guffaru, Shakkur Ali etc. often employed by Sahibs. They were all Ladakhis and very helpful for their respective Sahibs during their Central Asian expedition.

Notes and References

1. Hedin, Seven : 'Trans-Himalaya (Discoveries and Adventures in Tibet) Vol. I, Greenwood Press Pub., New York ; 1969 : 39-40.
2. *Ibid.*, 41.

3. *Ibid.*
4. *Ibid.*, 42.
5. *Ibid.*
6. *Ibid.*, 43.
7. *Ibid.*, 44.
8. *Ibid.*
9. *Ibid.*, 45.
10. Basgho-gompa : Bazgo-monastery.
11. Hedin, Seven ; *op. cit.* : 45-46.
12. Spittol monastery : Spituk monastery belongs to Gelug-pa order.
13. Robert : He was an employee of Seven Hedin caravan.
14. Meteorological observatory : This observatory was located at Leh. Today one can see its ruined condition in front of the Moravian Mission School, Leh.
15. Hedin, Seven ; *op. cit.* : 46.
16. *Ibid.*, 48.
17. *Ibid.*, 49-50.
18. *Ibid.*, 54.
19. *Ibid.*, 55.
20. *Ibid.*, 56.
21. *Ibid.*, 56-57.
22. *Ibid.*, 57.
23. *Ibid.*, 57-59.
24. Kardang Pass : Khardong la pass. It lies at the height of 18,380 feet and one of the highest pass in Ladakh.
25. Stokpa peeps : Stok Kangri, It lies about 21,000 feet.
26. Soravar Singh : Zorawar Singh, he was the General of Dogra Army and occupied Ladakh in 1834.
27. Hedin, Seven, *op. cit.* : 59.
28. Yigmet Kungak Singhei Lundup Thinlis Zangpo Sodnam Nampar Gelvela. He was the dethroned King of Ladakh and would be Jigmet Namgyal.
29. Tibetans : Actually they were Ladakhis.
30. Hedin, Seven ; *op. cit.* : 59-60.
31. Semo-gungma : Tse mo-monastery; it is near Leh palace.

32. Diva = Dukhang or temple hall.
33. Sakya - tubpa = Sakya - thuva or Buddha.
34. Hedin, Seven ; *op. cit.* : 60.
35. *Ibid.*, 61.
36. Mani ringmos : Mane - Ringmos ; they are long Mane walls.
37. Stagna - gompa = Tagna monastery. It belongs to Drugpa Kargyud pa order.
38. Hemis : This is the popular monastery in Ladakh and belongs to Drugpa Kargyud order.
39. Singrul : It would be a halting place for travellers.
40. Drugub = Dur - buk.
41. Tankse = Tangtse.
42. Hedin, Seven ; *op. cit.* : 65-71.
43. *Ibid.*, 72.

20

Journey to Ladakh by Ganpat in the Beginning of Twentieth Century

Ganpat visited Ladakh in the beginning of 20th century A.D. He called Ladakh as Lamaland; and marched to Ladakh from Srinagar during spring. He passed through the long meadows and glacier valley of Sonamarg lying between 8,500 to 9,000 feet. Next to Zoji-la pass, which was then difficult to cross during day time as there were chances of snow avalanches. He remarks :

> "Since snow is late and heavy on the pass, we shall have to be under way very early—perhaps at midnight, when snow is hard and frozen and the avalanches are less to be dreaded, the avalanches that make the Zoji such a place of ill omen in the spring months."[1]

New Country : Zoji La is a gateway of Ladakh, after crossing this pass we feel as if we are in a new country of hard rock and stone. Ganpat explains in his words as :

> "When daylight finds us over the pass, following the snow fields towards the bleak, huddled buildings of Macchoi, we know we are in a new country, that Kashmir has been left behind. The trees are gone, the hills are hard the softness of the Nature has deserted us. We have come into a new world of hard rock and stone, of immense distances and of great heights a land where the sun scorches by day the water chills into ice at night, where life is hard and luxury unknown, and where Nature's moods are quite other than those she shows to us in the softer lands we have left."[2]

Civilized People : Journey to Ladakh in olden days was not easy task as it had stony tracks, without tree shade, villages had come across after travelling a long distance; yet it was fascinating when travellers came across to civilized people of Ladakh. Ganpat explains :

> "When we march onward day after day over the stony tracks above the rushing torrents, with hardly over a tree to shade us, and where more often than not the discovery of a village marks the end of the long day's march, we understand better something of the charm of all we have left. And yet, all the same, there is a fascination of this new ganuntness, a fascination more apparent perhaps to us civilized people than to others. One feels somehow that one has been stripped of much that hampers vision, one is alone with nature-naked in front of life—and one understands oneself the better of it, now that the conventions of life have gone, that the veils and curtains have been drawn aside and we have been set down in immensity to see ourselves as the giant hills must see us—if their vision is microscopic enough to see us at all—infinite—simal dots in an immensity of space. And yet these countries seem not to breed at all the atmosphere of atheism that is produced so continuously by the overcrowded ant-heaps of civilization. One realizes, if one thinks at all, and most of us do in places like these, that there is something behind it all—that it is the creation of an artist and still more, that the artist spark is alive in each and all of us, to fan or let die as we will. It is the infinitesimal dot that counts more than the giant hills."[3]

Ladakh is a centre of hotch-potch people : Ganpat when reached at Kargil, he noticed, as it was a edge of Buddhist Ladakh. Thereafter upto Purigh it was the part of Baltistan, inhabitants belonged to Dards and Mongolian race, but by faith—Muslim of Shia sect. However, Muslims in Ladakh had three quarter population. Ganpat didn't know the real concept of Buddhism, as he said Buddhists were devil-worshippers. In fact, his statement in not true. In Buddhist monasteries we can see mask dance performed by lamas of the concern monastery. They wear mask of different Buddhist deities during annual festival to do tantric dance. Ganpat says :

> "Ladakh is filled with a hotch-potch of people—Mussulmans who are three-quarters of Buddhists, Buddhists who are really animists or devil-worshippers."[4]

Purig is the boundary of two religions : When Ganpat visited Ladakh he acknowledged that Ladakh had two main religions viz. Islam and Buddhism. Buddhists were in majority beyond Purig, whereas Skardu and Kargil had Muslims in majority. Altogether Buddhist monuments were scattered throughout in Ladakh. Today we can see this old tradition of Buddhism is still intact in Ladakh.

Ladakh is the roof of the world : Ladakh has low density of population with massif mountains Kz, Gasheabrums, Teram, Kangri, Nubra peaks etc. which have heights between 20,000 to 27,000 feet. Not only this it has wide desert fields with large area of least vegetation. It is therefore, considered roof of the world. Ganpat has following views in this regards :

> "I think more correctly Ladakh could lay better claim to being the actual roof. This little, forgotten country, some two hundred miles broad from south to north, by about three hundred log from east to west, contains a great portion of what is the biggest massif of mountains in the world. The Karakorum (Karakoram) range for practical purposes forms the northern boundary between Ladakh and Chinese Turkestan runs well to northward; but since there are no inhabitants, no villages far several hundred miles, nobody has ever worried their heads much about the actual frontier of these parts."[5]

Two Great Valleys : Through many nallas irrigate the land of Ladakh, yet broadly speaking Ladakh contains two great valleys—The Indus and The Shyok. Leh is more or less the centre of Ladakh, where the height of the valley is 11,000 feet along Indus and 10,500 feet at the bank of Shyok rivers.[6]

Glaciers are the life blood of Ladakh : In Ladakh, mostly small and big valleys are surrounded by glaciers, during summer come down in the form of water and irrigate the barren land in the lower parts where people grow wheat, barley, grim, vegetables, and even orchards of fruit—apricot, apple, mulberry and walnut. Ganpat remarks :

> "The glaciers, whence come down the waters which are the life-blood of Ladakh and the surrounding countries. Irrigation is the solution of Ladakh's problems; whenever water can be led down in the little carefully built and carefully maintained channels there are fertile fields and often artificially planted trees—little cases of green among the barren red and brown and chocolate hills—orchards of fruit—trees in the lower parts of the Shyok and Indus, apricot and apple, mulberry and walnut."[7]

Ladakh was once under sea : In Ladakh one can still see big lakes like Panggong, Tsomo Riri etc. on the high altitude ranges; these are the remains of the old sea under which present Ladakh was lying. Ganpat has the following opinion :

"At some comparatively recent of the earth's history Ladakh was under sea, later on, when it emerged, it was covered with an ice-cap sweeping right down from the North Polar regions. That ice-cap has been melting more or less continuously ever since, during the 100,000; 200,000; 300,000; or whatever number of years the latest geological text-books favour as the time that has elapsed since the world's most recent freezing."[8]

Ladakh is a magic land : Ladakh has varies faces; here landscapes have different colours; at one time it has blue-black, next brown-granite and so on. Ganpat remarks :

"I think you will find that Ladakh will give you things just as picturesque and just as attractive and in addition, throw over you a charm that is all its own—a charm, a magic that I have found in no other land."[9]

People of Ladakh : Primarily Ladakh consists three races—Balti, Bhoto and Dard. Baltis are dominated in Kargil district, Leh has Buddhists or Bhotos in majority. Besides, Dards are surviving in some parts of Leh and Kargil districts, e.g., Da, Hanu, Garkon, Bima etc. Ganpat explains :

"The inhabitants of Ladakh are primarily Tibetans; race, history and religion alike continue to make them truely the same as the inhabitants of Greater Tibet. Ladakh lying as it does directly across the main trade route between India and Central Asia, has inevitably been an open country, interested to some extent in, and directly influenced by, northern and southern neighbours. Besides the Tibetans of true stock there are two other classes in the country; one is the mixed population mostly to be found about Leh, the Arghuns, offspring of the unions between Ladakhi women and Kashmiri or Yarkandi fathers, Mussalmans all by virtue of their fathers; the other is Dards, a small survival of the Aryan races which at one time held Ladakh, before they were swamped by the waves of Tibetan incursions."[10]

Ladakhis have sturdily built : Ladakhis are normally five foot four and have relatively big lungs, so that, they do not feel breathing problems. Ganpat remarks :

"Ladakh is, as one would expect from the altitude at which he lives, a man of comparatively small stature, through there are exceptions. The average height is probably not much above five-foot-four, and the women are considerably shorter. They are, as one also expects of people of the high countries, very sturdily built. I should think in the course of centuries they have actually developed chests and lungs relatively far bigger than ours to compensate for the rarity of the atmosphere."

Polyandry is a thorny one : Buddhists had a tradition to follow polyandry system. This theory was practicable, because in those days Ladakh didn't have sufficient fertile land and to control population growth this system was a natural law. Ganpat has the following opinion in the regards :

> "The world has seen polyandry—the woman with two or more husbands—in many forms and in many ages and places, but it has been of sporadic occurrence. The eldest son of a Ladakhi family marries a wife either of his own volition, or else or arranged by the parents of both sides. The offer of his hand and fortune includes also the hand of his brother, or of two brothers next in age, but not their fortunes, since they have none. Any further brother have to go out into a cold world and even their own living. The lady being duly married takes on both or all three brothers, and the children for all official purposes are the children of the eldest. But I believe, in respectable families, when the eldest brother is at home the others are expected to keep out of the way. (In fact Polyandry) is a natural law to keep down the increase of population in a barren country."[12]

Woman is dominant in her household : Ladakhi woman is free in nature, she has full control over her house, trade and other related activities. Ganpat also agrees with this statement as :

> "The Ladakhi lady is complete head of her own household, and the men are well underneath her extremely capable thumb. She has her own money; she trades on her own; her word is very much law. And, lastly, when she meets you on the roadside she passes the time of day freely and cheerfully which is most attractive to anyone who has spent long years in the veil-cursed East."[13]

Ladakh had very few vegetables : Ladakhis didn't grow vegetables much, however, barley-meal then was common form. Now they grow these in good quantity. Ganpat says :

> "The barley is used in many forms, as puddings, cakes, and in a kind of short bread which will keep good for a year or more. There are very few vegetables in Ladakh, but those who can get them use large quantities of dried apricots, which grow in

abundance in the lower valleys at places such as Nubra or Hundar. Both the tea and the barley-meal are consumed from the little wooden bowls that all carry in the bosoms of their loose robes, the bowls often being lined with thin beaten silver but the well to do prefer their tea in China handleless cups on silver saucers, which are brought from China and Lhassa (Lhasa). There is chang, which is a fermented drink made of barley. The Ladakhi brews it and drinks it in large quantities, and contrives sometimes to get drunk upon it, which argues a perserverance that might be devoted to a better cause."[14]

Ladakhi ornaments : Like other ladies of India, Ladakhi women are fond of ornaments. Their ornaments are made of gold, silver, turquoise, corals etc. Ganpat remarks :

"Firstly, she braids her hair into innumerable plaits, and then she fastens onto it two large flaps of black astrakhan, one on each side, which look like elephants ears on a small scale. Between these she puts a long strip of scarlet cloth cut like a snake, with the expanded hood on top of her head, the head over her forehead, and the tail down her back. On this is sewn every turquoise she or her mother or grandmother—for it is an heirloom—have managed to buy or get, and finishes off the snake's tail with rows of coral beads. She may, if she has more money than most, intersperse the big turquoises with filagree gold ornaments sewn on to the red cloth. Her ears bear bundles of silver earrings and from the astrakhan ear-flaps droop gold or silver chains, while about her waist is a girdle, from which hangs an openwork brass or gold disc, as big as a saucer, suspending her household keys and manicure and toilet instruments. Her wrists are girt with large bracelets of shells—these from India mostly—and about her throat will be all the necklaces of gold or silver or corals or cheap beads she can afford. Lastly, if she be well-to-do, the usual goatskin cap will be replaced by a rich worked shawl of Bokhara. The Chang-Thang women of the East, in addition, fish off the peragh—the turquoise snake—with a bar of silver across their forehead from which little metal pendants and silk tassels fall to the level of the eyes."[15]

Islam has certain hold : In Ladakh Islam was not propagated forcefully, it spread peacefully by marrying with Buddhist girls. Ganpat has the following opinion in this regards :

> "Islam—the religion of Mohammad—has a certain hold in the country, more particularly in Leh itself and in the Shushot (Chushod) villages in the Indus valley, and it is slowly extending, producing a strong effect, in that, the two extremes of polygamy and polyandry meeting, the resultant product seems to be monogamy. This is due probably to a mutual unconscious compromise in the many mixed marriages that place, since the Mussulman husband refuses to share his wife with other men, and the Ladakhi woman objects to sharing her position with any others of her sex."[16]

Leh was the centre of Christian missionary : In past Moravian missionaries did academic and welfare works for poor Ladakhis in the beginning of 20th century A.D. There were very few Catholic missionaries visited Ladakh. In recent past this missionaries are doing well. Today Catholic has one popular school 'St. Peter' at Chushod village. Now let us see what Ganpat speaks :

> "Leh has always been a Christian missionaries, they probably owe their position to the most excellent medical work they have done. One of the main reasons perhaps for its popularity as a mission centre is that it seemed to offer a starting-point for mission work in the long-closed land of Tibet. Similarly of race, of speech and of religion would seem to point to it as an ideal training-ground for missionaries who hoped to go farther a field into Tibet proper."

Dalai Lama for Buddhism is like Pope for Roman Church : In Ladakh Buddhist monasteries are broadly divided into Red and Yellow sects, both are partially related with Dalai Lama, as one can finds throne in every monastery for Dalai Lama. Ganpat has the following views :

> "They are, moreover, in closer touch with Lhassa (Lhasa), which is to Lamaism what Rome is to Catholicism, and the Dalai Lama, who is to Buddhism who the Pope is to the Roman church, and who is invariably of the yellow sect."[17]

Anyone can become Lama : In Ladakh anyone can become Lama, but usually Ladakhis sent their children for monkhood at young age. In monasteries they learn ritual practices and Buddhist philosophy teaching from their respective teachers. Ganpat says :

> "A lama is made, not born. Anyone may become a lama, even in late life—though more usually he enters monkhood as a child, even as a baby, and to have a child become a lama is

probably as much to the Ladakhi family as to the Southern Irish family would be the entry of a son into the priesthood (Lama) learns the ritual of the services but is generally ignorant of the identity of the myriad gods and bodhisats whose images and paintings fill his monastery. He learns also to play the religious instruments—the big warming-pan-shaped drums, the little clarinets, the great telescopic brass and copper trumpets, six or seven or eight feet long. He learns also to spin the "dorje's" the thunderbolt symbols of Lamaism—which are the main mask of the lama; learns also to play the little double-sided drums, which are turned in the hand and so beaten by a small weight on a string as they twist backwards and forwards—little double drums, of which the best are made from the brainpans of two human skulls, and like the dorjes are mighty weapons against demons. He is taught also how to make the ceremonial offerings of chang and barley, to build the pyramids of butter and parched grain which are piled up on festival days; learns too the charms against evil spirits which will form so much of his work later on when he goes out among the laity. There are the arts and crafts to be learned—the painting of the scriptures by use of wooden and metal blocks, the fashioning of images in metal or wood or plaster, the painting of the wall frescoes, without which no monastery would be complete. Again these are horoscopes to be learned, the manner of selecting auspicious days for weddings, the selection of names for children, the choice of methods of disposing of the dead—an important business this, upon which may depend the hereafter of the departed spirit."[18]

Kashok's spirit is that of Buddha : In Ladakh Kushok is popularly known as rinpoche, he after parinirvana can be born only as a Kushok, therefore, free from the wheel of life cycle. Ganpat says :

"A Shushok (Kushok) in greater Tibet termed a 'Living Buddha' and the Dalai Lama is the greatest example of what in Ladakh is called a Skushok; after death can be reborn only as a Skushok—he is free of the chain of life. His spirit is that of Buddha, of a personified attribute of Buddha or of some famous Bodhisat (Bodhisattva)."[19]

Chortens of Ladakh : In Ladakh we can see chortens on the road side in which people of Ladakh put burnt body ashes. Ganpat explains :

"Once the body has been burnt, the ashes and bones pounded into little shapes and, after being kept one year in the house, placed in one of the many chortens which fringe the Ladakh villages—owned generally in common by groups of families or by monasteries for their monks. The lamas hold services for the deceased on certain days after death. The number of such services, and the number of lamas who perform at them, is naturally proportioned to the rank and wealth of the deceased and the amount which the relatives are prepared to pay."[20]

Monasteries in Ladakh : Ladakhis called Buddhist monasteries as Gonpas. They are normally built in solitary places, isolated hills in side valleys, or if in the vicinity of a village then upon the highest point. It is always the biggest and best constructed buildings in the locality. In some monastery we can see nuns, they are normally engaged in menial tasks. However, monks have their separate cells. Each monastery has many temples, decorated by Thankas, statues, religious books and beautiful paintings. Ganpat says :

"In the interior of the monastery are always to be found at least two large rooms—the first, which if there are two storeys is more usually on the lower, forming the monastery library, where in rows of pigeon holes repose the sacred books. On the walls of this apartment are mural paintings. In the second room, the 'Lha khang' or gods' house, will be the various images of those deities specially worshipped in the monastery."[21]

Women do much work in the field : Like other Himalayan states, women in Ladakh do maximum agricultural work. One can often see them with conical baskets laden with vegetables, fruits in order to sale them, in fields they are laden with manure to fertile their land. Ganpat remarks :

"Moving about in the fields you see the figures of women in dull, ragged garments and gaudy peraghs of turquoise, with conical baskets upon their backs, laden with fruit, or may be manure; or perhaps with that most treasured and somewhat rare possession, a Ladakhi baby. (They) do much of the field work in Ladakh, for along the main routes anyway, the men are more often occupied in their immemorial trade of carrying."[22]

Old and well established custom : In olden days Central Asian traders passed through Ladakh. Along the trade routes at every haltage Ladakhis awaited them for carrying their luggage. Ganpat says :

"... for along the main routes anyway, the men are more often occupied in their immemorial trade of carrying Ladakh lies athwart the Central Asian trade route, and its people have been carries from the dawn of history. From April until late November you meet the men on the road with their little ponies, their dzos, and higher up with their yaks, laden with the bales of Central Asia. So old and well established is the custom that it is officially recognised and organised today, is that each village or group of villages has to provide its quota of men and animals to convey merchants and travellers at fixed rates, from stage to stage. As a matter of fact, they do not always adhere to the rates or stages, preferring often to take up contracts to transport merchandise over a long journey, at a slightly lower average rate, rather than hold to their right of going not more than one day's march at a somewhat higher rate of pay."

Mud houses in Ladakh : Today we can see cemented buildings with glassrooms. Earlier it was just opposite, Ladakhis had glassless mud houses, except kitchen other rooms were dark. Ganpat describes :

"He builds himself a house of mud and stone, with a flat roof of peeled poplar—trunks, crossed with a layer of window wands, supporting a flat roof of mud, and since it hardly ever rains it keeps over his head, year in, year out. It is a small house and probably windowless—or if there be a window, glassless, and it is generally closed by a wooden shutter to keep out the wind. The kitchen is, of course, the chief room, and sometimes it is well worth seeing."[24]

Leh stands a real town : Ladakh had only one big town—Leh, it was the centre for Central Asian traders. It possessed a bazar where buyers and sellers of the Central Asia came and purchased their goods according to the demand. Ganpat made the following picture of the Leh market during his visit to Ladakh :

"(Leh) has many features which mark it out from the villages of Ladakh. It possesses a bazaar, a genuine bazaar, with shops where you can buy almost anything you want—if that is, your needs are comparatively simple. It has moreover, a real place—a tall, many-storeyed buildings, standing upon the hill which forms a background to the town. It is the mart where the incoming trade from Central Asia meets the upcoming trade from India and the cross-current of the Tibetan trade. In August and September, Leh bazaar is packed with the merchants and droers of half a continent and serais are filled with skull-capped, long-coated and long-booted merchants of Kashgaria, and with the pilgrims on their way to or from the Indian coast, whence sail the streamers to the Haj parts—the gates of Mecca and Madina—sacred places to the Mussalman."[25]

Lion's Mouth River : The Indus river flows down side of Leh town. Ladakhis belief that this river emerge from Lion's mouth shape part of rock near mount Kailash-Mansarowar lake. Ganpat's views that :

"The great 'Lion's Mouth' river, as the old Ladakhis called the Indus, for according to the Tibetan belief, the four great rivers they know each emerge from the mouth of some fabled beast."[26]

Mud avalanches : Today in Ladakh particularly houses in urban area are made of concrete cement, but in past all houses were made by mud bricks. When Ganpat visited Ladakh, he felt as if Leh town came under mud avalanches, he remarks :

"The valley slopes upwards at the rate of some hundred feet to each mile of stony, sandy going—a great fan, which conway, I think, attributed to mud-avalanches in the past before Ladakh settled down to the state of physical equilibrium which marks it today, in striking contrast to Gilgit, where the mountains are still trying to find their balance."[27]

Khardong pass opened in June : Today Khardong pass open throughout the year, earlier was opened during June month every year. Ganpat says :

"I crossed the Khardong this year with the first caravan, and the date was the 13th June. It was no child's play to force the pass, with its heavy covering of winter snow hiding the glaciers that dip over the north side, and made the 17,400 feet (18,380 ft.) of the Khardong—just about 6000 ft. above the altitude of Leh—a difficult and tiring ascent, where the unladen ponies had to be man-handled over with ropes, and in the worst places pulled over the snow on tent-flies and suleetash spread out, to make a way, like the grass."[28]

Bungalow of British Joint Commissioner : During nineteen century, trade through Ladakh to Central Asian countries was supervised by British Joint Commissioner, who had a dak bungalow and big garden near Leh bazaar. Ganpat remarks :

"(At the winding street of Leh bazaar), come out into European quarter: Here are the little bungalows of Moravian mission,

> and at the farther end, the dak bungalow and the big garden and house of the British Joint Commissioner, who, with his confrere, the Wazir or Governor of Ladakh, an official of Kashmir state, manages the treaty road to Central Asia."

Polo game : Traders in every evening during summer played polo-game in the street of main Leh bazaar. Ganpat says :

> "Shadowed evening you may come back and watch the polo—the national game of Baltistan and, to a lesser degree, of Ladakh—played in a dusty side street, with no apparent rules or time, where the exponents of the game dash backwards and forwards, in a cloud of dust, on their little ponies. True maids of all work, those ponies—carrying loads, carrying master, or playing polo to the strains of the local band—two drums and a charinet—all contributing of their loudest and, therefore, of their best."[29]

Morning bazaar at Leh : As I said Leh was the popular market of Central Asian traders, in the morning they exchanged their goods and in evening played polo game. Ganpat remarks :

> "In the morning you may stroll about the bazaar and watch the types that collect there—Kashmiris, Ladakhis, men of Yarkand and Kashgar, of Turfan and Khotan, Tibetans of Lhassa, Chang-Tang nomads, Indian moneylenders of the Shikarpur district—true sons of the horse-leech-and last, but by no means least, the regular soldiers of the Kashmir army, Gurkhas of the Bodyguard Regiment, which generally has a company stationed in Leh."[30]

Population of Ladakh : In Ladakh we can see the traces of three ancient races—the Dards, Mons and Mongol. These races are partically or fully Buddhists, the other race of 14th century A.D. is Balti. Today Baltis population is almost half of the total population of Ladakh. Ganpat mentioned about the former Buddhist races :

> "The population of Ladakh is made up of the three races : the original Aryan Dards—the Brokpa, as the Ladakhis call them; the Mons, the early Buddhist people from Kashmir; and the Mongol stock from Tibet, who now form the majority of the inhabitants. The Mons we know almost as little; they have been far more submerged than have the Dards, who in places still exist in complete colonies, whereas the Mons are now to be seen only as survivals in the lowest occupations, such as itinerant musicians, leather workers and the like."[31]

Tibetan Calendar : In Ladakh all the big monasteries organise their annual festivals according to Tibetan calendar which has a series of cycles of sixty years. Ganpat says in details :

> "The Tibetan calendar consists of a series of cycles of sixty years, each year being designated by a combination of one of the five elements: fire, water, earth, iron and wood; and of one of twelve animals. Thus, the first year of the cycle is the 'wood mouse' year the thirteenth is the 'Fire Mouse' year, the fifth is the 'Earth Dragon', the forty-fourth is the 'Fire sheep' year, and so on. The months into which the year is divided are known also by the names of the animals. At the expiration of each cycle of sixty years a new one is begun, using the same system."[32]

Hemis Festival : In Ladakh Hemis festival is not only popular among Ladakhis, but equally well known among travellers since early days, as this was the only festival which celebrate during summers. Ganpat describes about this festival in the following way :

> "The big Hemis festival is thronged with people from the Indus valley, from Leh, and from the outlying districts, and Leh business seems to come to a very definite standstill. The Hemis gompa, a tall building under a cliff, surrounded by a cluster of smaller dwellings; a five-storeyed block, whose roof is surmounted by the folded umbrella-like erections and the streamers of yaks tail which are the signs of a monastery. Here the crowd will be getting dense as you begin to pass through the little camps, where the sightseers have settled down—camps in name only, since but few of them have any form of tent. A camp means merely the spot where they have dumped their possessions and set up a fireplace, where one of the women is busy making tea in a great copper pot. Farther on you pass the willow plantation where the distillers and sellers of chang have congregated, within easy walk from the gompa, so that audience can quench their thirst during the intervals between the dances."[33]

In brief I may say Ganpat though didn't visit repotest parts of Ladakh, attracted very much by Ladakhi custom and trade. Initially he made no hesitation to say Ladakh a land of topsy-turvy customs, later by the Buddhist tradition here, he bound to say Ladakh a land of magic where it has a great natural beauty prevail with ancient Buddhist culture.

Notes and References

1. Gompertz, M.L.A. : 'Magic Ladakh : An intimate picture of a land of topsy-turvy customs and great natural beauty', Seeley Service Ltd., London, 1928 : 31.
2. *Ibid.*, 31-32.
3. *Ibid.*, 32-33.
4. *Ibid.*
5. *Ibid.*, 39.
6. *Ibid.*, 41.
7. *Ibid.*, 43.
8. *Ibid.*, 43-44.
9. *Ibid.*, 48.
10. *Ibid.*, 52.
11. *Ibid.*, 58-59.
12. *Ibid.*, 61-62.
13. *Ibid.*, 62.
14. *Ibid.*, 64-65.
15. *Ibid.*, 67-68.
16. *Ibid.*, 99.
17. *Ibid.*, 109.
18. *Ibid.*, 111-112.
19. *Ibid.*, 112.
20. *Ibid.*, 117.
21. *Ibid.*, 124.
22. *Ibid.*, 143.
23. *Ibid.*, 144.
24. *Ibid.*, 149-50.
25. *Ibid.*, 160.
26. *Ibid.*
27. *Ibid.*
28. *Ibid.*, 162.
29. *Ibid.*, 168.
30. *Ibid.*, 169.
31. *Ibid.*, 176-77.
32. *Ibid.*, 194.
33. *Ibid.*, 198.

21

Phyang Monastery : A Drigung Order of Ladakh

In olden days Central Asian traders often passed through Phyang village. It was then the capital of Ladakh[1]. Though Bagan was King Tashi Namgyal[2] strengthened Namgyal dynasty in Ladakh, the founder of Namgyal dynasty. Later he erected a long flagstaff at the right bank of the Phyang brook[3].

During 16th century A.D. King Jamyang Namgyal[4] was suffered by leprosy, he had consulted Ladakhi Amchis[5] and oracales[6], but was unable to cure. At last he invited Lama Danma Kunga Trakpa, who was then at Mount Kailash. He sent his messengers there. To know the details about king's health Lama Danma decided to visit Ladakh. Subsequently, met king and by spiritual power treated his disease. Thereafter king was feeling improvement in his health day by day. Thus, very much impressed by Lama Danma, and insisted him to become his foremost teacher. Lama didn't accept, however, said that he would be happy if he could establish one monastery of his sect in Ladakh. King felt happy with this proposal, requested him to take land anywhere in Ladakh and to build monastery as soon as possible.[7]

After sometimes Lama Danma Kunga Trakpa went out towards north-west side of Leh in search of a suitable land, riding on yak he travelled 16 km and reached at a big field[8]. He stopped there for a while, had an aerial view, again walked towards the centre of the field. He pitched his tent, went for prayer and meditation. Then marched towards a peaceful place near a hillock, here he again went for meditation. After sometimes he saw 'Achi-chos-Don' at the top of hillock, weaving a flag, riding on a blue horse. It was a very auspicious movement. Later without any doubt he decided to establish monastery on the hillock.[8]

Next day Lama Danma informed King Jamyang Namgyal about his decision. King became very happy with this, he ordered his ministers to provide all possible facilities to Lama Danma for the construction of monastery. Later he bequeathed three regions—Shyang, Sgomang and Yuru to him and put Phyang, Taru, Snemo, Basgo, Leh, Shyang, Sara, Khema, Digar and Yungru villages under his control for ritual practice.[9]

In conclusion King Tashi Namgyal made an effort to select Phyang for religious side. Probably in his later days one Lhakhang was established near hillock. During 16th century A.D. with the kind support of King Jamyang Namgyal. Phyang monastery was established by Lama Danma on the hillock at Phyang village.

Notes and References

1. According to Ladakh Chronicles, The Phyang Taktse (Tib. Phyi dbang stag rtse) palace was built during the time of the early successors of Nyathi Tsenpa of the Yarlung dynasty. Thus, it apparents that Phyang was then the capital of Ladakh.
2. Tashi Namgyal = Tib. bka - shis - rnam - rgyal.
3. Jina, Prem Singh & Konchok Namgyal ; 'Phyang monastery of Ladakh', Indus Pub. Co., New Delhi, 1995 : 28.
4. Jamyang Namgyal : Tib. Jam - dbyangs - rnam - rgyal.
5. Amchis : Tibetan Doctors.
6. Oracales : Lhas or Lhamos.
7. Jina, Prem Singh ; *op. cit.* : 30.
8. *Ibid.*
9. *Ibid.*

22

Historical Background of Lamayuru Monastery of Ladakh

Lamayuru monastery is 124 km far away from the Leh town, towards Leh-Srinagar highway, and situated on steepy rock at 11,520 feet from the sea level. In olden days the Lamayuru was under a big lake, latter by the spiritual power of Madhyantika[1] emptied it. During 10th century Naropa[2] via Zangskar visited Lamayuru, later went for meditation in a cave. To know that Naropa came Lamayuru for meditation, Lotsava Rin-chen-bzang-po[3] also decided to visit there, but didn't find him. So, he made five lhakhangs in the form of mandala, i.e., one in the middle, others at the north, south, east and west of it. Through the ages the centre lhakhang converted into the present monastery others are down side of it. Among them Singhe-Lha-Khang is the only temple which has Rin-chen-bzang-po's period wall paintings. The rest of Lha-Khangs have lost their paintings. However, one can see old paintings in the nearby chortens.

Zamar Influence : When Rin-chen-bzang-po initiated to propagates of Buddhism in Ladakh and its adjoining areas, Ladakh established cultural and religious contact with Tibet. Consequently, religious changes in Tibet effected the monastic system of Ladakh. During the 12th century A.D. Zamar tradition[4] became powerful, thus Tibetan Government came under its influence. So much so Lamayuru, which was then one of the main monastery in Ladakh also adopted this tradition.

Sponsorship by Tibetan Government : The Lamayuru was emerging as a powerful monastery in Shyam side[5] of Ladakh during 13th-16th century A.D. It had then complete autonomy in Ladakh established its direct relations with the neighbouring countries. Subsequently got its close contact with Tibet Government. The Abbot[6] of Lamayuru then annually sent gifts to the head of Tibetan Government, in its response received 60 khal[7] food stuffs every year.

The role of Baba Mohammad Khan : During 16th century Baba Mohammad Khan, the famous leader of commercial embassy, known 'Lopchak', was responsible for transporting goods from Tibet to Ladakh and to issue permit in this regards. In Tibet he was fully responsible to supply all goods and services to Lamayuru monastery.

Holy Site : It is said that during 16th century Lamayuru monastery was declared a holy site for all sects and kind of human beings; even criminals could seek shelter, as a result the monastery was popularly known 'Tharpa Ling'.

Support from Neighbouring Countries : The monastery had good relationship with its neighbouring countries. As a result the kings and emperors of these countries always ready to help and preserve the traditional culture of the monastery. Moorcroft in this regards rightly point out that :

> "The monastery of Lamayuru is invested with the privileges of a sanctuary, which they assert have been confirmed to it by edicts from the Emperors of Delhi and their governors of Kashmir. Documents which they showed me, with the real of Aurungzeb, Fidai Khan and Shir Khan, were however, only to the purpose of directing that Gelums should be disturbed in their religious usages, and that their lands should not be encroached upon. A similar injunction has lately been obtained by them from Ahmed Shah, the Shiah Raja of Balti, drawn up in more explicit language, and a still more liberal spirit. At the request of the acting superior I left with him a paper expressing my acknowledgements to his hospitality."

Drigung Ka-gyud order in Ladakh : During 15-16th century A.D. Drigung Ka-gyud order became popular in Tibet. Later Denma Kung Trakpa founded Phyang monastery near Leh and put Lamayuru monastery under its direct control. Subsequently with the help of these monasteries Drigung pa order spread in Chang-Thang and Shyam areas of Ladakh. After sometimes lamas of Drigung order started to go to Tibet for higher studies in Buddhist Philosophy, who after completing their studies in Tibet returned to their respective monasteries in Ladakh with gifts. They then offer these to the obbots. Chorje Catang pa statue in Lamayuru monastery is among such popular gifts which was brought here from Tibet. It is explained that this statue can speak and fulfil the desires of devotees.

General Zorawar Singh Invasion : In July 1834, General Zorawar

Singh with his 5000 soldiers started an adventurous career of conquests from Kishtwar towards Purig. While marching inside Ladakh he faced little resistance by Ladakhi soldiers, particularly on 16th August he fought bravely against Ladakhi soldiers. At Sanku severe fight took place. Ladakh army finally dislodged from their positions and suffered a great defeat. In this way Dogras occupied Suru-Kartse area. To stop the victory movement Ladakh King Tse-pal Namgyal again sent his troops to Kargil; pitched battle thus took place at Pashkyam. This time also Dogras won the battle. Thereafter, Dogras didn't get much resistance upto Leh. Hence, at last General Zorawar Singh occupied whole Ladakh. During this period Lamayuru monastery was helpless, nobody came forward to safe its property. Hence, was also destroyed by Dogras. But, later renovated by the devotees.

Comos in Lamayuru : It is said that before the invasion of General Zorawar Singh, Lamayuru monastery had comoling in which comos were resided in good number. William Moorcroft visited this monastery in 1820, remarks :

> "Lamayuru is the site of a very large establishment of Gelums and Chumas, accounting, according to some accounts, to five hundred. They do not all reside together, but are dispersed amongst the people, as in every house there is a chamber appropriated to the deity, and to a Gelum, whose business it is to place food and lights before the image repeating prayers and beating a drum."

Present Position : Today Lamayuru monastery has its own administration, and only the main monastery of Drigung order in Shyam area. It has many sub gonpas viz. Skrubuchan, Da, Hanu, etc. Its old chamra has been renovated and near to it a big temple is constructed. However, Comoling is still in ruined condition. A link road has also been constructed upto the temple passing through the ruined comoling. Like other big monasteries of Ladakh, Lamayuru also organise annual festival, in which lamas of the monastery perform cham.

Notes and References

1. Mathyantika : He was great Siddha who flew from Kashmir to Lamayuru by his spiritual power, and emptied the Lamayuru lake from Nagas.
2. Naropa : Mahasiddha Naropa visited Lamayuru monastery earlier to Rin-chen-bzang-po during 1st half of 10th century A.D.

3. Lotsava-Rin-Chen-bzang-po : It is said under his leadership a school of scholars and translators arose to render from Sanskrit into Tibetan not only Sutras and Tantras but also many extensive commentaries attached to these work.
4. Zamar Tradition : Tradition of composing 'doha' (gur), a type of verse or song spontaneously made up by tantric practitioners as the direct expression of their personal feelings and realisations.
5. Shyam side : The area below Nimo.
6. Abbot : Head lama of the monastery.
7. Khal : A unit of measuring weight of crop.

23

Lingshed (Tib. ling shed) Monastery of Ladakh

Oral history traces the roots of Lingshed Gonpa to the 10th century. Paintings in the monastery are similar to those monasteries built by Lochava Rinchen Zangpo in Ladakh. Now I'll discuss in details about this monastery in the following paragraphs.

The monastery is popularly known Tashi Od par[1] among Buddhists of Ladakh. Rinchen Zangpo visited Lingshed via Vamla and built one storeyed Avalokitesvara statue. Later he built two temples, one at Lingshed and other a few distance away at Yung Chung. Besides, he brought Buddhist texts called Bum written in golden ink.

In 1085 Zangskar Locava Phagspa Shesrab arrived in Lingshed. During his journey from Zangskar to Lingshed, he came across an interesting incident that—

> "On way to Lingshed, when he reached at Phakasta mountain's top, saw a bright light from the Rinchen Zangpo's temple. He followed the light, soon reached there and, was very much impressed by the structure of the temple, later decided to build temples in the same design."

In 13th century A.D. Siddha Nakpa Jogi[2] visited Lingshed. He liked this place for meditation. Thereafter went to west of Lingshed near Karche[3] for meditation in a cave. After sometime few lamas of this area also accompanied him. He built Bigang Ikhung Lhakhang in Lingshed. As a result lama population increased considerably. In the passage of time Lingshed monastery developed under the Drug pa K'a gyud tradition.

It is explained that—

> "According to an old tradition Lingshed monastery used to give its land to villagers on rent for cultivation. Normally these

villagers after cultivation had to give some percentage of crop production to the monastery. Once Lingshed gonpa society decided to give its land on rent to an old lady who had her land nearby to gonpa. Now lady also started to cultivate gonpa land. She was happy with the production. After couple of years she thought how nice it would be if she could occupy gonpa land. Accordingly she stopped to give percentage of crop production to gonpa. As a result gonpa society asked her to leave its land. She denied. At last gonpa society intimated if she would not leave gonpa land, society bound to go to court, then she had to leave the possession. But was not happy with this decision. So, one day by seeing the opportunity she diverted water stream towards the cave, finally cave was collapsed."

Today after excavation many old ritual items have been recovered from this cave. It was a great loss to gonpa as it had been decorated by beautiful wall paintings.

Later King of Ladakh Rinchen Namgyal[4] inspired Lingshed gonpa society to build a new establishment, accordingly it was constructed in Lingshed village east of the cave at 'Sung-dung'. The monastery was built according to monastic tradition and decorated by beautiful paintings. But misfortunes never come alone, it was destroyed by the Mongolian force. The ruins of this still can be seen.[5]

During 15th century cang cems shes rab[6] visited Lingshed. He repaired some portion and named it Tashi od par.

At present Lingshed monastery has the following temples

Chok-khang (Tib. Tshogs Khang)

Statues

(i) Chamba (Maitreya) : Clay of one storey in height.

(ii) Buddha : Clay of one storey in height.

Besides, Sugdan statue of brass metal is also placed in the temple. For statues Gonpa imported brass metal almirah from China. This dukhang has 20 beams.

The walls of the temples in the monastery are decorated by wall paintings of protectors.

Lhakhang Tashi Otpal (Tib. lha Khang bkris, ad 'bar)

In this Lhakhang one can see Avalokitesvara Mandala made by wood pieces. On walls 84 Siddha and Choskyong[7] are depicted.

On First and Second month of Tibetan calendar during *Purnamasi* devotees from Zangskar and Lingshed gather in Lhakhang and offer prayers.

Cham Khang (Tb. byams Khang)

It has one storeyed high clay statue of Chamba (Tib. byamspa). Besides, has wall paintings of various incarnation of Naris Chyang (Tib. mng'a ris tshang).[8]

Sojong Khang (Tib. gso sbyong Khang)

It is explained that this Dukhang was initially built by Locava Rin chen bzang po during 10-11th century. It has Avalokitesvara statue. Among wall paintings we can see various mandalas and images of 84 Siddhas. During Yarnas people and lamas offer prayer.

Gyal Khang (Tib. rgyal khang)

In this temple one can see five clay statues known gyal po (Tib. rgyal po). Besides, there are many brass statues.

Kangyur lhakhang (Tib. bk'a 'agyur lha khang)

Statues

(i) Dolma (Tib. rje btsung sgrol ma)
(ii) Padmasambhava

Paintings

(i) 16 Arhads (Tib. gnas brtan bcu drug)
(ii) Smanla De she gyat (Tib. sman bla bde gshegs brgyad)
(iii) Tung kyi lha - 35 (Tib. ltung bshags kyi lha-35)
(iv) Chela Namsum (Tib. The lha rnams gsum)
(v) Choskyong (Tib. chos skyong)
(vi) Gyaltsen zee (Tib. rgyal (chen bjhee)

Text : This temple has complete set of Kangyur Pothis.

Shar gyi zim chung (Tib shar kyi gzimes chung)

Statues

(i) jovo rinpoche (Tib. jo bo rin po che)
(ii) Paldan lhamo (Tib. dpal ldan lhamo)
(iii) Gonpo jhaljee (Tib. mgon po jhal bjhee)
(iv) gonkar (Tib. mgon dkar)
(v) shugdan (Tib. shugs ldan)
(vi) Shar chogs (Tib. shar phyogs)

(vii) guru (Tib. gu ru)
(viii) chosgyal (Tib. chos rgyal)
(ix) Brass dolma (Tib. sgrol ma)

Text : Sumbum of je yab sras sum (Tib. rje yab sras gsum). It has 36 pothis.

Zimphung (Tib. gzims phug)

In this room skyabje Nari Rinpoche (Tib. skyabs rje mng'a ri rinpo che) stays during his visit.

Gon dag (Tib. dgon bdag)

Here skyabje Nari Rinpoche (Tib. skyabs rje mng'a ri rinpoche) stays during his visit to monastery.

Rin Chen Zang po's (Tib. rin chen bzang po) cave

At the east of Lingshed village, about 4 km. one can see Rin chen bzang po's cave. In this cave Rin chen bzang po went for meditation. Thereafter, many lamas continued this tradition. It is said that in this cave there were many sacred papers written by mim miyan (Tib. mim rin or by god and goddess), but once a shepherd came there, who took them out and tored them. As a result heavy flood came and destroyed the cave.

Present position of the monastery : In 1988 Lama Nawang Tondup built a new temple nearby to the monastery.

At present Lingshed monastery has about fifty monks and following facilities have been provided to monks.

1. Teachings on tantric texts, sand mandala and other rituals.
2. The Gonpa has finished the work for making the initiation crown and clothes, known as Wang dzas. It has taken the Gonpa four years to complete this work.
3. The Gonpa provides basic modern education to young monks.
4. The Gonpa committee has decided to set up a school of Sutra philosophy for all monks of the monastery.
5. Geshe Ngawang Jangchup gives teachings on taught Buddhist texts to the monks of the monastery.
6. The Lingshed Como Gonpa was inaugurated in the summer of 1996, since then 21 nuns have joined the Gonpa. They practice daily life of nuns consists religious activities, learning and writing Bodhi language. In 1997, 10 small (5' x 6.6") and 10 big (8' x 10') residential rooms were built for nuns.

Notes and References

1. Tashi od par : Tib. bkra shis 'aod 'abas.
2. Siddha Nakpa Jogi : Siddha nag paa dzho gi.
3. Karche : Tib. dka rtse.
4. Rinchen Namgyal : Tib. rin chen rnam rgyal (1470-1500 A.D.).
5. Jamyang Gyaltsen (ed.) : 'Lingshed Gon shis od par', in ta 'The History of Ladakh Monasteries', 1995 : 825.
6. Shes rab : Tib. 'aphags pa shes rab.
7. Choskyong : Tib. chos skyong.
8. Jamyang Gyaltsen (ed.) ; *op. cit.* : 827.

24

Yarkand Troops of Sultan Said Invasion on Ladakh in 1531 A.D.

In 1531 Sultan Said of Yarkand decided to invade Ladakh and Balti country. He divided his troops in two divisions, one of which—under the joint command of his son Iskandar, and his minister Mirza Muhammad Hydar, whilst the other under the command of Said himself.[1]

Sultan Said Died : On April 1531 A.D. Sultan Said command one thousand men and penetrate Balti country—situated between Badakhshan and Bolor. The Sultan unfortunately suffered so severely from difficulty of breathing in the passage of the highlands—later died and buried somewhere in lower valley.[2]

Yarkandi Troops Victorious Career : In the last month of Hizari 938, i.e. about May of 1531 with an army of 4000 men, after crossing Karakoram, came in Nubra valley. Mirza Hyder with his master ordered 4000 men to attack Nubra. Consequently, Yarkandi troops under plan adopted guerilla activities and spent five months in Nubra. They started plundering, slaughtering, captivating and converting them to Muslim till the whole country devasted. In this way Mirza Hyder was able to convert a major portion of Nubra into Islạm. Today Thang, Takyasi, Parchathang, Turtuk, Chulugkha, Bogdang, Hunder etc. are the Muslim Shia sect; and probably would be converted from Buddhists into the above sect.[3]

Prince Iskandar and Mirza Hyder defended by Dards at Dras : After having been full controlled over Nubra valley, Mirza Hyder with the permission of Iskandar decided to march Kashmir via Leh. Therefore, left a few men of the army at Nubra and marched ahead. They arrived Zojila in December. The pass was closed due to heavy snowfall. The inhabitants at Dras when came to know the facts that Yarkandi troops did not get chance to cross the Zojila pass easily, they decided to defend Yarkandi troops. H.W. Bellew remarks :

> "Mirza Hydar, with the youthful Iskandar and the other four thousand of the force, minus a small detachment left in Nubra, set out to make their way into Kashmir. They arrived at the Zojibal pass about November or December and found it deep in snow, and defended by four hundred of the enemy—apparently people of Dras. These, however, were soon put to fight by the overwhelming number of their assailants, and the Yarkandis, hurrying on, reached Srinaggar (Srinagar) on the second evening, camping only one night midway; thus fighting a battle, and marching at least seventy miles within the space of forty-eight hours."[4]

Marriage Ceremony : When Yarkandi troops entered into Kashmir, they were welcomed by Kashmiris. King of Kashmir not only gave them good accommodation, but also offered his daughter for marriage to Yarkand prince. Bellew says :

> "At Srinaggar (Srinagar) they were hospitably received by the king, one Muhammad Shah, who enlivened the monotony of the winter months by celebrating a marriage between his daughter and the Yarkand prince."[5]

Return to Capital : Yarkand prince after enjoying winters in Kashmir decided to return Yarkand, but due to high altitude effect prince bound to stay in Ladakh. Bellew described the above incident in the following way :

> "In the ensuring spring the crescentaders issued from their respective retreats. The rigours of the winter in Balti, it would seem, somewhat chilled the fervour of Sultan Said's religious zeal, for he set out forth with to return to his capital. On reaching the elevated plateaux he was again seized with his former ailment, and though hurried on by double stages towards the place where the difficulty of breathing or *dam* is known to cease, he expired midway, only a few mile from the Caracoram (Karakoram) pass, just twelve months after he had set out on this ill-fated expedition."[6]

Said ordered Mirza to carry victorious banner of Islam into Lhasa: Staying a few days in Ladakh, Prince Said before departure to Yarkand from Nubra ordered his Minister Mirza to continue victorious banner of Islam into the neighbouring countries of Ladakh. According Mirza set out from Ladakh to Lhasa. The route to Lhasa pass through high passes, as a result many Yarkand men of Mirza army died because of cold and high altitude effects. Bellew remarks :

> "On his departure from Nubra Said had ordered Mirza Hydar to prosecute the *ghaza*, and carry the victorious banner of Islam into very metropolis of the infidels—to Aorsang or Ouchang, or Hlassa (Lhasa) itself. Consequently the Kashmir division set out from Maryol (Maryul) on the enterprise delay, as the goal of their ambition was distant a journey of two months. The force endured incredible sufferings and losses from cold, privation, and effects of altitude, and after wandering about for two months were compelled to retreat on Maryol before they had accomplished half the distance to their destination."[7]

Seized Kalasiay for and invaded Rang Shigar : As I said Prince Said when got high altitude effect, he decided to return to Ladakh. Here he got the information about the death of Sultan Said, and, revolution thereafter in his favour. So, he again thought to go to Kashgar, but because of winter it was not possible. On the other side his army division returned to Ladakh after covering a half and unsuccessful expedition of Lhasa. By the time due to sever cold deaths took place and his force reduced to five hundred men. Now, Prince Said had to arrange food and accommodation not only for himself, but for five hundred men. Consequently, he ordered Mirza Hydar to invade Rang Shigar, seize Kalasiya fort. Bellew says :

> "They now learned of the death of Said, of the revolution in Kashgar, and the accession to the throne of his eldest son, Sultan Rahid, by the murder of Mirza Hydar's uncle, Sayyid Muhammad Khan—who had seized on the government in favour of Iskandar—and of the recall of Iskandar with the army, and of the proscription of Mirza Hydar. The winter was now setting in, and the joint commanders decided on sharing what fortune provided together. By deaths and desertions their force had been reduced to five hundred men. With these they seized the fort of Kalasiya or Cala Shiya, and in it held out till spring, subsisting on the ten thousand sheep they had captured on their way down. With the opening of the roads they invaded Rang Shigar, and after ravaging the country for two months finally returned to Maryol."[8]

Returned to Yarkand : Both the Commanders of Yarkand army remain in Ladakh about two years, later Iskand returned to Yarkand with his four men and Mirza returned in 1531 via Rashgam, Pamir, Badakshan with his 23 men. Bellew made the following remarks in this connection :

"On the approach of the third winter Mirza Hydar and Iskandar, with their following reduced to fifty men, set out together to seek a safer retreat. By the time they reached the Caracoram (Karakoram) their men reduced to twenty seven. Of these, four returned with Iskandar to Yarkand, and the rest followed Mirza Hydar on his venturesome journey by an unknown track through Rashgam and Pamir to Badakhsham."[9]

Thus, Yarkand invasion on Ladakh ended in 1533. In this mission Yarkand army forcefully converted Buddhists into Islam and got success in the propagation of Islam in Ladakh for the first time.

References

1. Bellew, H.W. : 'Kashmir and Kashgar : A narrative of the journey of the Embassy to Kashgar in 1873-74', London : Trubner & Co. Ludgate Hill ; 1875 & Reprinted in India by Asian Educational Services, New Delhi; 1989 : 95.
2. *Ibid.*, 96.
3. *Ibid.*
4. *Ibid.*, 97.
5. *Ibid.*
6. *Ibid.*
7. *Ibid.*, 97-98.
8. *Ibid.*, 98.
9. *Ibid.*

25

First Indo-Pak War on the Land of Ladakh

As soon as India got independence Jammu and Kashmir state also came under the control of Indian Government. But Pakistan Government could not able to digest this happenings and invaded Kashmir valley from the north and north east direction. Indian army immediately rushed and defend the valley. However, had to solve the following important tasks :[1]

(a) Reopening the road from Srinagar to Leh and removing the menace to the Buddhist district of Ladakh.

(b) The relief of the Punch garrison.

The Zoji pass was the big hurdle to cross on road during winter as it experiences heavy snowfall. It lies 64 miles north east of Srinagar and dominated by high peaks on either side is about two miles long, debounching into the Gumri basin.

Raiders held three ridges around the Zoji La : It was winter season, Indian troops though had full controlled the western side, but was worried to cross Zoji La. The raiders could attack them as they were in the better position. On the other side the first and foremost task before the Indian Army was to clear enemy positions from the high ridges surrounding to the Zoji La and to advance towards Kargil so that communication with Leh could be restored. The Information Department of the Government of India thus got the following information :

> "Indian troops effectively controlled the western approaches to the Zoji La, but the raider held three ridges around the pass. These three ridges, named by the Indian troops 'chabutra', 'Machin-gui', and 'Mukund', had to be cleared of the enemy before the Indian Army could advance towards Kargil, an

important junction of the raiders line of communication from the north Ladakh."[2]

Gorkha and Maharatha battalion marched towards Zoji La : In Indian Army Gorkhas and Maharathas did many bravery deeds and in every event got success to defend the country. Therefore, both the above said battalions moved towards Zoji La pass in September without any hesitation. Let us see what Information Department recorded :

"The first attempt to break through the Zoji pass was made early in September while Patialas were ordered to hold to their positions flanking the Zoji-la, one battalion of Gurkhas was to carry out a diversion along a left hook to Dras via Botkulamgany, and a company of another Gurkha battalion, setting out from Pahalgam, was to demonstrate towards Suru. Maharathas and Jats were to carry out a frontal assault."[3]

Finally tank marched over Zoji La : It was November, though sky was cleared by interminantly snow fall was being noticed over the high ridges. Indian Army moral was very high, therefore, according to the orders all the deputed Army personals were ready to fight against enemy boardly. Here follows the reports of Information department :

"Day October, fortunately the weather cleared up in time, and under the nature cover of cloud, the tanks moved out at 10 A.M. on November 1. It was snowing as the tanks moved the Zoji-La track. From the jeephead, the road constructed by our sappers meandered forward for two miles, whether any track existed beyond that point nobody knew. The tanks moved forward, crossed Zoji La and gingerly stepped on the 'no man's land' in the Gumri basin. Solely relying for guidance on air reconnaissance reports, the tanks forged ahead through snow-drifts, glaciers, mountain streams and over boulders to reach the foot of Chabutra Hill."[4]

Bachhan Singh, the driver of Tank besides enemy fire reached Gumri : When Bachhan Singh was driving tank over Zoji La, enemy opened fire, Bachhan did not stop, he opened the mouth of tank gun; as a result, 25 enemy bunkers were being destroyed and finally he reached Gumri. The Information Department of Government of India has the following information in this regards :

"The enemy opened up barrage of fire, which ricochethed harmlessly off the tank armour. Then the tank guns barked and systematically destroyed about 25 enemy bunkers and seized full control of Gumri by mid-day. Behind the tanks, the infantry

> moved in without much opposition. The credit for taking the first tank through the snow-covered pass goes to Acting Lance Duffardar Bachhan Singh of Rampur, Mandar village, Mansal Tehsil, Patiala State. Driving his tank through snow-covered and boggy tracks over rock like glaciers and through streams of melted snow, Bachhan Singh advanced through a hailstrom of enemy fire from the ridges around, while the guns of the remaining tanks gave protection to the infantry marching into Gumri."[5]

Enemy never thought that tank could be taken through Zoji La : On November Bachhan Singh according to the orders marched over the Zoji La with his tank, it was snowing heavily and Bachhan Singh without any hesitation marched ahead. When enemy saw that Bachhan Singh moving towards their bunkers they opened fire. Bachhan Singh knew this fact, therefore, he fought bravely and at last reached Gumri. Bachhan Singh says :

> "When we received our marching orders at 10 A.M. on November 1, and started off to break through the enemy defences at Zoji La, it was snowing heavily and the enemy could not spot us. He did not even imagine that tanks could be taken through the pass. A track had been made by our sappers working through the night 500 yards beyond the pass, but we had no idea what lay ahead. We did not know whether the glaciers over which we had to take our tanks would be able to stand their weight or would bury us all under many feet of snow. We took a chance, and driving over the glacier; we soon descended into Gumri basin. The enemy then spotted us and immediately opened up a barrage of machine-gun, anti-tank rifle and Bren-gun fire. He also opened fire with a 3.7 howitzer, but without effect. A few small arms bullets which hit my tank glanced off and my tank remained undamaged. The gunner of the tank thereupon opened fire on the enemy bunkers and crossed over and occupied the lower slopes of Gumri, cutting off the enemy from behind. We reached Gumri at the end of two hours."[6]

Enemy encircled by Indian troops at Machhoi : Indian troops on 1st November marched further ahead of Zoji-La pass and reached Gumri by 9 at night. However, Colonel Sukhdeo Singh did not agree to stop here, and under his command Indian troops climbed throughout the night and finally encircled the enemy from all sides. The enemy had only one option that to surrender before the Indian Army. Here follows the actual story :

> "The enemy was surprised and demoralised by the sight of the tanks in Gumri, which he had never expected. About 9 P.M. on November 1, Patialas under the command of Lieutenant Colonel Sukhdeo Singh, set out from the Gumri basin walking surreptitiously throughout the night, a company of Patialas reached Machhoi and covered the enemy from behind. On finding themselves encircled on all sides, the hostiles were completely demoralised. Those who tried to flee were good targets from our riflemen, other surrendered and saved their lives. On the 'North Ridge' our troops found a dismantled 3.7 howitzer. The enemy was obviously trying to carry it in parts while running away to safety."[7]

Enemy concentration at Batkundi ridge : After capturing the Machhoi post Indian troops marched towards Matayan under the command of Lieutenant Colonel Girdhari Singh and finally controlled all the ridges over the Dras and cleared the Srinagar-Leh route. Here follows the details :

> "The Patialas rested at Machhoi on 2nd November as they were on dry rations for more than 40 hours and the Rajputs under the command of Lieutenant Colonel Girdhari Singh pushed towards Matayan, six miles to the north-east of Machhoi Matayan eventually fell into our hands on November 4 at 3 P.M. Our patrols here discovered strong enemy concentration at Batkundi ridge, which rises from Pindras to the west, where the enemy had dug-outs, stone caves and bunkers constructed on the Japanese pattern. Another ridge behind named 'Anant Ridge' after Lt. Colonel Anant Singh Pathania, commander of a Gurkha battalion, who captured the ridge later, was also infested with enemy gun positions. This ridge along with the 'Brown feature' controlled the entrance to Dras. Our troops could not take the risk against such strong enemy positions. They had to wait for eight days for the tanks to arrive from Gumri. There was no road and it was not possible to build one during winter. The commander took a chance and drove the tanks through Gumri nullah in knee deep water and over huge boulders and ultimately reached Matayan without a break down. At 10 A.M. on Nov. 14, our troops supported by armour attacked and secured the lower slopes of Anant ridge. At 7 P.M. the same day a two pronged attack was mounted, one on the Anant ridge and the other on the track at the foot of the

> Brown feature, which leads to Dras through Gumri nallah and Dras river yet another diversionary drive was simultaneously made on the Batkundi ridge to enable the two main prongs to by pass the ridge and reach their objectives."[8]

In conclusion Indian troops not only captured all the enemy pots surrounding to Zoji-la pass, but they moved further upto Alchi near Leh and supported commander Hari Chand and evacuated Shyam Elakas from Pak troops and thus freed Ladakh from the enemy.

References

1. Defending Kashmir, The Pub. Div. Ministry of Information and Broadcasting, government of India ; 1949 : 73.
2. *Ibid.*
3. *Ibid.*, 75.
4. *Ibid.*, 75-76.
5. *Ibid.*
6. *Ibid.*, 78.
7. *Ibid.*
8. *Ibid.*, 79.

Brown feature, which leads to Dras through Otmi nallah and Dras river yet another diversionary drive was simultaneously made on the Batkundi ridge to enable the two main prongs to by-pass the ridge and reach their objectives.[8]

In conclusion Indian troops not only captured all the enemy posts surrounding on Zoji-la pass, but they moved further into Alchi near Leh and supported commander Hari Chand and evacuated Skardu blokas from Pak troops and thus freed Ladakh from the enemy.

References

1. Defending Kashmir, The Pub. Div., Ministry of Information and Broadcasting, government of India, 1949 : 75.
2. Ibid.
3. Ibid : 75.
4. Ibid : 75-76.
5. Ibid.
6. Ibid : 78.
7. Ibid.
8. Ibid : 79.

26

Ladakh and Its Boundary Demarcation Dispute

In 1846 Lahul and Spiti was taken away from Ladakh region and came under the British control. Ladakh remained with Maharaja Gulab Singh Kingdom. H.E. Richardson gave the following information in this regards :

> "A group of Hill states from Tehri to the borders of Ladakh was taken under British protection. In 1846 when Kashmir was made over to Maharaja Gulab Singh, Spiti and Lahul were detached from Ladakh and incorporated in the administered district of Kangra. Ladakh itself, as a dependency of Kashmir, came indirectly under British influence."[1]

In this way the relationship of Tibet with border districts of Himalayan frontier got effected. These districts then did not have permanent envoys from Tibet, however, had trade and grazing connections. Tibet still had its special position and influenced over ties of religious homage, trade, racial affinity, and a degree of common interest.[2]

Boundary Demarcation : In 1846 at Peking a proposal was passed, under which it was decided that Joint Anglo-Chinese Commission would demarcate Ladakh and Tibet boundary. His Holiness XIIIth Dalai Lama was not happy with this proposal. Richardson covered the following information in this connection :

> "Nevertheless, press from India could not always be resisted and in 1846 a specific but fruitless overture was made at Peking, linked with the proposal that the boundary of Ladakh should be demarcated by a joint Anglo-Chinese Commission. Informal roundings were made on several subsequent occasions but the

cause was not one very close to the heart of the British Legation and it was, in each case, deemed to be either useless or inexpedient to put the matter to an official test. At last, in 1876, the negotiation of the Chefoo convention offered a suitable opportunity for including a separate article, which the Chinese were in no position to resist, agreeing to provide facilities for a British mission of exploration across Tibet from India to China or in the reverse direction. What had happened was that the Tibetans had flatly refused to accept the proposed mission and the Chinese were quite unable to compel them. This cannot have caused much surprise to the British Legation in China but the belief that the Chinese exercised actual authority in Tibet died hard elsewhere and standard English works on history reflect the view that it was only about 1898 that 'the control of the Ambans was visibly weakening'. In fact, although the last rags of influence and prestige were stripped from the imperial representatives at Lhasa in 1895 by the assumption of power by the XIIIth Dalai Lama and by the disaster to Chinese morale in the Sino-Japanese war of 1894-95, there had been no real Chinese control in Tibet in the previous thirty years. Even when that came to be appreciated in India it took some time more to appreciate the depth of distrust which made the Tibetans prefer the light yoke of their ineffectual overlord to the dangers inherent in official relations with their pushing British neighbours."[3]

Boundary position between Ladakh and Tibet : In 1899 the Indian Government made a detailed description about the boundary position between Kashmir and China. So far the boundary demarcation between Ladakh and Tibet is concerned towards Southward of Tibet. In seventeenth century it was shown, Lanak La, the frontier point between Ladakh and Tibet. This border point was confirmed in the Tibet-Ladakh Treaty of 1842. Richardson made the following description :

"In 1899 the Indian Government conveyed formally to the Chinese Government a description of the frontier between Kashmir and Sinkiang as running along the Kuen Len Mountains to a point east of longitude 80°, as had been shown on Indian Survey maps for many years. It is not proposed to examine the Indian frontier, westward of the point, with the Chinese province of Sinkiang but only the Indo-Tibetan frontier of which that point marks the north-west corner. From there the boundary between Ladakh and Tibet runs roughly southward in a traditional line dating back to the seventeenth century and confirmed in the Tibet-Ladakh Treaty of 1842. In its northern sector it passes through high, uninhabited country so far as the Lanak-La which is a well-established frontier point between Ladakh and Tibet confirmed by travellers from William Moorcroft in 1820 onwards. It is unlikely that anyone on either side ever had a closely detailed knowledge of the frontier in that little—visited desert north of the Lanak-La, known as the Aksai Chin, or that the Kashmir authorities ever had cause to exercise active jurisdiction there. The line in general had never been subject to dispute with the Tibetan Government and the frontier nor claimed by the Indian Government's Survey officers from 1865. Southward of the Lank-La the frontier was surveyed in 1846 and the traditional line embodied in Indian Survey maps."[4]

Ladakh : An integral part of India : In 1947 when India got independence all the princely states came under the main body of free India. Ladakh, automatically came under the control of India. Richardon says :

"On the transfer of power in 1947 some adjustment was needed in the juridical basis of the relations of the new India with the border regions. The paramountcy of the British crown over the Princely States was replaced by a policy of absorbing them into the main body of India by accession. The circumstances in Kashmir were exceptional but the upshot, so far as the Indo-Tibetan frontier was concerned, was the Ladakh, from being a protected state, was converted into an integral part of India although with a form of administration somewhat different from that of the regular Indian states."[5]

Kashmiri Merchants have monopoly over Pashmina Trade : Just after Ladakh-Mughul was during 1681-83, a trade treaty between Tibet and Ladakh was established in 1683 under which wool imported from Tibet through tribute mission and the whole as such exported from Ladakh to Kashmir valley. Since then Kashmiris have monopoly over wool trade till date. Richardson describes :

"This treaty terminated the war... included the cession to Tibet of the Province of Ngari, commercial stipulations mainly connected with the imported trade in wool, and the dispatch to Lhasa every second year of a sort of tribute mission. This liability was taken over by Kashmir when that state annexed Ladakh in 1842, and continued to be discharged down to 1950. The mission was known as the Lopchok."[6]

Peace Treaty between Tibet and Ladakh : This treaty indicates the officers of Tibet and Ladakh/Jammu & Kashmir were agreed to maintain peace, friendship, unity and keep open of the route for wool, shawls and tea. (Appendix-I)

Chinese Road across the Aksai Chin and Indian government Objection : The peace along the Indo-Tibet border along Ladakh was maintained till 1958. In 1950 Chinese forces invaded Tibet from Khotan by the Aksai Chin route as it was occasionally used by the explorers before the invasion. The Indian Government did not know about the road as built by China across the Aksai Chin in the north-eastern corner of Ladakh. However, during 1960 or so Indian Government came to know that China actually built the above said road, therefore, immediately made an objection to the Government of China for illegal building road along the corner of Ladakh. The Chinese replied and claimed that the road was built in its territory. Indian Government again made objection and said the areas shown in the Chinese maps are not right in all respect, so it requires changes after a proper survey. Thereafter Indian Government did not pay much attention and only show Aksai Chin area in Indian maps. Richardson has the following opinion in this regards :

> "Thereafter there was general calm along the whole frontier until in the autumn of 1958 it was discovered that part of a new Chinese road between Western Sinkiang and Tibet had been built across the Aksai Chin in the north-eastern corner of Ladakh. The Chinese force which invaded Tibet from Khotan in 1950 travelled by that route and it was probably used occasionally after that for supplies before being converted into a regular motor road. The remoteness of the area from effective Indian control is reflected in the fact that the existence of the road does not appear to have been known to the Indian Government until two years after it was actually built. The Indian Government protested to the Chinese at the violation of their territory; and the Chinese replied by bluntly claiming the territory as their own and adjecting to Indian interference there. This repudiation of Indian frontier in the west probably stimulated Nehru in December 1958 to open a correspondence with Chou En-lai about the new Chinese maps in which old territorial claims had been repeated. He remained Chou of his

assurance in 1956 about the Mc Mohan Line. Chou replied that the frontier between Indian and Tibet had never been delimited and that there was no treaty of any kind between the Chinese Central Government and the Government of India about their frontiers. He attacked the Mc Mohan Line as a product of British aggression but was willing for practical reasons to take 'a more or less realistic attitude towards it'. He did not claim that the Chinese maps were right in every respect but considered that changes could only be made after a proper survey. He added that Chinese opinion was surprised by the frontier claimed in Indian maps, particularly in the western section. Here may be seen the first hint that a bargain might, perhaps, be arranged of part of Ladakh against the Mc Mohan Line; but the Government of India paid no attention to that veiled suggestion and flatly restated its position, claiming the border as shown in its own maps."[7]

Chinese troops crossed Mc Mohan Line : The dispute between Indian Government and Chinese along the Mc Mohan Line did now solve. At last on 26 August 1959 Chinese troops crossed Mc Mohan Line and drove out the Indian Police pickets from the border. Richardson says :

"On 26 August 1959, some 200 or 300 Chinese troops crossed the Mc Mohan Line in the region of the upper valley of the Subansiri and drove out the picket of Indian border police manning a forward post at Longju. Nehru declared it to be a clear case of aggression and ordered the Indian army to take over responsibility for the defence of that part of the frontier. Within a few days Chinese incursion into Ladakh were reported."[8]

Heated Exchange through Letters between Indian and Chinese Prime Ministers : Indian Prime Minister softly replied Chinese P.M. that he did not examine his letter fully. However, Chinese P.M. flatly rejected Indian Government claim over the Ladakh border. Richardson pointed out that :

"Nevertheless, in a very short time he found it necessary to reaffirm both the validity of the Mc Mohan Line and Tibet's treaty—making competence at that time. He did this in a letter dated 26 Sept. 1959 to Chou-En-Lai, replying to one from Chou which had not been fully examined at the time of Nehru's statement of 10 Sept. In his letter, dated 8 Sept., Chou persisted in his rejection of Indian maps of the Ladakh area and his reassertion of Chinese claims there. He also, in a flood of unconvincing explanations, unmistakably went back on the assurance he had previously given about his acceptance in practice of the Mc Mohan Line."[9]

United Nations Debate : At the end of September 1959, there was an idea to solve the border dispute by negotiation came in air. But suddenly Chinese troops attacked India and serious clashes were taken place between Indian army and Chinese force in Ladakh. Chinese in fact wanted to stop any possibility of negotiation over the Ladakh border. Richardson reports :

> "By the end of September passions had begun to abate and the idea of arranging negotiations was in the air. But the storm broke again with even greater fury when on 21 Sept.—the last day of the United Nations debate on Tibet. The Chinese put out a version of the affair completely contradictory to the Indian account; and irreconcilable national attitudes were hardened still further by the exchange of strong words. The Chinese went so far as to utter barely veiled threats that unless the Indian Government accepted Chinese claims in Ladakh they themselves would not refrain from action south of the so called Mc Mohan Line."[10]

In conclusion though China occupied a large portion of Ladakh, yet India not accept Chinese claim over Ladakh. Today, the situation has been changed considerably. China now ready to solve border dispute peaceful and amicable manner with India. On 21st October 2004 Chinese high officials came to India to discuss border dispute. I hope, Government of India will able to convince them in a logical manner.

References

1. Richardson, H.E. : 'Tibet and its History', Oxford University Press, London ; 1962 : 73.
2. *Ibid.*, 73-74.
3. *Ibid.*, 75-76.
4. *Ibid.*, 224-25.
5. *Ibid.*, 225-26.
6. *Ibid.*, 245.
7. *Ibid.*, 228-30.
8. *Ibid.*, 230.
9. *Ibid.*, 231.
10. *Ibid.*, 232.

Appendix-I

Treaty between Tibet and Ladakh, 1842 (Translation)

As on this auspicious day, the 2nd of Assuj, Sambhat 1899 (16th or 17th September A.D. 1842), we the officers of the Lhasa Government Kalon of Sokan and Bakshi Shajpuh, Commander of the forces, and two officers on behalf of the most resplendent Sri Khalsaji Sahib, the asylum of the world, King Sher Singhji and Sri Maharaj Sahib Raja-i-Rajagan Raja Sahib Bahadur Raja Gulab Singhji, i.e., the Mukhtar-ud-Danla Diwan Hari Chand and the asylum of vizirs, vizir Ratnum, in a meeting called together for the promotion of peace and unity, and by professions and vows of friendship, unity and sincerity of heart and by Sahib, have arranged and agreed that relations of peace, friendship and unity between Sri Khalsaji and Sri Maharaj Sabib Bahadur Raja Gulab Singhji and the Emperor of China and the Lama Guru of Lhasa will hence forward remain firmly established for ever; and we declared in the presence of the Kunjak Sahib that on no account whatsoever will there be any deviation, difference or departure (from this agreement). We shall neither at present nor in future have anything to do or interfere at all with the boundaries of Ladakh and its surroundings as fixed from ancient times and will allow the annual export of wool, shawls and tea by way of Ladakh according to old established custom.

Should any of the opponents of Sri Khalsaji and Sri Raja Sahib Bahadur at any time enter our territories, we shall not pay any heed to his words or allow him to remain in our country.

We shall offer no hindrance to traders of Ladakh who visit our territories. We shall not, even to the extent of a hair's breadth, act in contravention of the terms that we have agreed to above regarding from friendship, unity and fixed boundaries of Ladakh and the keeping open of the route for wool, shawls and tea, we call Kunjak Sahib, Kairi, Lassi, Zhoh Mahan and Khushal Choh as witnesses to this treaty.

Quoted from Aitchison's Treaties Vol. XIV, p. 15.

27

A Clash of Civilisations for 14th Lok Sabha Election-2004 in Ladakh

Four-Ladakh Parliamentary Constituency had recorded 1,72,963 voters. (Appendix-I) The number of the electorate in Buddhist-dominated Leh district has risen from 79,553 in 2001 to 89,094, thus registering an increase of 11.30 per cent. These comprise 72 per cent of the total population of the district, which stands at 1.19 lakhs.[1]

Similarly, in the adjoining Muslim-dominated Kargil district, the number of the electorate increased from 73,972 in 2001 to 83,969 at present, registering an increase of 12.04 per cent. This comes to 71 per cent of the total population of Kargil district, which has been registered as 1.17 lakh. However, as per the national average, the number of the electorate comprises 60 per cent of the total population.[2]

Therefore, inflation in voters lists started after 1998 when National Conference candidate Syed Hussain was elected to Lok Sabha from Ladakh, thereafter, both communities have been trying to outsmart each other for long. In late 80s, when Ladakh Buddhists intensified their agitation for the grant of Union Territory status to Ladakh, they were not supported by the people of Kargil.[3]

Finally, Leh got an autonomous hill development council in 1995. Kargil got the similar council after the PDP-led coalition came to power over a year ago.[4]

This time Ladakh Parliamentary election took place on 10th May 2004. I, alongwith three polling officers were deputed for 83/Dumkhar Doo polling station. Here follows the details :

1. Polling Station : 83/Dumkhar Doo
2. Total Voters : 522

3. Presiding Officer : Dr. Prem Singh Jina (Uttranchal)
4. Polling Officer-I : Sonam Lhargyal (Leh)
5. Polling Officer-II : Anwar Hussain (Kargil)
6. Polling Officer-III : Abdul Wahid (Leh)
7. Police Person : Riyas Ahamad (Kashmir)

On 8th morning about 9 o'clock our bus started for election duty. There were six polling parties in my bus : Urbis, Leh Do, Dumkhar Doo, Dumkhar Barma, Dumkhar Gongma and Tagmachik. I had collected polling materials on 7th; my two polling officers Sonam Lhargyal and Anwar Hussain purchased food stuffs and vegetables from Leh market. In this way we were fully prepared for the election.

About 10 A.M. we arrived at Nimo. It is situated at the bottom of Magnetic Hill and at the bank of Indus river, which receives a tributary from Zangskar valley. Here we took halt for sometime, and had light refreshment.

Our next halt was Kha-la-tse, we reached here afternoon at 2.30. Our polling officers have had their lunch, but I didn't as I had already taken heavy breakfast. About 3 P.M. our bus marched ahead. After travelling half an hour Tagmachik polling station party dropped at the road site. My polling station was next to come. Abdul Wahid my polling officer was sitting on the front seat next to driver. It was now his duty to stop bus at my polling station, but he forgot to tell driver to stop bus at Dumkhar polling station. Then we moved ahead towards the next polling station. I asked :

"Wahid! where is our polling station ?"

"We left our station, driver says, he'll return our station after Dumkhar Gongma, because bus cann't turn from here."

Before reaching Dumkhar Barma, I saw huge rock near the Micro Hydel Power station. It would be about 1000 m. high from the base. This village is in the middle of Dumkhar, therefore, called Dumkhar Barma. Barma means middle in Ladakhi language. This village has 200 voters.

Dumkhar Gongma was further ahead of about 15 km. from Dumkhar Barma. It was Kaccha road and driving was very difficult. Any how we were climbing and further climbing in the middle of huge rocks. At one place, I saw stone avalanches. I was informed that :

> "The road between Dumkhar Barma and Dumkhar Gongma becomes dangerous after rain, during the period of snow melting; as constant occurrence of stone avalanches take place. Villagers and travellers of this country have to face one of the most dreaded dangers."

We reached near Dumkhar Gongma village. It has 600 voters. Here our bus driver could not able to turn the bus, thus most of the polling parties got down. The bus driver then drived bus back about 500 m. Here he got a place and turned the bus towards Dumkhar Doo. We all again sat at their respective seats. As our bus moving down slope, we were facing intermitent jumps. At last we arrived our polling station in late evening about 6 o'clock.

Next morning about 10 A.M. I went to the polling station along with my polling officers; made all arrangements, by 11 o'clock we returned to our rooms. Anwar Hussain said, "We should prepare our lunch." Anwar Hussain started preparation for lunch, my other officers went out for walk, last night I didn't have sound sleep, therefore, went for rest. Our polling officers came late, we took lunch together after at 2.30. Later I gave primary instructions to my subordinates about election duty, then we all took complete rest. In the evening villagers came to me, he inquired about the available facilities. We all had our bag and baggage, so we did not demand anything. However, two police constables who came here for election duty from Jammu demanded to supply some blankets. Goba spent about an hour with us, so I asked, 'Kindly let me know how the name of village Dumkhar Doo derived? He replied : "In olden days there was a palace on a big boulder, so the name of village derived from Dom (boulder) and Khar (palace). As Domkhar has three portion, that is upper, middle and lower part; the upper part is known Gongma, middle part-Barma and lower portion is Doo." "Is Domkhar has monasteries? Yes, it has Drigung and Drugpa monasteries but Drugpa in majority."

Table 27.1. Voting at 83/Dumkhar Doo polling station on 10/5/2004

Sl. No.	*Time*	*Hour*	*No. of Voters casted their votes*
1.	7 A.M.-9 A.M.	Ist two hours	009
2.	9 A.M.-11 A.M.	IInd two hours	091
3.	11 A.M.-01 P.M.	IIIrd two hours	153
4.	01 P.M.-03 P.M.	IVth two hours	107
5.	03 P.M.-05 P.M.	Vth two hours	073
	Total		**433**

Note : 433 has included 03 E.D.Cs.

On 10th morning about 6 o'clock we all have had heavy breakfast and went to polling station. I inspected electronic voting machine and, by 6.45 A.M. I showed the E.V.M. control unit machine to the polling agents of candidates, and declared that control unit machine showed us clearance that is every candidate has zero number of vote. When agents were satisfied I asked them to put their signature on the 'Declaration Form'. Thereafter, I sealed the control unit by paper seals. Initially in the first two hours only nine voters casted their votes, later hours brisk voting was recorded, in between 11 A.M. to 1 P.M. it was reached to its peak, during this hours 153 voters casted their votes. Thereafter, this trend went downwards (Table 27.1).

This time four candidates, including two independents were in the fray. Their names are as follows :

1. Ghulam Hassan Khan, National Conference (N.C.) candidate, a sitting Member of Parliament (M.P.)
2. Sonam Paljor, B.J.P. nominee.
3. Thupstan Chhewang, Independent candidate (nominee of Ladakh Union Territory Front)
4. Wazir Mohammad Wali, Independent candidate.

At Dumkhar Doo polling station female voters were far ahead than male; as 243 females voters casted their votes.

In Dumkhar Doo polling station number of voters increased tremendously during last 14 years as compared to 1988 (Table : 27.2)

Table 27.2. Number of voters at Dumkhar Doo Polling Station in Leh-Ladakh (1988-2002)

Sl. No.	*Year*	*Number of Voters*	*Total*	
		Male	*Female*	
1.	1988	166	90	256
2.	1989	181	111	292
3.	1991	225	113	338
4.	1995	241	115	356
5.	1996	253	133	386
6.	1997	261	143	404
7.	2001	287	181	468
8.	2002	296	197	493

Source : Marked copy of voters issued for Dumkhar Doo Polling Station, 2004.

Nevertheless, like Dumkhar Doo Polling Station, voting was smooth and peaceful throughout in Ladakh, with about six polling stations snow-bound in the Leh Assembly segment. Voters were seen standing in long queues in most of the polling stations in Ladakh.

Ladakh constituency comprising the twin districts of Leh and Kargil, the polling station of Fastan was the highest booth at a height of 17,000 feet. The Thugje-Gonpa polling station of Chang-Thang sub-division of Leh district had a minimum of 11 voters, while the Chuchot (Chu-shod) Gongma polling station had the maximum of 1,515 voters.

On 11th May 2004 we have had our breakfast at 8 o'clock and by 10 A.M. came down at road side. About 11 A.M. our bus arrived, we then travelled by bus back to Leh, but soon after travelling a few distance stopped for the Tagmachik polling party. Then moved to Kha-la-tse. Here we had lunch and about 1 o'clock marched for Leh. At 2 P.M. we came to Nimo, and after taking tea and light refreshment moved further to Leh. About 3.30 P.M. reached election material centre at Leh.

At the materials collection station I first filled a form in which I gave the details of my polling station. Thereafter with a copy of it I went to stand in queue at counter No. 1. Here I submitted the following items/ statutory cover.

1. EVM used at the polling station
    a. Control Unit
    b. Ballot Unit
2. The cover containing the accounts of votes recorded and paper seal account, i.e., 17-C.
3. The cover containing the declaration by the presiding officer.
4. The cover containing the presiding officer diary.

At the next counter the following materials were collected :

1. Sealed cover contained the marked copy of the electoral roll or the list of CSVs.
2. Seal cover containing the Register of voters.
3. Sealed cover containing voters slips.
4. Sealed cover containing used tendered Ballot papers and the list in form 17-B.
5. Register.

At the third counter the concerned authorities received the following materials :

1. Cover containing the copy or copies of electoral roll (other than the marked copy).
2. Cover containing the appointment letters of polling agents in Form 10.
3. Cover containing the Election Duty Certificate in Form 12-B.
4. Seal cover containing the list of challenged voters in Form 40.
5. Cover containing the list of blind and infirm electors in Form 14A and the declaration of the companions.
6. Cover containing the declaration obtained from electors as to their age and the list of such letters—(Annexure-XI).

7. Cover containing the receipt book and cash, if any in respect of challenged votes.
8. Cover containing unused and damaged papers seals.
9. Cover containing unused voter slips.
10. Cover containing unused and damaged special tags.
11. Cover containing unused and damaged strip seals.

The last counter collected the following materials :

1. Handbook for Presiding Officer.
2. Manual of Electronic Voting Machine.
3. Indelible ink set (with topper having been secured on each phial effective with molten candle or was applied thereon to prevent leakage or evaporation).
4. Self inking pad.
5. Metal seal of the presiding officer.
6. Distinguished mark rubber stamp.
7. Arrow cross mark rubber stamp for marking tendered ballot papers.
8. Cup for setting the indelible ink.
9. Arm band for presiding officer.
10. Arm band for polling officers.
11. Polythene bag.
12. Polling agent hand book.

On 13th May 2004 counting took place, at late evening election result of Ladakh constituency was declared. The Ladakh Union Territory Front candidate, Thupstan Chhewang gave a crushing defeat to his nearest rival Hassan Khan of N.C. by a margin of 25,713 votes.

In this Parliamentary election 1,29,093 (73.52%) voters of Ladakh casted their votes. Thupstan Chhewang bagged 66,839 (51.72%) against the total of 41,126 votes (31.82%) the N.C. candidate managed to get followed by the independent candidate from Kargil, Wazir Ali, who got 18,117; while as the B.J.P. candidate Sonam Paljor got only 2,849 (2.2%) votes.[6]

However, the official announcement of the final result was delayed as ballot boxes from the three polling stations in remote Zanskar (Zangskar) area were not arrived in Kargil in time due to some technical problems the helicopter sent to collect the ballot boxes from remote areas in Zanskar failed to get to the Shun, Shade and Stog polling stations. The three polling stations comprised only 147 votes. Thus, the election commission direction was sought in this regard before the official declaration of the result.[7]

This time Thupstan Chhewang got 9,844 votes from Kargil district. According to the sources Kargil people voted in favour of Thupstan

Chhewang personality, they hoped that newly elected M.P. of Ladakh would definitely works for the development of whole Ladakh without any Leh-Kargil biases.

Wazil Ali, the independent candidate from Kargil was also happy as he did not want N.C. to win. He bagged 18,117 (14.01%) votes and considerably cut down the vote size of the Hassan Khan in Kargil. Therefore, helped Thupstan Chhewang to win the election. Now Ladakh people have many expectations from Thupstan Chhewang, so he has to think peacefully for the economic development of Leh and Kargil together; otherwise in the next election people of Ladakh may cast their votes against him. Any how it's a good victory of Buddhist candidate after a long time.

References

1. Sharma, Arun : 'A Clash of Civilisations in Ladakh', *The Indian Express*, March 25, 2004.
2. *Ibid.*
3. *Ibid.*
4. *Ibid.*
5. Morup, Tashi : 'Thupstan's crushing defeat to N.C. M.P.', *The Kashmir Times*, Jammu, May 14, 2004 : 5.
6. *Ibid.*
7. *Ibid.*

Appendix-I

However, official records speak that 4-Ladakh Parliamentary Constituency has 1,72,963 voters. Here follows the details :

4-Ladakh Parliamentary Constituency

Sl. No.	*Assembly Segment No.*	*Name*	*No. of Electors Male*	*Female*	*Total*
1.	47	Nubra	6,078	5,989	12,067
2.	48	Leh	39,542	37,385	76,927
3.	49	Kargil	29,107	32,940	62,047
4.	50	Zangskar	1,039	11,603	21,922
		Total	**85,046**	**87,917**	**1,72,963**

28

Life and Works of Ven Kushok Bakula

His Holiness Bakula Rinpoche was born on 19th May 1917 at Matho palace. His father Nawang Thayas and mother Ishey Wangmo were simple and god fearing.

It is said that before the birth of Kushok Bakula Rinpoche Ishey Wangmo went to Matho Nangrang, from lha she asked :

"Kindly tell me something about my future."

"You are lucky and have long life, you should not worry about your future."

When Kushok Bakula was small child, his mother asked Matho Devi :

"Kindly tell me about the future of my child."

"Your child is the incarnation of Nythi trampo. He will become a great leader of Ladakh."

To listen this Ishey Wangmo forgot all worries and passing her time in domestic works.

Incarnation of Kushok Bakula : Bakula Rinpoche earlier incarnation was in Zangskar. He got perinirvana at the age 63 years. Lamas of the Spituk monastery then went for prayer. Some of them even went to Matho Nangrang and asked about his incarnation. Finally they got the information that Ishey Wangmo's son had some characteristics resembled to Bakula's earlier birth. They came to Matho palace and after some test convinced that Wangmo's son is the incarnation of Bakula. Later they sent the details of Bakula Rinpoche to His Holiness 13th Dalai Lama in Tibet for his confirmation. Dalai Lama replied in affirmative and named Thupstan Gyaltsen.

Education : In 1922 Bakula Rinpoche became 5 years old. Spituk lamas then requested Ishey Wangmo :

"We want to bring your child to Spituk monastery; as he is the incarnation of Bakula, so his throne is vacant at the monastery, after performing ritual ceremomy we offer him his throne. He will be returned within one year to you."

"As you wish, I have no objection."

At the age of 6 years, Rinpoche came to Matho. Later he brought to Matho monastery. Here Lobzang Tsulthim Chosphel Rinpoche of Rizong monastery became his teacher. He taught him Bodhi and Buddhist culture and civilization.

In 1926, at the age of 10 years Bakula Rinpoche went to Tibet via Kashmir-India alongwith Chagzot Lobzang Chetan, Tondup Chokzugpa, Lobzang Rikdol and Geshes Paljor. In Tibet he stayed at Spituk Khang Chan of Tashilunboo monastery. Thereafter, went to Lhasa and met 13th Dalai Lama, who gave special protection and for his safety appointed one guard. Later he studied Pherchin, Uma etc. from different Tibetan Gurus.

In 1936 thirteenth Dalai Lama gave him Seela diksha and new name Lobzang Thupstan. Thereafter under Geshes Lopon he studied Kangyur, Stangyur, Lamrim, Zot etc. Thence, on the occasion of Galdan or Gadan Monlam he was offered throne and called for Tibetan debated with Galdan or Gadan Geshe Gildun Kalzang. He answered all the questions wisely, later awarded Geshes Lharampa degree in 1940.

Return to Ladakh : When Spituk lamas came to know that Rinpoche Bakula got the highest Tibetan degree in Buddhist Philosophy, some lamas went to Tibet and requested him :

"His Holiness you have Geshes Lharampa degree. In the Spituk monastery we need your valuable service, therefore request you to return to your monastery in Ladakh."

Bakula Rinpoche accepted the request and returned Ladakh alongwith Spituk lamas via Chang-Thang which took four months. In Ladakh, public and lamas welcomed and offered him head lama throne at the Spituk monastery.

Pakistan Attack : In 1947, just after India got independence Pakistan raiders attack India, and occupied most of the Kargil and Skardu areas, Leh was only left free, it was almost certain that they could soon occupy Leh. The Kushok Bakula alongwith some rich people of Ladakh went to the hillock and offered pray to safe Ladakh from enemy, later by God sake Indian army under the command of Major Prithi Chand reached Leh and defend the country.

In Ladakhi Politics : On June, 1949, Pandit Nehru, then the Prime Minister of India visited Leh alongwith Sheikh Mohammed Abdullah. He advised Bakula Rinpoche :

"You should join politics, by joining politics you can help your people more energetic way."

Bakula Rinpoche accepted Pandit Nehru's advice and joined politics in 1949, later visited Hemis and witnessed Hemis Tse-chu (or Tse-cu) alongwith Nehruji and Sheikh Mohammed Abdullah. In the same year he became the president of National Conference Party for Ladakh district. In 1962 first J&K State Assembly election in Ladakh was held. Rev. Kushok Bakula contested as a National Conference party candidate and won the Ladakh Assembly seat by big margin. In 1971 mid-term parliamentary election Rev. Kushok Bakula contested as a Congress candidate and won this lone seat of Ladakh. Later he was nominated as Member of Parliament for Rajya Sabha.

Land Abolition Act : In 1949 Government of India passed 'Land Abolition Act' under which no religious institution in J&K state should have more than 120 canals land. Rev. Bakula made campaign against 'land abolition act' in this connection he went to Srinagar, met Sheikh Mohammed Abdullah. But, didn't get proper response, then went to Delhi, there met with Dr. Ambedkar (Law Minister), Dr. Rajinder Prasad (President of India) and Sardar Patel (Home Minister) and persuaded them logically that how 'land abolition act' could harm Buddhist religion and society of Ladakh. Thereafter Congress Government at the centre called an urgent meeting and discussed on 'land abolition act'. The concerned authorities in Ladakh then directed to withdraw the above act immediately.

To remove corruption and loan exemption : During British Government, every Ladakhi family had to provide men and animals for transport to government officials under the 'res' system. This rule was continued after independence. The poor Ladakhi farmers didn't have sufficient money to purchase animals for the above purpose, therefore, they had to take loan from the moneylenders in high rate of interest. As a result once loan taken from them means to invite death, this was the popular slogan in those days. However, because of poverty they were bound to indulge themselves in the debts and die in debts. To understand this problem, Rev. Bakula launched a campaign against corrupt government officials and moneylenders. At last government agreed to exempt all kinds of loans against poor Ladakhis. Moneylenders also exempted their loans. In this way by the efforts of Bakula Rinpoche, Ladakhi farmers got relief from the greedy government officials and moneylenders.

Education Improvement : Till 1949, Ladakh did not have High School. Students after passing their Junior High School Examination used to go to Srinagar for Higher education. Therefore, an urgent need was then required to provide facilities for Ladakhi students to get high level of education in Ladakh. Bakula Rinpoche in this connection approached to State Government and requested the concern authorities to provide educational facilities in Ladakh.

To Preserve Buddhist Culture : During olden days young lamas used to go to Tibet for higher studies in Buddhist philosophy. In Tibet they studied Buddhist philosophy in Drepang, Sera, Galdan (or Gadan) and Tashilunboo monasteries. Some of them returned to their respective monasteries in Ladakh after passing out the highest degree like 'Kachen' Geshes etc. In 1959 after the occupation of Tibet by China this tradition came to an end. Therefore, to preserve Buddhist old culture and tradition, Rev. Bakula established Buddhist school in Leh and inaugurated it on 23 December 1959. He request to all big monasteries to send their monks for education in this school. Initially 10 Gonpas sent two monks each to this school. Later he met Pandit Jawaharlal Nehru and requested him to take this school under Central Government control. Nehru accepted Bakula Rinpoche proposal. Later under the department of culture, Government of India gave full financial support. Today, this school is known as Central Institute of Buddhist Studies and fully financed by Department of Culture under Ministry of Culture, Government of India progressing very well. It has feeder schools in all big monasteries of Ladakh.

Padma Bhushan Award : Rev. Kushok Bakula was from a royal family, but instead to lead his life luxuriously he decided to remain in monastic life and decided to work for the welfare of poor people of Ladakh. He dedicated his life in building up the public infrastructure; opening of Vishesh Kendriya Vidyalya in Delhi and Central Institute of Buddhist Studies, at Choglamsar in Leh was the mind of Bakula behind them. His promotion of education in Ladakh, perhaps be his great contribution for the development of education in Ladakh, as a result of his contribution for the Economic and Social Development of Ladakh he was awarded Padma Bhushan by the Government of India.

Polar Star Award : In 1990 Government of India appointed Kushok Bakula as a Indian Ambassador to Mongolia. He worked in the same post for 10 years. During this period he helped Mongolian government to strengthen Buddhism in Mongolia. He established a tradition to celebrate Buddhajayanti every year in Mongolia and helped in the formation of New Buddhist Association. He brought one big Buddha statue from India and gave to Mongolian government as gift. In this way through Rev. Kushok Bakula's contribution towards Buddhism in Mongolia. On 26th June, 2001 he was conferred the 'Polar Star' by the President of Mongolia.

On 4 November 2003, this great leader passed away, but we remember him for his remarkable contribution in the development of Ladakh. In this event I also remember him for his encouragement which he gave me, when in 1981 I presented my Ist paper on 'Tourism in Ladakh', in the 'All India Conference' organised by the Central Institute of Buddhist Studies, Choglamsar, Leh-Ladakh, he asked me a question on Buddhist antiques. That time I was unable to give the right answer. Prof. Jagarnath Upadhya said Dr. Jina highlighted some good issues which need to be studied. Then Rinpoche said to the scholars that Dr. Jina pointed out some advered impact of tourism which the State Tourism Department and District Administration of Ladakh should carefully study while promoting tourism in Ladakh. Later all the monasteries in Ladakh carefully preserved their antiques and in this direction, Department of Culture, Govt. of India started to give required grant to the Gonpa welfare societies in Ladakh and other parts of the Himalaya.

29

Some Ladakhi Personalities

Scholars have always attempted to describe the cultural heritage of Ladakh, but there are very few example when anyone made an attempt to tell something about the personalities. I have endeavoured to find some about whom my writing would give some worthful information.

Sonam Wangyal : He was born in a poor family of Chemre on 26 January 1925. As he brought up in a rural background, unable to get higher education. In October 1947, Pakistan invaded Kashmir and Ladakh. To defend the country Pandit Shridhar Kaul raised a volunteer force and in the meanwhile gave information about all the activities of enemy to Pandit Jawaharlal Nehru, then the Prime Minister of India. Sonam Wangyal then went to Pandit Kaul and expressed his desire to join the volunteer force/ home guards. Pandit Kaul advised him to continue his education. He wrote a letter to the Prime Minister of India and requested him to give scholarship to Sonam Wangyal for his higher studies. Prime Minister accepted the request and recommended scholarship grant to Sonam Wangyal. He got admission in the S.P. High School, Srinagar. After passing matriculation examination he returned to Leh and joined Rev. Kushok Bakula's party. Later under his leadership he launched a vigorous campaign against the corrupt administration, the moneylenders and other vested interests. During course of agitation against Kashmir Government he was arrested several times. Ultimately Government came on an agreement table and settled down framers half the debt and loan cases. The Rinpoche was pleased by his pioneering efforts and advised Ladakhis to give him their support. Thus, Sonam Wangyal gained the full sympathy of the people of Ladakh and was elected Ladakh district President of National Conference. Later in 1957 he was elected Member of the Legislative Council of Jammu and Kashmir State, and continued in this position till 1967. In 1967 state elections, he was elected from Leh constituency and inducted as Minister of State of J&K government. Subsequently, in the 1972 Assembly election, he again won from Leh. In 1982, a campaign was launched by Ladakhis to declare the Scheduled Tribes. Sonam Wangyal was actively participated in this movement and went on hunger strike for 16 days in January. In 1984, he again went on hunger strike for five days. Mrs. Indira Gandhi, then the Prime Minister came Leh and assured the protesters that Ladakh would be given Scheduled Tribe Status, and asked Wangyal to withdraw his hunger strike. In 1989, Ladakhi Buddhist Association launched campaign that Ladakh to be given Union Territory status, Wangyal favoured this demand and proposed that in this movement Muslims should also participate. In 1992, Ladakh Buddhist Association invited Muslims to fight jointly for granting Ladakh Autonomous Hill Development Council—Leh. Wangyal was very happy with this decision. In November 1998 he passed away. Sonam Wangyal in fact a great social reformer of Ladakh, he will be remembered for his sacrifices to uphold communal harmony and social justice.

Abdiel Jeva Kundan : He was born in 1926, Chuterantak Leh; got his primary education from Leh, later went to Srinagar for higher education. In Kashmir he studied in S.P. College and Amar Singh College. During fifties he came in Government of India Service and joined as pilot officer ground in the Indian Air Force. In 1960 became Flight Lieutenant. Thereafter, he joined Indian Frontier Administrative Service and posted to NEFA as Assistant Political Officer. In 1964 he went to USA under Government sponsored training programme in Wiconsin University. He returned India in 1965 and posted at Leh as Additional Deputy Commissioner, but within three months transferred to Poonch, as Special Commissioner. He was called back to Ladakh as Development cum Deputy Commissioner in 1967. After his two years tenure he went to Delhi as Education Secretary, then Sale Tax cum Excise Commissioner. Now he came in I.A.S. cadre and posted Manipur in 1973 as Hill Commissioner, then Development Commissioner. In 1975, he returned to his home state J&K as Managing Director for Industries in Srinagar; but again in 1978 he went to North-East as Chief Secretary for Mizoram State. He was again called in the Centre as Joint Secretary in the Finance Ministry in 1981. This was followed as Additional Secretary to the Planning Commission. In September, 1986, he retired from this post. After retirement his health deteriorated day by day. In 1998 he got serious health problem which eventually led to his death on April 21, 1998.

Colonel Rinchen : Chewang Rinchen was born in a farmer's family of Nubra valley in 1930. His house name was 'Stakre'—which means tiger—this title was given to his great grand-father by the King of Ladakh. Like his great grand-father Rinchen had war skills. In 1947, when India was celebrating Independence day, Pakistani raiders entered into Kashmir and Jammu regions. In those days Ladakh district had Leh, Kargil and Skardu areas. On May 10, 1948 Pakistani raiders occupied Skardu and Kargil areas, then Ladakhis had no hopes to safe them from Pakistani cruel forces. Fortunately Indian Government sent force under the command of Major Prithi Chand. Chewang Rinchen was then only 17 year young boy. He joined the force and took rigorous training, and posted at Nubra. This time he had only one sten gun and some ammunition. In Nubra with the group of local volunteers he was able to guard the valley. On August 25, 1948 he was promoted to JCO in 7th J&K Militia. Thereafter he raised Nubra Guards Company to operate guerrilla war against Pakistanis. During 1960-62 he fought bravery against Chinese force, as a result he won Sena Medal. In 1971, Pakistan launched a major attack on Indian fronts. Rinchen moved ahead with his men and captured Turtok from Pakistani forces. Government of India awarded him MVC. On September 1, 1986 he retired from the Indian Army as Lt. Colonel. In January 1990 he was given the honorary title of Colonel. This brave soldier passed away in 1997.

Eliezer Joldan : Eliezer Joldan was born in Leh in 1916. He passed Junior High School from Leh, then went to Srinagar for higher studies. He passed graduation from S.P. College in 1940. Thereafter got admission in BT, equivalent to B.Ed. After teacher training course he was appointed as a teacher in Leh. In those days Ladakh had serious shortage of trained teachers. In 1970, the Governor of J&K State conferred him State's Best Teacher Award. He worked for the poor and disadvantaged children in government school, he believed that though teachers have no power, they have high position in the society.

Bibliography

1. A tribute to Eliezer Joldan ; Ladags Melong, Vol. I, Issue I, July 2001.
2. Kundan is no More ; Ladags Melong, Vol. I, Issue I, August 1998.
3. Ladakh's Last Salute to its Hero ; Ladags Melong, Vol. 2, Issue 2, Autumn 1997.
4. Life of Shri Sonam Wangyal (1925-1998) ; Sonam Wangyal Memorial Committee, 2002.

30

Tso Mo ri ri (Tib. mtso mo ri ri) is the Lake for Birds Attraction

Tso Mo ri ri lake is located in Chang-Thang region of Leh district. As a matter of fact the whole Chang-Thang belt is covered by pasture lands where very long and wide fields are comparatively wet because of the existence of many big lakes popular among them are : Tso-Mo ri ri, Panggong Tso, Tsokar, Satsaphik Tso, Tatsang Tso, Shigwol-Tso and Yage-Tso. Therefore, with the scenic beauty the whole region is attracted by different specie of migratory birds, who spend summer season at high altitude wet-lands lie Lungbarma, Dungti, Staklung, Pugga, Tsokar Basin, Hanley, Phoktsey, Loma, Nyoma marshes, Lalphari.[1]

The lake Tso Mo ri ri is 215 km. from Leh at 14,081 feet ASL. It is about 25 km. long and 6-7 km wide and has its surface area is about 160 sq. km. To the south lies Korzok and Hanley valley in the east, which one of the longest marshes in Chang-Thang plateau and has ecological importance as black necked crane (Grus Nigricallis) annually during summer comes here for breeding.[2]

In Ladakh, the marshes of Chang-Thang are good breeding place for the migratory birds during summer. According to the local inhabitants, tall and stately with dark necks and a shiny red patch on their heads, as few as three to four of black necked cranes are fly into the Ladakh region during April and May.[3]

These summer time birds and local inhabitants of Hanle valley have good relationship. The people here are Buddhists and don't kill these, instead welcome them. Therefore, black necked crane pair during summer without any hesitation enjoy and with an air of fervent delicacy the male and female crane point their bills upwards and stretching out their wings, their tall slender legs chalk out pironettes as gracefully as Nureyev would have done in one of his ballets. Their sense of companionship and trust is legendary and it is with a complete sense of wilful abandon that the pair mate. When the mating dance is over, it is time for gestation. A short tenure and two eggs are laid. Brownish and perfectly oval in shape, both male and female incubate the eggs. But these are stressful times, for when darkness falls over the Hanley Valley, there are predators for whom the eggs present a tasty morsel. All going well, after hatching eggs for one month tiny chick peer out. The Hanley valley has shallow watery marshes which are suitable for mating grounds for cranes. In a couple of years back, Black necked cranes prefer to visit this valley in good number, today their number reduced to a few.[4]

Tso mo ri ri and its surrounding areas are important breeding place for some exquisite species of birds including Bar-headed geese (*Anser Indicus*), Great crested grabe, terns, gulls, ruddy shelduck, teals, and sand plovers.

Danger to migratory birds

1. Today Tso mo ri ri lake and its surround areas are opened for foreign tourists, as a result massive development taken place, roads being built and tourists frequency increased up to the higher limit during summer season. Consequently the area of the bar-headed goose's habitat is gradually shinking. Not only this the water at the surrounding is being diverted for purposes of irrigation and as a result the marshes are slowly drying. It will only be a matter of time before the fish and other aquatic species perish. This threat to the habitat means to change the place by cranes.[5]
2. Nowadays foreigners are allowed to visit Tso-Mo-ri-ri who unnecessary take photographs of birds and disturb them.
3. The wide infrastructure development around the lake, and human pressures cause the frequent movement of taxies and other vehicles, such activities disturb the solitude atmosphere, thus the area of the bar-headed goose's habitat is gradually shinking.
4. The unregular flow of tourists and their tents of bright colours surrounding to the lake also harmful for the healthy ecological condition. As they knowing or unknowingly throw mineral water bottles, wrappers etc. which shine brightly and effects the activities of imported birds of many rare endemic and migratory species viz. Bar-headed geese, Black-Necked cranes,

great crested grabe, terns, gulls, ruddy shelduck, teals and sand plovers.

5. From the last couple of years one can see tin sheds of paramilitary forces along the banks of the lake attract stray dogs who eat the eggs of migratory birds, thus irritate the movement and behaviour of these birds.
6. The movements, hussel and bussel of paramilitary forces also effects the behaviour of birds.
7. The tin sheds as being constructed reflect the sun light during days which effects birds behaviour while they fly or when they search a marshy place for breeding.
8. During summer when unwanted helicopter of army fly and lands around the lake side, disturb the birds who incubate their eggs. According to an information on June 2001, one helicopter landed at the nearby place of Tso-Mo-ri-ri, many Bar-headed Geese where then incubating their eggs, it was estimated that out of 200 geese, only 95 remained on the resting site after the helicopter hovered over their nests.[6]
9. It has been observed that Black-Necked cranes earlier laid eggs at the Peldo site of Tso-Mo-ri-ri, now because of hectic activities of men-animal, motor-helicopter movement, they changed their place as they didn't get success to build their nest.

The Changing Behaviour of Habitat : Today it has been noticed that because of unwanted human activities along the banks of Tso-Mo-ri-ri lake, migratory birds bound to change the place. In this direction many of them migrated towards the banks of Indus river. However, could not satisfied to lay eggs and incubate them. Therefore, it is a great danger for such rare birds who come here after flying 200 km per day.

Recommendations

1. To restrict foreign tourists activities and prohibit them for photography. In case they are permitted, their taxies should not be allowed to park at the nearby area of Tso-Mo-ri-ri lake.
2. Construction of huts/tin sheds should be made far away from lake area, if they are constructed they should be green-wash.
3. Tourists, army personals and others who visited lake area should be educated properly about birds behaviour and tell them how to keep clear, clean and hygienic atmosphere at the surrounding of lake.

4. Strictly prohibit stray dogs and other predators around the breeding sites of birds.
5. To prohibit the grazing of wild and domestic animals around the lake, as they disturb the breeding and feeding of these birds.
6. There should be proper supervision or watch is required during summer season along the lake area.
7. Nobody is allowed to throw any kind of things at the nearby lake area.
8. Time to time garbage should be cleaned.

References

1. Bedi, Rajesh and Naresh : 'The Many Faces of Tso Murari', Swagat, pp. 52-56.
2. *Ibid.*
3. *Ibid.*
4. *Ibid.*
5. *Ibid.*
6. Mohammad Abass : 'Tsomoriri birds in danger', Ladags Melong, Oct. 2002 : 27-28.

31

Eco-friendly Relation in Hemis High Altitude National Park

Hemis National Park is situated at the south-west of Leh town. The park covers an area surrounding to Hemis monastery including high mountains capped with snow and sparse vegetation.

Though Hemis Park has short period of green vegetation as it has sky-touching mountains, dry climatic condition cause high winds in every afternoon. Thus during winters the temperature goes down to 40-45°C below zero.

The Park ranges from 3400 m to 5150 m with thin air containing less oxygen percentage. As a result of this hard climatic condition, the wild life have strong body with high percentage of red cells in their blood. The popular species among them are—Snow leopard, Tibetan Argali Sheep, Ibex, lynx.

As we know the Hemis National Park is the home of snow leopard. In recent years its number declining throughout the world where it is found. Therefore, there is an urgent need to conserve this endangered specie. In Ladakh people do not poach snow leopard for fur, yet there has been growing concern as every year hundreds of domestic cattle viz. sheep and goats killed by snow leopards. Thus to come out from this problem there is an urgent need to improve animal husbandry practices by the herders such as :

1. Villagers will have to make covered or predator proof pens for their livestock.
2. At night pens should be properly guarded and at the side of these fire wood should be placed in such a way that all pens would be properly looked.

3. During cold the fire wood would help villagers to guard their livestock properly, sometimes if they leave fire wood outside the pens, snow leopards due to fear unable to harm livestock. Thus, villagers may gradually leave the place and can sleep well during night or they may no longer have to stay awake.

Fig. 31.1 shows the further details. We can understand that when villagers will proper fence and construct covered pens for their livestock viz. sheep and goats, snow leopards will unable to kill them. This will help to safe the livestock life in one hand and on the other snow leopards for their survival will kill blue sheep, Tibetan Argail etc. In this way an healthy environment may take place where men and animals together live in a harmonious way.

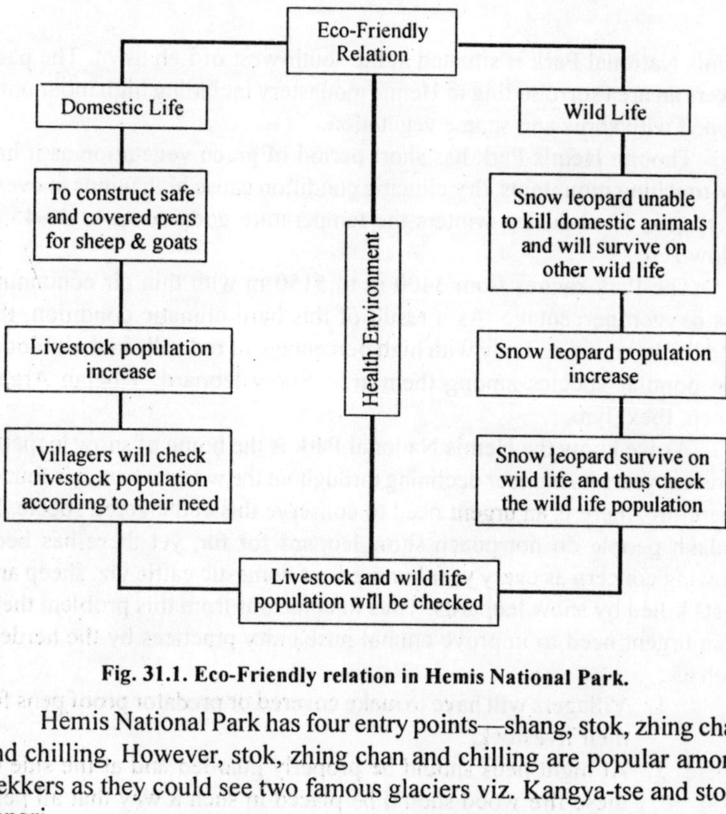

Fig. 31.1. Eco-Friendly relation in Hemis National Park.

Hemis National Park has four entry points—shang, stok, zhing chan and chilling. However, stok, zhing chan and chilling are popular among trekkers as they could see two famous glaciers viz. Kangya-tse and stok-kangri.

Today every years 3000-4000 foreign trekkers pass through Markha valley. Now locals are well aware about their habits and thus can invite them to their dwellings, thus could earn some money for their services in terms of boarding and lodging. This practice will help to keep the environment of wild life as they may not disturb the flora and fauna of the nature. Hence, locals and foreigners together are responsible to preserve the natural habitat to Hemis National Park by improving their eco-friendly habits.

Today every years 3000–4000 foreigner trekkers pass through Markha valley. Now locals are well aware about their habits and thus can invite them to their dwellings, thus could earn some money for their services in terms of boarding and lodging. This practice will help to keep the environment of wild life as they may not disturb the natural home of the nature. Hence, locals and foreigners together are responsible to preserve the natural habitat to Hemis National Park by improving their eco-friendly habits.

32

Pashm Trade : Past and Present in Ladakh

Pashm is a softest animal fibre for textile industries. Ladakhis called it 'lena'. In this paper I will discuss Pashm production, past and present Pashm trade through Ladakh to Kashmir, and finally suggested how to increase Pashm production in Ladakh.

Pashm, commonly called Pashmina, in international market is known 'Cashmere'. It is one of the costliest and softest animal fibres known to the textile industries. The fibre has three times the insulating value of the finest wool on a comparable weight basis. It has 90 per cent of the strength of the finest Merino wool fibre and 60 per cent of Mahair. Therefore, we can say it is a delicate fibre.

In Ladakh we have world class Pashmina production. Besides, China, Iran, Tibet, Mongolia, Himachal Pradesh (India), Uttranchal (India) and Afghanistan also spun top class-fine and soft yarn.

Now let us discuss, how Pashmina is internationally known as 'Cashmere'. It is explained that in ancient time Kashmiri traders had monopoly in Pashmina trade. From Pashmina they made fine quality of shawls. In India their shawls did not have good demands, so they searched international market in European or cold climate countries. As a result they got good demands from England and European countries and likewise got trade mark 'Cashmere'.

During early days traders from Rudok, Rupshu, Chang-Thang, Tibet carried Pashmina to Ladakh which then exported to Kashmir. The first reference of this trade appeared in the middle of seventeenth century. Francois writes :

> "Trade caravans did go from Kashmir via Ladakh to Central Asia and on to China. They returned bearing, among other

things, the products of Ladakh, including a quantity of a very fine wool of two kinds, the first from the sheep of that country, and the latter which is known by the name of touz and resembles, as already observed, the beaver, and should rather be called hair than wool."[1]

Ladakh history also tells us, when Deldan Namgyal was the king of Ladakh, Mongolian forces entered into Ladakh. As he was a weak king, he asked military help from Mughals to expel the enemy army. Aurangzeb was then the Badshah of Mughal Saltanat. He agreed to help Ladakh King under some conditions. Among others he made an agreement with king Deldan Namgyal that he has to open the trade routes from Ladakh to Kashmir and resume the supply of Pashmina and toosh to Kashmir.[2]

By the middle of 1680, the 'Shawl Wool' (Pashmina) trade had become a matter of such important as to be the subject of the most significant clause of the Treaty of Tingmosgang, which was to define Ladakh's relations with Tibet on the one hand, and Kashmir on the others. As a result four Kashmiri merchants were to be settled at Spituk village near Leh to procure Pashm from the high plateaux, no other Kashmiri was to be admitted to the pashm-producing areas. Thus pashm trade became an area of mutual dependence between Ladakh and Kashmir. This tradition was resumed till 1883 as Ladakh King appointed Pashmina Agents known 'court merchants' or *khar tsong* who sold the whole pashmina in the hands of Kashmiri Sunni Muslim merchants, settled at Leh. They then descended the whole consignment to Kashmir valley.[3]

In 1715 Ippolitio Desider visited Ladakh, saw white long and extraordinary fine wool, which was sold to Kashmiri merchants. He says :

> "It is a source of great richness of Kashmir involved a large number of agents kept by Kashmiri merchants in Ladakh to collect the Pashm, paying the primary products, a most miserable price."[4]

William Moorcroft visited Leh in September, 1820. He evaluated that Pashmina did not have much commercial value for Ladakh. The only important thing is that Pashmina, which later exported whole to Kashmir. He remarks :

> "One of the most important articles of the trade of Ladakh is shawl wool, of which it forms, in some degree, the source, but in a still greater, the entrepot between the countries whence the wool is chiefly supplied Rodokh[5] and Chan-Than[6], and that in which it is consumed Kashmir."[7]

He also observed that in those days there was a Treaty between Ladakh and Kashmir Government under which Pashmina producers of Chang-Thang had to sale their wool to authorised Kashmiri or Ladakhis. He estimated that during 1820, the quantity of Pashmina was 120,000-240,000 pounds in Ladakh, which as a whole exported to Kashmir through the hands of number of middlemen viz. Bakal[8] who first collected Pashmina from producers, later disposed to Pashm Furosh[9]. The agreement of buying and selling of Pashmina between these two only finalized by the intervention of Mokim[10], who after the final deed received a commission of three anas[11] per Tarak.[12]

He further reported that : "(Shawl wool) whence comes at Le'[13] is sold by the importers to the merchants at that city, by whom it is sent on to Kashmir. The Raja and Khalun[14] deal extensively in this trade, but it is also shared by merchants, both from Kashmir and Turan. About eight hundred loads are annually exported to Kashmir, to which by ancient custom and engagements, the export is exclusively confined, and all attempts to convey it to other countries are punished by confiscation. In like manner it is considered in Rodokh[15] and Chang-Thang as illegal to allow a trade in shawl wool except through Ladakh; and in the letter country considerable impediments are opposed to the traffic in wool from Yarkand although it is of superior quality and cheapness."[16]

In 1847, Cunningham estimated that Ladakh imported 55 per cent Pashmina from West Tibet 12 per cent from Yarkand and Ladakh itself had produced 33 per cent.

Ladakh got good revenue out of this, as it was Rs. 4,100/- in 1847, from the importers, later 8 per cent of the total imported Pashmina exported to Kashmir and Panjab. Ladakh also got revenue from the exporters, it was then estimated Rs. 3,000/-. (See table)

Thus according to Cunningham shawl wool was the important article of Ladakh trade between the Chinese province and India.

The following Table 32.1 shows the details :

Table 32.1. Pashm Trade through Leh in 1847

Pashm Produced	*Munds*	*= lb*	*= kg*	*Value (Rs.)*	*Rate of duty/maund*		*Value of duty (Rs.)*
					Import (Rs.)	*Exp. (Rs.)*	
Ladakh	2,400	76,800	34,909	76,800	—	—	—
W. Tibet	4,000	128,000	58,128	128,000	8 as	—	2,000
Yarkand*	875**	(28,000)	12,727	28,000	2.4 as	—	(2100)
Total	**7,275**	**232,800**	**105,818**	**232,800**			**4,100**

(contd.)

(Contd. Table 32. 1)

Pashm Produced	*Munds*	*= lb*	*= kg*	*Value (Rs.)*	*Import (Rs.)*	*Rate of duty/maund Exp. (Rs.)*	*Value of duty (Rs.)*
Pashm Exported							
Kashmir	3200	102,400	46,545	102,400		8 as	1600
Punjab	3200	102,400	46,545	102,400		12 as	1400
Total	**6400**	**204,800**	**93,090**	**204,800**			**3,000**

* Imports from Yarkand are not computed by Cunningham in the final tally of exports.

** Figures in brackets are inferred from given figures.

Source : Cunningham 1854: 239, 248, 249, 250, 253 & cf. Rizvi.

According to Aitchison during 1867-72 white Pashmina was Rs. 13-Rs. 25 per maund higher than back, and total collected Pashmina from domestic or from Central Asian countries was exported to Kashmir and Punjab. However, under the 1846 Amritsar Treaty Ladakh had to export 80-90 per cent of the total collected pashmina to Kashmir per year (Table 32.2).

Table 32.2. Pashm Export from Ladakh to Kashmir during 1867-72

Year	*Colour*	*Rate/maund at Leh (Rs. as p.)*	*Quantity (maunds and seers)*	*Value (Rs.)*
1867	—	47.12.3	408.00	19,490
1868	White	50.0.0	694.37	34,747**
	Black*	37.8.0	155.33	5,843
1869	W	50.0.0	614.00	30,700
	B	25.0.0	92.39	2,025
1870	W	60.0.0	348.04	20,886
	B	40.0.0	58.19	2,339
1871	W	65.4.4	871.04	56,858
	B	—	96.14	4,052
1872	W	75.0.0	241.25	18,122
	B	60.0.0	88.07	5,290. 8 as
	Total	—	**3669.22**	**200,252.8 as**

* Black : means clearly, natural colour or khudrang.

** This does not include 1500 maunds exported to Kashmir on behalf of the Kashmir government in 1868.

Source : Aitchison, 1874 : 192

But due to difficult tarrain the quantity of import and export varied. The following table shows the details.

Table 32.3. Comparative Statement of Import and Export of Pashm in Leh-Ladakh during 1867-72

Year	*Total Pashm imported*		*Total exported*	
	Quantity (maunds & seers)	*Value (Rs.)*	*Quantity (maunds & seers)*	*Value (Rs.)*
1867	585.00	27,625	421.00	21,140
1868	1449.11	72,463	960.20	96,078
			+1500.00*	+75,000**
1869	528.28	26,435	865.03	46,631
1870	1,084.04	63,206	449.29	25,814
1871	1,220.39	59,047	1,003.38	62,748
1872	918.32	64,060	433.32	30,687
Total	**5,781.34**	**312,842**	**5,634.02**	**301,098**

* This figure is not included in the tables, but added a footnote to the table of exports from Leh to Kashmir. In the context of the rest of the figures of looks wildly improbable.

** Figure calculated by multiplying 1500 maunds of pashm by Rs. 50, the rate for white pashm during the year in question.

Source : Figures consolidated from import and export Tables given in Aitchison & Cf. Rizvi; op. cit.

Table reveals that during 1868 total exports from Ladakh was 2460.00 maund out of which 1500 maund pashmina was from Kashmir government quota. Besides a negligible quantity that is 30 maunds and 30 seer was exported to Baltistan over the six years. The grand total export was 3669.22 maunds to Kashmir plus 1500 maunds to Kashmir on government quota, plus 30.30 maunds to Baltistan, plus 433.50 maunds to the Punjab, which equals 5634 maunds and 2 seers, or 147 maunds and 32 seers less than the total import. Pashm cannot be stored for long as its raw state, there need not be absolute parity in the figures for import and export for a particular year.

In those days Amritsar was the main centre for woollen industries, therefore Kashmiri merchants after fulfilling their Pashm requirement, further exported the same to Punjab and other nearby parts of Hindustan (Table 32.4)

Table 32.4. Export of shawl wool from Kashmir during 1886-94

Year	*Shawl Wool (Rs.)*	*Year*	*Shawl Wool (Rs.)*
1886-87	12,10,012	1890-91	1,96,250
1887-88	12,68,500	1891-92	85,250
1888-89	6,07,510	1892-93	2,19,275
1889-90	7,08,300	1893-94	22,850

Source : *Lawrence, 1895 ; 388. The figure for 1873-74, ibid., 377 in. cf. Rizvi ; op. cit.*

We understand from the above table that during 1898-1900, Tibet exported 80 per cent pashm of its production to Punjab, the rest to Ladakh (Table 32.5).

Ladakh imported only 13-20 per cent pashmina from Tibet and the same quantity from Yarkand (Table 32.5)

Table 32.5. Comparative Statement of Imports of Pashm into Punjab and Ladakh during 1899-1900

Year	*Value of Pashm imported*		
	From Tibet into Punjab (Rs.)	*From Tibet into Ladakh (Rs.)*	*From Yarkand into Ladakh (Rs.)*
1898-99	85,825	20,930	23,030
1899-1900	113,575	23,422	25,795

Source : *Lamb 1960, Appendix H (347), and Appendix (I) 348. Figures taken from the Punjab External Land Trade Reports & cf. Rizvi ; op. cit.*

During 20th century it had been observed that there was 50 per cent margin between Chang-Thang and Leh Mundi. Thus Pashmina brokers earned handsome money from this business. Table 32.6 shows the details.

Table 32.6. Pashm price according to main merchants in two mundies : Chang-Thang Leh during 1925-1960

Name of Merchant	*Period*	*Price of Pashm in Chang-Thang (Rs.)*	*in Leh (Rs.)*
Tonyot Shah	1925-60	1/ser	10/seer
Chaudhri Ghulam Ahamed	1925-60	1½ to 2/Bhatti	12-13/8 Bhatti (Ladakhi Pashm)
	1925-60	2½/Bhatti (Best quality Pashm from Tibet)	18-20/8 Bhatti

Contd.

Contd.

Name of Merchant	*Period*	*Price of Pashm in Chang-Thang (Rs.)*	*in Leh (Rs.)*
Akhon Mahdi Ali	1925-47	2-3/Bhatti	1-4/kg (Depending on quality)
Mohammad Asghar	1940-60	2-2½/Bhatti 4-5/Bhatti	4-5/Bhatti
Rigzin Namgyal Kalon	1940-47	12 as to Rs. 2/Bhatti	5-9/Bhatti
Abdul Hakim Shanko	1947-60	4-5/Bhatti	10-12/Bhatti
	1947-60	50-60/Bhatti (Higher side)	160-200/Bhatti (Higher side)

Source : *VII-A/10-11, C/31, IX-A/3-5, 6/52; X-A/14, B/14-15, D/13; XI-A/16, B/8-11, XXII-A14/7; LXXIV-A/53, B/54, C/58 & Rizvi ; op. cit.*

Shamma traders from Shyam side of Leh were also involved in Pashmina business, they annually visited to Chang-Thang and exchanged wheat/barley with Pashmina/wool. According to Shamma informants they got Rs. 5-10/Bhatti marginal benefit. Table 32.7 shows the details :

Table 32.7. Prices of Pashm according to Shamma informants during 1915-60

Shamma	*Duration (approx.)*	*Price of Pashm in Chang-Thang*	*in Leh*
Sonam Nurdup (Nyurla)	1915-60	Rs. 1/seer	Rs. 7-8/Bhatti
Tsering Namgyal (Ting mosgam)	1935-60	5-7 pau/Rs.	Rs. 10-14/Bhatti
Tashi Phuntsog Tsakan (Nyurla)	1935-60	— Approx. 100%	Reckoned to get
Stobdan (Nyurla)	1945-60	Rs. 4/Bhatti rising to Rs. 12/Bhatti	Rs. 10-12/Bhatti rising Rs. 22/Bhatti
Tashi Phuntsog (Nyurla)	1945-60	—	Rs. 22 max. before the transborder trade came to end

Source : *XX-A/3, XXI-A/3, 6; XXIII-A/3, 4; LXX-A/68; LXX-A/4-5 & Rizvi; op. cit.*

* In the market at Gartse the price of pashm was invariably double that of wool & Cf. Rizvi; *op. cit.*

We come to this conclusion that before 1900 Pashm came to Ladakh freely from Yarkand and Tibet, later this tradition did not continue and maximum Pashmina was supplied to Ladakh by Chang-Thang. During Maharaja Pratap Singh Arghuns[17] were the main commission agents in Leh who collected Pashm from Chang-Thang and sold it to Kashmiri merchants.

Classification of Pashm producing goats : It is an established fact that there is no breed of goat specially called as 'Pashmina Goat'. In fact, a wide range of goat breeds in the world bear marketable goat down, during a particular season of the year. Zoologically goats can be classified into five species[18] :

1. Capra hircus,
2. Capra ibex,
3. Capra causcasica,
4. Capra pyrenaica, and
5. Capra falconeri

The origin of pashmina or commonly called as 'Cashmere goat' has been traced to capra falconeri or to capra hirus. Later being domesticated in three centres : Kirgizia (North-east), Himalaya (South-east) and Mongolia (West) of the world (Fig. 32.1).

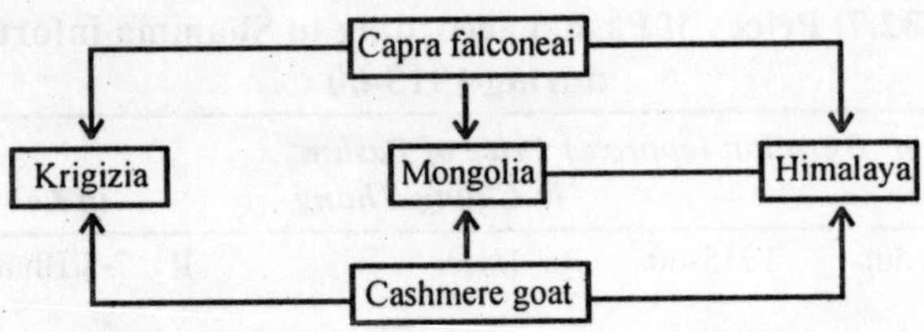

Fig. 32.1. Pashmina goat rearing centres of the world.

Production : As per a rough estimation world produces about 8000 tons of raw pashmina, out of which China alone produces 60%, Mongolia 20-25% and others 20-25%.[19]

Ladakh produces 35000 kgs of raw pashmina from 1.5 lacs of Changra goats of Chang-Thang area and there is potential for producing more than 25000 kgs of Pashmina from the goats in non-conventional areas of the region.[20]

Animal : The body weight of Cashmere goats varies from 11 kgs. to 70 kgs., depending upon the country of origin. The size at withers very between 60-70 cms. These goats have a thick, heavy outer coat of long, straight, coarse medulated fibres, and an undercoat of short, non-medullated 'down' finer than wool, having a spinning count of 70 S-100 S and an intermediate fibre with an interrupted medula.[21]

The under coat is generally removed by combing. However, now in developed countries like Australia and New Zealand various equipments have been devised. The animals are shorn and fine wool is sorted out. The details of equipments are often guarded as trade secret. These stiffness. The separation of the 'down' fibre is done by different.[22]

In Ladakh, Pashmina producing goats though do not have not have good pashmina goat breeds as comparison to Tibet and Chinese Turkistan, however grow next the skin beneath the outer coat of hair, which is cut once a year. William Moorcroft and Trebeck gave the following reports in this connection :

> "The wool is that of a domesticated goat, and consists of the under fleece, or that next the skin beneath the outer coat of hair; the breed is the same in Ladakh as in Lassa[23], Great Tibet, and Chinese Turkistan, but the wool is not so fine as in the breeds of the districts on its eastern and northern frontier. The fleece is cut once a year, and the wool."[24]

Factors affecting the growth of Pashmina : The goat produce pashmina in responses to a variety of stimuli—the main being change in the day length, environmental temperature, breed status etc. are other possible reasons for down growth. Quite interestingly, nutrition has not been found to have any meaningful role in the growth of pashmina.

To the above context a little research on the affect of feeding on pashmina growth was conducted at Upshi Farm during 1992-94. A group of young females were kept exclusively on dry lucern hay and another group of the same status was kept on lucern as well as the palleted feed allowed. It was found that there was no remarkable affect on Pashmina growth by the controlled group.[26]

The Changra goats are generally white with a variety of horn patterns like turned upward and backwards, laterally drawn normally heterohelicle character, sickle shaped in females. The ears are erect, head is small, the most slightly concave and both sexes are boarded. The animals are medium size, the males weights 35-45 kgs. and females 20-35 kgs.[27]

Individual animal production of Pashmina : The average Pashmina production in females are 200-250 gms/goat/year whereas in males it is 250-300 gms/goat/year. (Table 32.8). There is instances in male producing 820 gms/goat/year at Pashmina Goat Farm Upshi, Leh (Ladakh). It has also been found that coloured goats produces more down than white ones. However, in general condition an average weight adult male produce 180 gms/goat/year pashmina whereas commonly it has been observed that at the Pashmina Goat Farm Upshi 185 gm/goat/year was the average pashmina production. (Table 32.9).

Table 32.9. Average Pashmina yield for the year 1999-2000 in Upshi Goat Farm

Sl. No.	*Item*	*Average Pashmina yield/goat/year (Gms.)*
1.	Adult male	362.10
2.	Adult female	209.11
3.	Young male	121.81
4.	Young female	132.53

Source : Compiled from pashmina goat farm Upshi, Leh (Ladakh).

Table 32.9. Pashmina Production during 1999-2000 in Upshi Goat Farm

Sl. No.	*Year*	*No. of Animals combed*	*Total yield of Pashmina in Kg.*
(1)	*(2)*	*(3)*	*(4)*
1.	1980-81	475	59.130
2.	1981-82	593	66.370
3.	1982-83	717	84.370
4.	1983-84	793	120.010
5.	1984-85	751	108.950
6.	1985-86	803	131.195
7.	1986-87	733	150.000
8.	1987-88	557	122.000
9.	1988-89	572	152.840
10.	1989-90	628	177.920
11.	1990-91	663	180.155
12.	1991-92	576	162.170
13.	1992-93	552	125.340
14.	1993-94	561	124.115
15.	1994-95	530	120.020
16.	1995-96	565	141.235
17.	1996-97	583	129.790
18.	1997-98	643	164.040
19.	1998-99	752	181.550
20.	1999-2000	751	139.325

Source : Compiled from Pashmina Goat Farm Upshi, Leh (Ladakh).

In Ladakh, Durbok and Nyoma Block of Leh have more than 50 per cent Pashm production of the total. Table 32.10 shows the details.

Table 32.10. Blockwise Livestock Population in Leh district of Ladakh during 1999-2000

Species	*Leh*	*Khalsi*	*Nubra*	*Durbok*	*Nyoma*
Pashmina goats	8,219	21,816	11,302	28,887	63,066
Non-Pashmina goats	14,906	50,848	40,137	—	—

Source : Compiled from Annual Progress Report, Upshi, Leh, Ladakh.

During 1998-99 Pashmina was produced 43,000 kgs. which was about 33 per cent of the total livestock production (Table 32.11)

Table 32.11. Monastery value of Total Livestock production during 1998-99

Sl. No.	*Items*	*Production (Kg.)*	*Rate per kg.*	*Monetary value (Rs. crores)*
1.	Pashmina	43,000	@ Rs. 1300/-	5.59
2.	Wool	1,92,000	@ Rs. 75/-	1.44
3.	Mohair (Angora wool)	13,000	@ Rs. 45/-	0.06
4.	Meat	8,10,000	@ Rs. 100/-	0.1
5.	Milk	6,77,800	lit. @ Rs. 12/- per lit	0.81
6.	Goat guard	16,100	@ Rs. 20/-	0.03
	Total	—	—	**16.71**

Source : Compile from Annual Progress Report, op. cit.

Thus, viewing to the study of Pashmina production in Ladakh, we may come to this conclusion that all the Ladakhi goats can produce Pashmina but only the nomads of 'Chang-Thang' or Eastern part of Leh district known 'Changpas' traditionally used their goat herds for production of Pashmina. In the rest of Ladakh goat rearing is subsidiary activity to agriculture farming and people do not collect pashmina in spite of the fact that their goats grow down in varying quantities during season. The reason for disinterest towards pashmina collection had been the poor price fetched by raw pashmina in olden time. Incidentally manure and not pashmina occupied the primary position of interests for rearing of goats in the areas of Leh, Kha-la-tse and Nubra blocks and the whole district of Kargil in Ladakh. However, the people of Chang-Thang collected pashmina in spite of the low price it fetched because livestock rearing had remained the mainstay of the economy of Chang-Thang through ages in view of the low possibilities of agriculture farming in Chang-Thang. People of Chang-Thang reared huge herds of goats and remained in migration on specific routes, demarcated socially in search of better pasture for their livestock. The social boundaries were never disregarded. The available pasture was sufficient for the number of livestock reared in Chang-Thang by the Chang-pass till 1959, but around the Chinese invasion of 1962, lot of people from Western Tibet migrated and the extra stocking of livestock on the limited pastures caused damage to the pasture land-especially the winter reserve pastures came under extreme level of pressure due to overgrazing.[28]

Combing Method : In Ladakh pashm is collected in a simple and traditional way. However, there are three methods of combing which are being used by west.[29]

1. *British Method :* Hair removed by carding and combing by circular combs and pashmina made up with noils, free of hair.
2. *American Method :* Based on carding and product is got as loose wadding. Cardin and combing is usually combined with blowing and suction.
3. *Shirlay Analyser :* Used for separating vegetable matter from cotton can also be used.

Pashmina Characteristics : The undercoat is known by different names such as Kashmir, Pashm, Pashmina, Tiflit, Hiftik, Tivit and Tibit. It is one of the finest natural fibres with an average diameter of 15.5 m. The percentage of undercoat by weight to outer coats varies in different goats as :[30]

Chinese breeds	:	22-88%
Indian breeds	:	20-60%
Soviet breeds	:	36-96%
Australian foral goats	:	5-58%
Scottish foral goats	:	13-60%

The pashmina has on equal weight basis, three times the insulating capacity than that of wool but by its structure it is weaker than wool and is more susceptible of wetting :[31]

(a) *Diameter :* The ideal average fibre diameter for a Pashmina should be 15.5-18 microns. Some advanced countries observed pashmina diameter much better. Here follows the details :[32]

1. American society for testing materials, 1959 : 30 microns.
2. Soviet state standard goat : 8-25 microns.
3. British manufacturers : 13-26 microns.

However, fine pashmina must have diameter 11-18 m. Fine fibres can be processed into uniform yarns and have better abrasion resistance than coarse fibres. Fibres diameter 8-24m., are best for knitwear and over 24m., used for fabrics.[33]

(b) *Colour :* Pashmina is available in white, off white, light greyish colours. White is most preferred, as it can be dyed into the desired hues and colour.[34]

(c) *Length :* The average fibre length of Pashmina should be greater than 40 mm. A maximum length has not be determined but a range of 20-65 mm is suggested. The ideal average is 50-55 mm. Spinning machines can handles shorter length fibres also but manual spinning requires fibres above 44 mm long, moreover 44 mm long is considered one of the fine fibre.[35]

It is interesting to know that the Ladakhi pashmina is by for best pashmina in the world. The average fineness of Chang-Thangi pashmina fibre was recovered to be 12-1333 microns observed under the dry laboratory conditions of fleece testing laboratory Upshi. The average diameter was found to be about 15 microns when a few samples were analysed under the standard humidity conditions, i.e., 65 per cent at Kiross Scotland.[36]

The pashmina produced by lower regions of Ladakh are a little more finer with average staple but the yield per goat need for the creation of a dehairing plant at Leh is strongly felt. Ladakh can think about exporting dehaired/scoured pashmina as tops rather dealing in raw pashmina. The scoured and dehaired status of pashmina can be traded as a value added material and tremendous benefit will accrue in the process. The Ladakhi pashmina can feed an average dyeing and spinning industry outside till value addition starts in Ladakh. The culture of dealing in raw pashmina has become outdated and should be given up sooner than later in the best interest of Ladakh.[37]

As the diameter of Changra goat in Ladakh down fibre was found to be around 15 micron recorded under standard controlled condition of humidity in Scotland, this material can be utilized by the knit wear industry. The pashmina produced in Skrubuchan area and all other areas (9000-12000 ft. level) were found to be finer compared to the Chang-Thangi pashmina but the yield per animal is less in these areas. Therefore, it should be planned to consider Nyoma sub-division of Leh district for well research and to carry a bigger stocking rate if the winter pastures are improved and managed soundly.[38]

For centuries, Ladakh remained as a hidden land, new ideas and techniques always took time to reach Ladakh. A few countries of the world got progressed with forward ideas regarding pashmina production, typing analysis, processing and end uses over the last few decade but Ladakh remained conventional even to this day. Old habits have to be sidelined and new ideas have to be welcomed if Ladakh has to regain its lost glory. In this connection the following pashmina production figures would be interestingly give some idea that how far India is lacking behind in term of pashmina production.[30]

China : 750 tonnes
Iran : 1000 tonnes
USSR : 750 tonnes

Though these figures are old but showed us that India does not stand anywhere in a comparative study of pashmina production.

Besides all impediments if we consider the pashmina quality, Ladakh is producing one of the best pashmina and thus may become a leader in producing the finest pashmina and store house of the best germplasm with potential to export the superior genetic material for improvement of a whole range of pashmina producing goat in the world. The following table 32.12 shows that pashmina produced from the Upshi (or Upsi) goat farm, Ladakh has better quality than Mukteshwar Farm of Uttranchal.

Table 32.12. Comparison of Pashmina production in IVRI Mukteshwar and Leh Upshi

	IVRI, Mukteshwar		*Upshi Goat Farm, Leh (Ladakh)*
(a) *Growth ;*			
Birth weight	—	2 kgs.	02 kgs.
03 months weight	—	5 kgs.	07.1 kgs.
12 months	—	18-19 kgs.	21 kgs.
03 year	—	36 kgs.	27 kgs.
Length (adult)	—	60-70 cms.	—
(b) *Pashmina yield*			
0-1	—	46 gms.	—
1-2 yrs	—	77 gms.	149 gms.
2-3 yrs	—	129 gms.	230 gms.
3 years and above	—	120-220	80-340 gms.
Fibre diameter	—	11-13 m	11.94 m

Source : *Wani, G.M. & Teli, A.A. : 'Sheep & Goat production in Ladakh : Goat for Pashmina Production; paper presented in National Conference on cold Desert, Ladakh, Leh ; 1986.*

History reveals that from times immemorial that Ladakh region and the Western Tibetan regions have been the homes of the pashmina bearing goats like many other areas of the Asiatic region. We have herds of high quality Changra goats with nomadic 'chang-pas' who have a migratory lot of people and remain in migration along with their livestock throughout of the year on specific routes. Chang-Thang region of Ladakh, at elevation ranging from 12,000 to 15,000 ft. has an estimated Changra population of 1.51 lacs. There are about 3.00 lacs of non-Changra goats in the areas of Zangskar, Nubra, Kargil and Shyam of Ladakh region. These goat are traditionally reared as a subsidiary to agriculture farming in spite of the fact that the goats like Changra are coming form the same larger genetic pool and can be considered as potential producer of Pashmina.[40]

The pashmina produced by Ladakh go to Kashmir or Himachal Pradesh in order to feed the shawl industries through middlemen or traders. These middlemen collect pashmina from the grower/producers at very cheap rates. The middlemen located in the areas and the growers normally transact business through barter system. The real benefit go to the middlemen and users of raw pashmina, the poor growers are always the exploited partner.[41]

Pashmina traditionally comes from Chang-Thang in Leh district. The annual production of raw pashmina ranges from 30,000 to 35,000 kgs. which is 80 per cent of the total produce of the country.[42]

Chang-Thang pashmina goats (Changra) is of great importance for vitalizing the economy of poverty stricken region of Chang-Thang in particular and Leh district in general. The pashmina fibre produced in Chang-thang region has fibre diameter of 12-13 microns and the staple length averages from 4-5 cm. The goat gurd hair percentage in raw pashmina ranges from 45-60% depending upon the region and type of goats.[43]

Status of Pashmina Industry in Ladakh : On the world scenario only a handful of companies specialize in dehairing Pashmina/Cashmina. Joreph Dewson, Seal International William Fein and Elders all in Braford, U.K., are the leading country dehairing the Cashmere wool. In Scotland, Jonstons of Elgin also dehairs for its own consumption. But in later part of eighties the Chinese reported to a speculative stock-pilling of Pashmina with a change in the trading policies. China then tried to set up processing units for textile value added products in order to tape the vast European market for its own benefit. Even now Japan, Italy, Belgium and USA are also consuming a large quantity of Pashmina by setting up of textile industries to produce excellent high valued luxury knitwear items.[44]

The potentials of Ladakh Pashmina/Cashmere needs further exploration as lot of scope still exists for export of the material to the user countries in the world. But the material should be dehaired and scoured besides proper laboratory analysis of Pashmina is necessary. The scoured and dehaired status of Pashmina can be traded as a value added material and tremendous benefit will accrue in the process. The culture of dealing in raw pashmina had become absolute and should be given up soon in the best interest of Ladakh. Moreover, only 5 per cent of Pashmina raw is utilized in Ladakh for making shawls. The entire process of shawl making is manual which leads to uneven, unattractive and poor quality products which ultimately do not fetch remunerative price in the market.[45]

The Role of Animal Husbandry Department of Ladakh for the Development of Pashmina Production : The following objects in this connection were made in Ladakh region.[46]

1. Increase in the pashmina yield from 200-300 gms, average for the female population and 400-500 gms average for the male population of Pashmina goats.
2. Increase in the present Changra goats population by almost 10%.
3. Conservation of all the goats to uniform colour.
4. Making availability of superior genetic breeding material either through breeding bucks by natural covering or through artificial insemination.

Pashmina Goat Farms in Ladakh : The State Animal Husbandry is running two goat farms in Ladakh for the development of Pashmina products.[47]

(i) *Pashmina Goat Farm Upshi :* The Pashmina goat farm Upshi (or upsi) was sanctioned as centrally sponsored scheme under All India Coordinated Research Project on goats and the project started functioning in March, 1973 under central allocation of grants. The farm was transferred to state sector in the year 1985-86. The farm is situated at Upshi 52 kms from Leh. The farm have irrigated canal and command area of 354 acres not of which 251 acres have been brought under alfa-alfa cultivation and plantation.

The livestock were purchased from different parts of the Chang-Thang and selective breeding programme was started. Selective breeding was undertaken so as to produce best males, superior in both quality and yield of Pashmina. The farm at Upshi has been able to increase raw-pashmina yield per animal from 180 gms to 260 gms at an average and the gains are passed on to public through distribution of improved bucks for upgradation of their goats. More than 2200 bucks have been distributed to the breeders for upgradation so far.

This project has distinction of producing more than 2800 qtls of dry alfa-alfa which is not self sufficient but also supplies fodders to Chang-Thang region.

(ii) *Pashmina Goat farm Khuril :* This is one of the oldest farm which was established during 1958 at Chushul village in Durbuk block, but later shifted to Khuril during 1962 due to Chinese aggression.

The farm was started by purchasing local pashmina goats and upgradation was carried out by selective breeding of indigenous Changra-goats. The Pashmina farm Khuril is located at a distance of 35 kms from sub-division headquarters of Nyoma. The farm is located at an altitude of 14,500 feet above sea level. The farm produces bucks of superior germ plasm for distribution amongst the breeders of Chang-Thang to continue the programme of selective breeding.

The farm has produced more than 2200 bucks which have been distributed to the breeders in Chang-Thang region. The technique regarding rearing of livestock have been adopted in village also.

The farm is of migratory nature and during summer it is stationed in Queng area and in winter it moves to Skakjung area near the Chinese border. At the time of kidding, the animals are kept at Khuril headquarters, where some feeding is given.

Pashmina Development Activities in Field[48] **:** The Chang-Thang region of Ladakh is famous for pashmina production. It comprises of two blocks: Nyoma and Durbuk.

(a) *Nyoma Block :* It comprises of 22 villages/hamlets and is the main traditional pashmina and wool producing area of Ladakh. It has about 2 lacs sheep and goats, producing meat, wool and pashmina.

The livelihood of people inhabitating this block is mostly dependent upon the income from sale of livestock and its products. The area is very elevated, windy and people migrated on specific routes along with all categories of livestock. Most of the area are above 12000 ft. from sea level.

Besides, this block has 10 goat extension centres and six First Aid centres. The main function of these extension centres are to provide high quality pashmina bucks, to provide health care, to make necessary arrangements for feed/fodder during winter season especially during crisis periods.

(b) *Durbuk Block :* It is also lies in Nyoma sub-division and comprises of 12 villages. The State Animal Husbandry Department has seven goat extension centres and one First

Aid centre. The main pashmina producing villages are Chushul, Kargium and Phobrang. The total population of pashmina goats are 40,000. The department provides breeding coverage, health cover and other incentives to the breeders through these goat extension centres.

Pashmina Development in Non-tradition areas[49] : It comprises of areas of Kha-la-tse, Nubra and even some parts of Leh. In Kha-la-tse block the areas of Lingshet, Fotoksar and Tia have the potential of producing pashmina from the goats. In Nubra block area of Digger, Tangyar, Khardong and Panamic can be brought under pashmina development. At present there are one lac goats which are being taken for pashmina is ensured. The department has schemes for provision of lambing sheds/feed and fodder banks and various other programmes under watershed programmes.

The State Animal Husbandry Department made the following issues in order to develop the Pashmina production in Ladakh.[50]

1. Need for change in breeding season, dosing and dipping at least once a year to reduce the parasitic location.
2. Need for exchange of germ plasm between families and areas to reduce the level of inbreeding in order to reduce the chances of harmful impacts in production parameters.
3. Need for purchase of bucks in good numbers from Korzok area for distribution in other areas in other to raise the genetic status of the goats.
4. Need for production of quality pashmina from non-traditional areas of Leh, Kha-la-tse, Nubra areas by tagful planning and exploring the genetic potentials of the non-Changra goats, and their upgradation.
5. Need for reduction of kid/mortalities by providing kidding lambing shed facilities for each families.
6. Need for shelter structure facilities in highland areas on migratory routes.
7. The breeders felt that the goats should wave the cost of medicine and there should be 100% subsidy on supply of medicine.
8. Need for sufficient qualities of Terramycin injection in other to combat the incidences of lung and intestinal problems.
9. Remunerative prive of pashmina by involving wool board.
10. Watershed development association, existing in Chang-Thang needs to be strengthen to make them function as small co-operative societies for handling pashmina business.

Over All Recommendation for the Pashmina Development

1. With an aim to focus on the various socio-economic upliftment of the breeders of Chang-Thang it is necessary that some quantity of the pashmina produced in the region is dehaired and value addition taken place here in the Ladakh region. Here follows the details :[51]
   - (i) The need for creation of dehairing facilities in Ladakh was urgent by felt.
   - (ii) The Secretary Wool Board J&K State suggested that some officers should be sent to the valley to acquire knowhow about dehairing and processing facilities available in Kashmir and would submit their report to the council within one month.
   - (iii) Various speakers wished that value addition of pashmina should be done at the source of raw pashmina to benefit the breeders.
   - (iv) The Chief Executive Councillor opinioned that the pashmina products should be diversified.
   - (v) The pashmina growers wanted to go value addition at village levels provided they were trained in the art.
2. Livestock Husbandry rather than crop cultivation has remained the main income generating sources for the inhabitants of Chang-Thang for ages by virtue of the importance of Pashmina fibre for shawl industry. This region has provided a unique place for Ladakh in the economy of Kashmir for centuries, as landscape and environment here helped to produce the finest pashmina in the world. Therefore in order to increase the undercoat density of S/P ratio, direct selection on S/P ratio requires trained technical staff and laboratory set up. In this direction Don goats could help us to advise a fool-proof method for selection. If this selection is done properly, it'll increase fibre length, body weight and fibre diameter. It is, therefore, necessary to frame a selection index. For establishing a selection index we may need various studies in Chang-Thang region, which could be undertaken on the farmers flocks. However, to make success this scheme, we need to have data recording system in the first hand, later to establish a buck rearing centre and germplasm centre for progeny testing of the bucks. No doubt we may use deep freezed semen for A.I.[52]
3. The pashmina growers can be benefited if processing of pashmina starts in Ladakh, unfortunately, for ages, Ladakh

remained a pashmina producer and could never became a pashmina user. Therefore utilization of pashmina in Ladakh is of paramount importance which will ultimately boost the economy of poor breeders. Recently on 30th September 2004 a processing unit of pashmina was inaugurated by Mrs. Sonia Gandhi, President Congress Party.[53]

4. Leh district has not been able to create appropriate reasonable facilities for scouring of pashmina dehairing the raw pashmina, machine spinning knitting and other activities related to value addition of pashmina. Even traditional methods of dehairing carding and spinning have not been improved over the decade in Ladakh. Therefore, Animal Husbandry Department and NGOs should think over this problem and make necessary steps in order to improve the pashmina growers' conditions and to increase pashmina production.[54]
5. Pashmina and pasture development are correlated. Therefore, in order to increase pashmina production, we have to think for the development of pasture. Here follows some suggestions in this connection :[55]
   (i) To make necessary arrangement for winter pasture reserves/fodder bank.
   (ii) Winter pasture reserves should be guarded to protected from skiyang and stray animals by providing pasture guards.
   (iii) The Chinese nomads who illegally transgress on the pasture of the Indian nomads should be driven away.
   (iv) Need for highly adopted pasture seeds for wild protein rich perrenial grasses.
   (v) Sprinkle irrigations need to be tried as gravitational canals causes soil erosions in view of the texture of soil of Chang-Thang.
   (vi) Pashmina growers should make Pashmina Co-operative Growers Society. Such society will be able to bargain for hiking the price level of Pashmina and remove the monopoly of pashmina brokers.

References

1. Janet, Rizvi : 'Trans-Himalayan Caravan', Oxford Univ. Press; 1999 : 53.
2. *Ibid.*

3. *Ibid.*
4. *Ibid.*, 55.
5. Rodokh : Rudok.
6. Chan-Tan : Chang-Thang.
7. Moorcroft, W. & Trebeck, G. : 'Travels in the Himalayan Provinces of Hindustan and the Punjab; in Ladakh and Kashmir; in Peshawar, Kabul, Kunduz and Bokhara; Vol. Sagar Pub. (Reprinted, 1971).
8. Bakal : Who deal Pashm trade from Ladakh with importers, treated as Pashm wholesellers.
9. Pashm furosh : Wool retailer.
10. Mokim : Pashm broker, who worked as Pashm agent on commission, through his presence retailers purchased Pashm from Bakal or Pashm wholesellers.
11. Three anas = 18 paise (16 annas = about 100 paise = Rs. 1/-).
12. Per tarak : A local measure of weight equal to five kg. & Cf. Rizvi, quoted from Moorcroft, MSS. D. 263/86.
13. Le' = Leh, the capital of Leh district of Ladakh region.
14. Khalun = Kalon = Prime Minister of Ladakh Kingdom.
15. Rodokh = Rudokh : It was one of the main centre of Pashmina growers, from where Pashmina was imported to Leh in large quantity.
16. Moorcroft, W. and Trebeck, G. ; *op. cit* : pp. 347-48.
17. Argluns : The offerings of Kashmiri/Yarkandi Muslims and Ladakhi Buddhist ladies.
18. Wani, G.M. and Teli, A.A. : Sheep and Goat production in Ladakh; (paper presented for National Conference, Desert Dev. Leh ; 1986).
19. Joseph, Dawson : International Broadford, U.K. 1996.
20. Animal Husbandry Deptt. Leh, Report on Pashmina Production—Brief note on Pashmina.
21. Wani, G.M. and Teli, A.A. ; *op. cit.*
22. Ibid and Aglink : 'Goats Rearing, Go-down Techniques' ; Willington, New Zealand ; Information Services, FPP : 8.
23. Lassa : Lhasa, the Capital of Tibet.
24. Moorcroft, W. and Trebek, G.; *op. cit* : 347.
25. Animal Husbandry Deptt., Leh ; *op. cit.*

26. *Ibid.*
27. *Ibid.*
28. *Ibid.*
29. Wani, G.M. and Teli, A.A. ; *op. cit.*
30. *Ibid.*
31. Ibid and Rydar, M.L. ; 'British Cashmere a small step rearer', Wool Record ; 1985 : 35-47.
32. Wani, G.M. and Teli, A.A. ; *op. cit.*
33. *Ibid.*
34. Animal Husbandry Deptt., Leh, *op. cit.*
35. *Ibid.*
36. *Ibid.*
37. *Ibid.*
38. *Ibid.*
39. Wani, G.M. and Teli, A.A. ; *op. cit.*
40. Animal Husbandry Deptt., Leh, *op. cit.*
41. *Ibid.*
42. *Ibid.*
43. *Ibid.*
44. *Ibid.*
45. *Ibid.*
46. *Ibid.*
47. *Ibid.*
48. *Ibid.*
49. *Ibid.*
50. *Ibid.*
51. *Ibid.*
52. Wani, G.M. and Teli, A.A. ; *op. cit.*
53. Animal Husbandry Deptt., Leh; *op. cit.*
54. *Ibid.*

33

The Role of Seabuckthorn in the Development of Cold-Arid Zone of Ladakh

In Ladakh barren and uncultivable land constitute about 47 per cent, cultivable waste land account 14 per cent of the total geographical area of Ladakh (Table 33.1) ; and can be used for Seabuckthorn cultivation if irrigation facility available.

Table 33.1. Land Use Pattern of Ladakh

Sl. No.	*Particulars*	*Area ('000 ha)*	*Percentage*
1.	Total area (as per village papers)	62	—
2.	Land under non-agricultural use	03	04.83
3.	Barren and uncultivated land	29	46.77
4.	Land under miscellaneous tree crops and groves	03	04.83
5.	Cultivable waste land	09	14.51
6.	Net area sown	18	29.06

Source : According to 1978-79 Revenue Records.

In Ladakh shrub Seabuckthorn can be found along the water beds or at the banks of streams and rivers, or grows throughout in Ladakh between 9,000 to 11,000 ft. ASL.

Seabuckthorn and Economic Development : Ladakh region has an extensive surface water, but due to extremely rugged terrain and dry temperate climate, only a fraction is used for irrigation. Hence, Seabuckthorn or popularly known thorny nitrogen fixing shrub can grow easily under the adverse climatic condition and can survive in less water availability.

Therefore, if Ladakhis will propagate Seabuckthorn in barren/ uncultivable through the watershed scheme, their economy will accelerate upto great extend (Fig. 33.1).

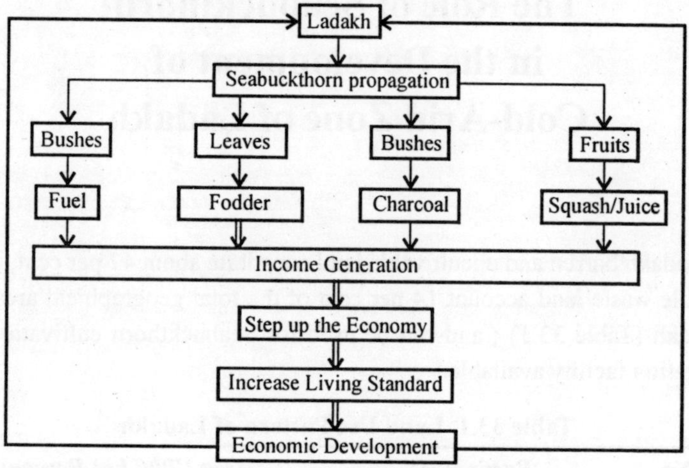

Fig. 33.1. The role of Seabuckthorn in the Economic Development of Ladakh.

Seabuckthorn and Environment : The term environment has no fixed solution. However, can be articulated as "It includes as much of what is external as can be reached in any given interval of time, and each localized population now draw its food and other materials for economic and social purposes from a described area, to keep natural culture intact and solve the human problems effectively."

Thus, Seabuckthorn is the only alternative for Ladakh region to normal the level of oxygen for animal beings (Fig. 33.2).

Nutrients Contents in Seabuckthorn : Seabuckthorn is a small deciduous thorny shrub belongs to the Elaeagnaceae family, known as *Hippophae*, Ladakhi called it *tsermang* and has high contents of vitamins as shown in the following Table 33.2.

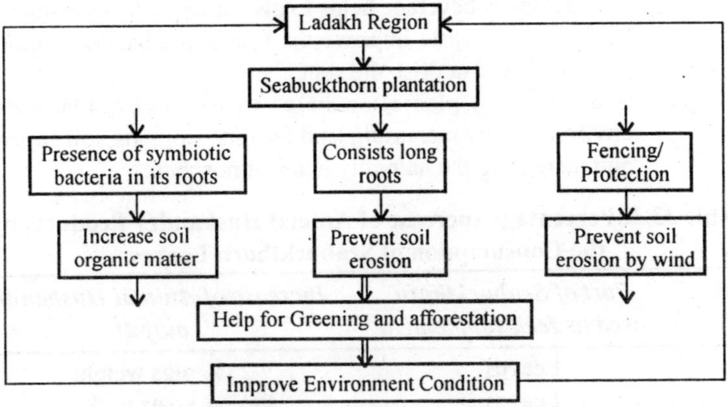

Fig. 32.2. Seabuckthorn and Environment of Ladakh.

Table 33.2. Vitamin Content of Seabuckthorn Compared with other Fruits/Vegetables (mg/100 gm)

Sl. No.	*Fruits/Veg.*	*Vit. A*	*Vit.* B_1	*Vit.* B_2	*Vit. C*	*Vit. K*	*Vit. P*
1.	Seabuckthorn	11.00	0.04	0.56	300-1600	100-200	1000.00
2.	Chili	04.33	0.05	0.03	1000-3000	—	2900.00
3.	Orange	0.55	0.08	0.03	100-150	—	—
4.	Tomato	0.31	0.03	0.02	11.0	—	—
5.	Carrot	4.00	0.02	0.05	8.0	—	—

Source : Lu Rongsen, 1990 and quoted Ladags Melong 1995 : 38.

Table reveals that Seabuckthorn has high contents of vitamin C (i.e., 4-100) times higher than any other fruit/veg. Similarly it has high percentage of vitamin A, Vitamin B_2 and Vitamin K.

Animal Husbandry and Seabuckthorn : Seabuckthorn leaves contain good quantity of nutrients and bioactive substances. The male plants do not bear fruit, therefore, their leaves normally used for fodder. Experiments show that by the consumption of leaves and seeds the fertility percentage among animals increased considerably Table 33.3.

Uses of Seabuckthorn

1. Seabuckthorn fruit has ample percentage of vitamins, minerals, flavonoids, anti oxidants and other bio-active substances, and helps to fight cold and enhances anti-aging substances in the body, and, to improve the health of weak children.
2. If one drinks Seabuckthorn juice regularly in some cases, feels relax in stressed muscles and improve memory power.

3. Seabuckthorn beverage helps to give strength to sportsmen.
4. Seabuckthorn paste improve the micro-circulation of blood capillaries and nourish the skin.
5. Seabuckthorn plantation helps to improve Ladakh dry environment by increasing land fertility, stopping soil erosion and increasing the humidity in the atmosphere.

Table 33.3. Percentage Increase of Animal Husbandry Products by the Consumption of Seabuckthorn Leaves

Sl. No.	*Part of Seabuckthorn used as feed supplement*	*Increase of Animal Husbandry output*
1.	Leaves	9-21% pigs weight
2.	Leaves	8-13% goats milk
3.	Leaves	24-28% poultry laying

Source : Tsewang Dorje ; Ladags Melong, 1995 : 38.

Seabuckthorn in the Field of Industry : M/s Compact International Ltd. was the first Seabuckthorn juice industry in India who have undertaken the task of extracting the juice of plant with the help of technical tie-up of UBF Company of Germany and further supported and collaborated by the Defence Research and Development Organisation (FRL), Leh. In July, 2002 Ladakh Food Ltd. (LFL) involves an expenditure of Rs. 4.85 cr. of which around 1.72 cr. would go to the equipment. With a direct employment to 76 persons, it aims to work 8 hours for 120 days a year to produce around 2,000 tonnes of various Seabuckthorn juices and oils. Thus, I may firmly say Seabuckthorn is the boon for Ladakh and its economy.

References

1. Pamphlets issued from Compact International Ltd. & FRL, Leh ; 2001.
2. Masood Hussain : 'Berry Shrub becoming Main Industry in Ladakh', *The Kashmir Times*; May 19, 2003 : 1.
3. Tsewang Dorje : 'The Undervalued Seabuckthorn : The Thorny Bush could provide vitamins, fodder and income', Ladags Melong ; 1995 : 37-38.

34

Danger to Pottery Works in Ladakh Himalayas

Ladakh, the land of the passes in Jammu and Kashmir State is often described as moonland and its terrain in one of the most elevated regions on earth. Meadows and mountain daisies give way to expenses of multihued rocky mountain ranges, some dark and smooth like an elephant's tortso, others craggy and copper coloured, enlivened occasionally with brilliant pink flowering dogrose bushes. The land as far as the eye can see, appear to be a succession of flat, dust ridden plains and barren mountains.[1]

Turning off from the main road towards the famed monastery situated at Likir village. The great Likir monastery, a multistoreyed white edifice dominates the spiritual and physical aspect of the village. Its head lama also controls the functioning of Alchi, the famed shrine nearby built between 1020 and 1035 A.D. Likir village is also the home of some of the indigenous crafts of Ladakh. Woodcravers and potters live here. Some of them did ornamental woodwork in the summer residence of His Holiness Dalai Lama, they also did the same work for the Likir monastery.

There are only a few potters in Ladakh. They are in Chilling, Sunda, Likir and Sumda. In fact, pottery works in Ladakh has a very poor condition. Today there is only one professional potter in the whole of Ladakh. He make the following articles :

1. Za-ma (Tib. rdzha ma) : Beer making (Small & big).
2. Pung ma (Tib. pung-pa) : Beer supply pot.
3. Phe-por (Tib. phye por) : Sattu pot.
4. Sango por (Tib. sang-por) : Incense bunners.
5. Kore (Tib. Ko-re) : Cup.

In Ladakh potters are known as zo-las (Tib. rdzo-las). They are well known for their production of clay vessels and incense burners all of which are an integral part of every Ladakhi home.

In Ladakh brew a popular barley (nas Tib. na-s) beer known as *Chang* which is stored in a wide mouthed container that narrows down to a thin neck before widening against in the same proportion as a common *Surahi* or water pot. This vessel is called *za-ma*. On marriage festive (bag-ston) occasions *Chang* is freely shared by all members of the family and stored for such days in *za-ma*.

The incense burner or phok spor is used in the prayer rooms of Ladakhi homes. Shaped like a large cup with a stand and a handle it is decorated with three clover shaped eyelets on the side. Oil containers and bowls are imperative in an area which subsists without the infrastructure of widespread electricity. Small pots are occasionally glazed. During research tour I came across a potter in Likir village he uses red earthenware clay which he dries himself from a nearly valley. Another clay is used to make a watery green glazed but this has to be carried from the high plateau of Chang-Thang a hundred or more miles away. His technique is a form of coil pottery. A small wheel is struck into the ground. After laying the clay on in coils he spins the wheel and beats the pot to coax if into shape. He makes only three varieties of pot.

1. One with a wide mouth flat rim for *Chang* (barley-beer).
2. A large one with a wide mouth which is filled with glowing coals.
3. A teapot which fits into the wide mouth and is kept warm by the coals inside.

He used dried cow dung as fuel. Since wood fuel is scarce, the dung and the pots are piled up and covered with a layer of earth, and the dung is set on fire there is no permanent kiln.

Among the crafts the art of metal work is highly developed in Ladakh. The silver and copper smiths of Chilling, Sumda and Zangskar display a high level of skill in their tea kettles and braziers and a common blacksmith sits in his front yard fashioning elaborate brass decorations to ornament a large iron stone.

However, potter from Likir employs typifies the true essence of the term 'dust into dust'. He resurrects the wheel when he begins his work using the abundance of clay around him. The fragments of pots and the vessels of his creation will eventually disintegrate and return to the earth waiting to be regenerated once again. It is almost as if, in the pattern of his work he is repeating the cyclical and thus infinite movement of the universe.

Potter of Likir uses only those products which emerge directly from nature or animal life for his subsistence. The leather of his horse's bridle, the barley he eats, the rough handspun and handwoven clothes he wears the goat hair used for the wool of his socks, the sunshine, the fine earth and water that combine with the dexterity of his hands to become vessels and containers for home use, reiterate his closeness him from his environment and he has no use for the technology of modern machinery or machine-made products which would create in him a dependence on factors far beyond his control.

In his small yard in Likir, nobody can discern that Likir village has any potter, as his life is almost same as others have. He starts his work with a simple way with no wheel and no demarcated work place. As he sits down he picks up a long bristled brush and wets a patch of ground before him. With a stick he pokes a hole into the ground and fixed a flint-shaped wooden piece into it. A small stone wheel no larger than a long playing record with a hole at the centre on one side is fitted on to this wooden peg and made a spin freely. A damp cloth is placed over this wide bowl shaped wheel, and an upturned rounded mug, the mould, is fixed on top of the cloth. The potter then moulds the clay into a round ball with his hands and places it over the mould, beating it into a conical shape with a wooden palette.

While it turns on the wheel a wooden stick is used to draw simple design lines below the rim. Another piece of clay is taken in hand, moulded, beaten and kneaded with a stone. On top of another stone shaped by hand, it is placed on to the lower piece which now forms the base of a cup. The edges are raised by pressing and turning and a cup shape is formed. The cup is then moistened with a brush while it is being turned on the wheel and its final shape emerges. A wooden palette with a sharp point gives a decorative edge to the top and base and the uppermost edge is made even with the help of the sharp palette. Wooden palettes of different curvatures are used to give pots their final shape. Strips of leather are wet and held around the top edge of the cup while the wheel turns so that a smooth surface is obtained. While copper, brass, silver tea kettles and braziers decorate the shelves of kitchens in larger and more wealthy homes in Ladakh, the simple village home still requires its full share of the earthern phospor and small oil containers made in this manner.

Sir Alexander Cunningham, perhaps the best documented authority on Ladakh wrote in 1853 :

> "The Tibetan Lamas are unrivalled amongst orientals as modellers in clay and workers in metal. A small medallion,

two inches square, which I possess, contains five figures surrounded by leaves and flowers of exquisitely delicate workmanship. It is formed of baked clay, but the edges are as sharp as if the work had been done by an European artist in plaster of paris."

As his work for the day is completed, Likir potter dismantles the apparatus that he had fashioned into a potters wheel. The flints and palettes are heaped in a corner against the side wall and the wet cloth is spread across a stone to dry. The hole in the ground is covered and the area cleared of oil and water bowls. Once again the small yard is overrun by the strutting cock, the dog, the horse and all nature quietly settles back into place. The process employed by Likir potter to live off the earth and create from it for the needs of his immediate society is probably amongst the most simple and most primitive that continue till today.

References

1. Ceramic Review ; 1981-83 ; 9-10.
2. Jettley, Jaya : 'A Potter in Ladakh', Sawagat, March 1988 ; 42-44.

35

Colourful 3-day Sindhu Darshan-2004 Festival in Ladakh

The major waterway of Ladakh is the Sindhu river, it is one of the longest rivers in the world with an astonishing length of 2900 km. Rising in south-western Tibet or emerging from the north of Mansarowar lake starting near Mt. Kailash, the Sindhu according to mythology, sprouts from the mouth of a lion, and is therefore known Sing-ge Chhu, Sing-ge in Sanskrit *Singh* means lion and *Chhu* in Ladakhi language for a flowing water body.[1]

The Sindhu river symbolises the power and after drinking its water one gets strength as if of lion. It enters Indian territory from Tibet at Demchok. Later flows past Batalik into Pakistan.

Inauguration Ceremony : This year Sindhu Darshan festival was started from 18 June to 20 June 2004, earlier it was organised 1-3 June. This year festival was delayed because of Parliamentary elections. The festival was inaugurated by Jammu and Kashmir Chief Minister Mufti Mohammad Sayeed.

Presence of VIPs : During the inauguration ceremony of Sindhu Darshna, many VIPs were present, popular among them—The Governor of Tamil Nadu, Ram Mohan Rao, Union Minister for Tourism, Renuka Chowdhary, Minister for Tourism, J&K, Ghulam Hassan Mir, Minister for Information Technology, Nawang Rigzin Jora, Minister for Sports and Youth Services, Haji Nisar Ali, Ministers for Tourism from Uttranchal and Delhi, Member of Parliament Thupstan Chewang, legislator Sonam Wangchuk Norboo, former M.P. P. Namgyal.[2]

Mixing of Water and Cultural Programme : The highlight of the festival was the mixing of waters from the Brahmaputra, the Ganga, the

Yamuna and the Godawari into the Indus. This shows the symbol of National Integration and brotherhood.[3]

On this occasion famous Bharat Natayam dancer, Sonal Mansingh gave a scintillating performance while the local Ladakhi dancers also received ample adulation from the audience.[4]

Pakistan Guests for the First Time : This year in Sindhu Darshan festival Pakistan guests for the first time arrived. It is said that they were invited by the Sindhu Academy, New Delhi.

Speaking on the occasion the Chief Minister of J&K State said that he supported free movement of people from one country to other and believed in dismantling the walls of hatred. He added—he was working towards forging greater interaction between the people that would ultimately lead to the end of suspicion and misgivings and promote friendship and amity. He further added :

> "Greater interaction of people on both sides will change their mindset," he said that he had taken up this matter with the former Prime Minister and the former Deputy Prime Minister. He was allowing people of Pakistan and Pakistan occupied Kashmir to visit Jammu and Kashmir like they go to other parts of the country and vice-versa. There would be needed to remove misconceptions among the people of both sides; as wrong notion had been fed to the people of Pakistan that people of Jammu and Kashmir were captives of the security forces. Likewise, some people on this side had this feeling that the real Islam existed in Pakistan alone. Therefore, if the people of both sides were allowed free movement all these misconceptions and wrong beliefs would go. He said he would take up this issue with the new Union Government also.[5]

Kashmir is the Show Window of Secularism : In Kashmir all castes and creeds live together without any hesitation. It is the example of Indian Secularism. During inauguration ceremony of Sindhu Darshan, the Chief Minister of J&K State said :

> "Kashmir was the show window of Indian secularism and democracy where people of all countries including Pakistan should be encouraged to visit and see the flowering of these two cherished ideals of the country."[6]

Ladakh Route for Kailash Mansarowar : The route from Ladakh to Kailash Mansarowar is comparably shorter than the present route via Pithoragarh in Uttranchal. Chief Minister of J&K on the inauguration said, he would persuade the Centre to open the Ladakh route for Kailash Mansarowar yatra in Tibet. He said, "The route from Ladakh to Kailash Mansarowar is easy, short and motorable compared to the Uttranchal route."[7]

However, Mufti Mohammad Sayeed made it clear that he did not want the present Uttranchal route to Kailash Mansarowar to be abandoned, but open up Ladakh as an alternate route for the pilgrims.

Promotion of Tourism : Last year because of Sindhu Darshan festival domestic tourists in Ladakh increased to a record level, that is, to 20,000. Mufti Mohammad Sayeed said :

> "There is tremendous potential of tourism in the region particularly of the adventure tourism."[8]

He said he would request the Central Government to throw open all the lofty mountains of Ladakh for trekkers and mountaineers and urged the Central Tourism Ministry to present the area as a package for the state bound tourists. He demanded that the flights to Srinagar and Leh from different parts of the country should be increased as the present flights to these two destinations were far too less than the demand.

Focused for Development : Ladakh has got tremendous development since it has been opened for foreign tourists as well as by Sindhu Darshan festival the percentage of domestic tourists has been increasing year by year, therefore, the living standard of Ladakhis also being increased upto high level. Focusing his attention on the development of Ladakh, the Chief Minister of J&K State said since the coalition government in the State assumed office, he had visited Ladakh for six time today. He added the government had ensured equitable distribution of resources and each reason was feeling as an equal partner in the development process. The government had empowered the Ladakh Autonomous Hill Development Council Leh and a similar council was set up in Kargil.[9]

Ladakh is the Best Place for Tourism : Since Ladakh has been very much popular destination for tourism among foreign and domestic tourists, now it has received some ecological problems. Speaking on the occasion of Sindhu Darshan Union Minister for Tourism, government of India, said that due care would have to be taken to preserve the ecology of Ladakh while opening it for more and more tourists. She added her Ministry was above politics and committed to the people of all the regions of the country irrespective of their political affiliations. She said her Ministry would showcase Ladakh as the best place in the country.[10]

Ladakh unaffected by any turmoil in J&K State : Tourism in Kashmir has been effected severely by terrorist activities whereas Ladakh remained unaffected. The J&K Minister for Tourism, Ghulam Hassan Mir said on the occasion of Sindhu Darshan Festival—Ladakh remained more or less unaffected during the long turmoil in Jammu and Kashmir. He said that while the Kashmir tourism suffered the greatest damage, it was encouraging the Ladakh continued to attract domestic and foreign tourists. He said :

> "Ladakh is culturally a very rich area, therefore, in order to increase tourism in Ladakh special package should be given to the interested tourists for Ladakh."[11]

Ladakhis are the true inheritors of Indus Civilization : Sindhu stands for peaceful co-existence and communal harmony. It is a symbol of India's identity and Indus civilisation which we can understand after visiting Ladakh and after taking bath in the pious river Sindhu. Speaking on the occasion of inaugural ceremony of Sindhu Darshan Festival, at Shey village, the Minister for Information Technology of Jammu and Kashmir State, Nawang Rigzin said "The people of Ladakh are the true inheritors of Indus Valley Civilization"[12]

To open Nubra Valley for Mountaineers : Initially during summer 1974 foreigners preferred to see Ladakhi culture and monasteries. Since tourist flux year by year increased tremendously. Leh converted into a densely populated town of Ladakh where the number of cemented buildings, Hotels, Guest Houses, vehicles, taxies etc. have been increased dramatically. These all together increase sound, air and water in and around the town area. Therefore, tourists particularly foreigners don't like to stay more in Leh town and prefer countryside and thus their interest diverted towards trekking and mountaineering, where they get more peace, enjoyment and adventure. Rigzin Zora on the occasion of Sindhu Darshan also pointed this matter and said :

> "The relations between Indo-Pak have been improved, the Centre must consider opening of Nubra valley for the mountaineers."[13]

Conclusion : Sindhu stands for peaceful co-existence and communal harmony, the Sindhu Darshan festival is the symbol of national integration. Therefore, both the State and Central Governments should think for the purity of this river and make all steps to avoid pollution. These good steps would definitely promote tourism in Ladakh.

References

1. Booklet 'Ladakh', 1990 : 3.
2. *The Kashmir Times*, Jammu; June 19, 2004 : 5.
3. *Ibid.*
4. *Ibid.*
5. *Ibid.*
6. *Ibid.*
7. *Ibid.*
8. *Ibid.*
9. *Ibid.*
10. *Ibid.*

36

Hemis Festival and Naropa Ceremony in Ladakh

2004 is a monkey year, important for events—Hemis festival and Naropa ceremony. The Hemis Festival was held on 28-29th June. On the first day, the rare thanka of Padmasambhava was unveilded after 12 years. It is a two-storey thangka, only exhibits after 12 years on the eve of Telo Hemis Festival. As a result huge number of domestic and foreign tourists visited Ladakh and attended the function. According to an estimation 20,000 domestic and foreign tourists came Ladakh in the June and July month.

Next to the Hemis Festival Naropa ceremony was undertaken from 1 to 3, July 2004. On this special function His Holiness, the 12th Gyalwang Drukpa or Gyalwang Drukchen Rinpoche, the supreme spiritual head of the Drukpa Kargyud lineage, gave preparatory teaching of the cakrasambhava empowerment to the general audience. On this occasion Drukchen Rinpoche donned the six sacred ornaments after 12 years. This was the third time when Rinpoche wore the ornaments and the ceremony shifted from Hemis monastery to the site of Druk Padma Karpo Institute at Shey village.

The six ornaments of Naropa consists :

(i) Head-gear
(ii) Apron
(iii) Arm-bands
(iv) Necklace
(v) Bracelets
(vi) Chest-bands and ear rings.

All the above ornaments are made of bone and used by Naropa himself in Vajrayana practice. These ornaments of Naropa symbolise spiritual realisation through the six yogas of Naropa.

It is explained that Marpa during 11th century visited India for the third time to receive teachings from Naropa. He was a Tibetan scholar, translator and great yogi, therefore, Naropa was very happy with his yogic activities, latter handed down the six ornaments to him, and made him spiritual regent in Tibet.

Marpa handed down the ornaments to his disciple Ngokton, and remained with the Ngokton lineage till the 7th Ngokton. Ngok Jangchub Pal the 7th Ngok offered these to Gyalwang Je Kunga Paljor, the 2nd Gyalwang Drukchen. Since then the six ornaments of Naropa have remained with the Gyalwang Drukchen lineage.

His Holiness Gyalwang Drukchen Rinpoche in addition to the six ornaments of Naropa, don the magnificent Black crown, women of the hair of one hundred thousand Dakinis and offered to Je Jamyang Chodak (1478-1523), the 3rd Gyalwang Drukchen, by the primordial Dakini Sukhasiddhi and gave the formal Cakrasambhava empowerment to the public the present Druchen Rinpoche first wore Naropa ornament in 1980, then 1992 and now this year on 2004.

37

World Music Festival : A Danger to Ladakhi Culture

This year two-day Music Festival was organised by Namgyal Institute for Research on Ladakhi Art and Culture and the Ladakh Autonomous Hill Development Council at the polo ground, Leh. On this occasion more than 60 international, national and local artists from the different discipline of music presented their classical and modern music programmes.

It is explained that the above festival not only boost tourism, also help to local musicians to interact with the world famous artists.

I do not know, how Ladakhi Art and Culture will be promoted by such Music Festivals, today it is my experiences that Ladakhi pop music does not encourage Ladakhi music at all, change is required according to time and demands of public but when such changes will harm to your culture, do you accept this ? Definitely you will say 'No'. Similarly we can accept Ladakhi music festival programme on stage, but when western music will be encourage here, it is not accepted, as our young generation by attracting western music, English songs easily follow their culture and forget their ancient and beautiful Ladakhi culture. How nice it would be if we say, "our Ladakhi music is the best of its kind and our music is the best in the world. Therefore, Westerners should invite us in their countries and learn our traditional and classical music."

In conclusion I may say Ladakhis should be very cautious when Western musicians are encouraged in Ladakh to perform western music in public. It will not promote Ladakhi music and cultural tradition of Ladakh, on the contrary Ladakhis will unable to preserve their culture.

37

World Music Festival : A Danger to Ladakhi Culture

This year two-day Music Festival was organised by Namgyal Institute for Research on Ladakh Art and Culture and the Ladakh Autonomous Hill Development Council at the polo ground, Leh. On this occasion more than 60 international, national and local artists from the different discipline of music presented their classical and modern music programmes.

It is explained that the above festival not only boost tourism, also help to local musicians to interact with the world famous artists.

I do not know how Ladakhi art and culture will be promoted by such Music Festivals, today it is my experience that Ladakhi pop music does not encourage Ladakhi music at all, change is required according to time and demand of public but when such changes will harm to your culture, do you accept this ? Definitely you will say 'No'. Similarly we can accept Ladakhi music festival programme on stage but why a western music will be encourage here, it is not accepted as our young generation by attracting western music, English songs easily follow their culture and forget their ancient and beautiful Ladakhi culture. How nice it would be if we say "our Ladakhi music is the best of its kind and our music is the best in the world. Therefore, Westerners should invite us in their countries and learn our traditional and classical music.

In conclusion I may say Ladakhis should be very cautious when Western musicians are encouraged in Ladakh to perform western music in public. It will not promote Ladakhi music and cultural tradition of Ladakh, on the contrary, Ladakhis will unable to preserve their culture.

38

Some Ladakhi Mountaineers

On 22nd March 1996 ITBP[1] Everest Expedition left from Delhi for Kathmandu on 30th March entered in Tibet. On 5th April 1996 they established Base Camp at Rongbok at an altitude of 17,200 feet. After this the following six more camps were established.

Table 38.1. Datewise Camp and Heights from the Sea Level

Date	*Camp*	*Height (feet)*
7-4-96	Camp-I	18,500
8-4-96	Camp-II	19,100
10-4-96	Camp-III	21,400
19-4-96	Camp-IV	23,100
3-5-96	Camp-V	25,750
9-5-96	Camp-VI	27,300

Source : Indian (ITBP) Mt. Everest Expedition 1996 (North Col.) News Magazine : 1.

On 10th May 1996, under the leadership of Harbhajan Singh 7 members team left camp-VI for the summit. Four members could not go beyond Step-I which was at an altitude of 27,880 feet. However, three Ladakhis : Inspector T. Samnla[2], NK Tsewang Palzor[3] and Ct Dorjee Morup[4] continued their ascent towards the summit. At 2.30 P.M. they reached successfully at the 'death zone' of Step-2 of 28,200 feet. At 6.00 P.M. they reached on the summit of Mount Everest. Unfortunately the happiness was short-lived as these great climbers faced very rough weather and were trapped in the blizzard and could not reach Camp-VI.[5]

Mountaineering in Ladakh : Ladakhis are tough climbers because Ladakh is a mountainous country and great portion of it lies in the biggest massif of mountains in the world. There are various mountain ranges viz.

the Karakoram, the Ladakh, Mustag and Kun-lun mountains. Between these ranges wide valleys are existed which are suitable for camps. The ridges and summits are fit for climbing. Here follows some mountain peaks which are important for mountaineers (Table 38.2)

Table 38.2

Sl. No.	*Mountain Peak*	*Height (feet)*
1.	Nubra Peak (or Saser Kangri)	25,180
2.	Shyok ridge	25,000
3.	Nubra Peak (or Saser Kangri)	24,600
4.	Kun Peak	23,410
5.	Nun Peak	23,219
6.	Tshomoriri Peak	21,000
7.	Gya Peak	21,000
8.	Stok Peak	21,000
9.	Rongo Peak	20,786
10.	Hanle Peak	20,650
11.	Zangskar Peak	20,000
12.	Lanak Peak	20,000
13.	Mustag Peak	20,000
14.	Baltal Peak	19,650

Source : Jina Prem Singh : 'Ladakh : The land and People', Indus Pub., New Delhi, 1996.

In 2004 I met the Hav. Chhering Tundup Sharapa, he retired from Ladakh Scout and at present working as security guard at State Bank of India, Choglamsar. In 1981 he was a member of Karakoram Expedition and scaled the Sisar Kangri-I peak. As a result Lt. Gen. A.M. Sethna gave him the following certificate.

Army Karakoram Expedition 1981 : For your invaluable contribution towards the success of the army Karakoram Expedition 1981, which crossed the seventy kilometers long Siachen Glacier, the longest in the Himalayas on Skis to reach Indira Col, the watershed between Central Asia and the Indian Sub-continent climbed Saltoro Kangri (25,400 feet), the highest in the Eastern Karakoram and Sia Kangri (24,350 feet), the Northernmost peak climbed by any Indian in India Hav. Chhering Tundup (Sharapa).

Sd.

Lt. Gen. A.M. Sethna

Vice Chief of Army Staff

Chhering Tundup Sharapa narrated about Karakoram Expedition in the following way : The High Altitude Welfare School, Gulmarg, Srinagar, selected 60 members team for Expedition in 1981. Col. N. Kumar of Kumaon Regiment was the group leader. Among others Ladakh Scout Armymen, Chhering Tondup came Nubra Base Camp on June 1981. Next day Tundup along with his members team left Partapur for Tirit village, which is 9 km. from Partapur. At Tirit they arranged poneys from villagers, then riding on horses along the Shyok river bank they covered 12 km. journey and arrived at Chati (Tib. Tse ti) village. At Chati they found 15 houses, after light refreshment and few hours rest again marched for Tangyer village of about 8 km. from Chati. Here they took night halt. The journey between Chati to Tangyer village was full of danger as they had crossed Shyok river at many places, while crossing the river they put their luggage on horse back and crossed the river by holding hands of each another. This time they found river was flowing upto the height of their shoulders. But they had courage, and crossed the river easily.

From Tangyer 30 members team of Chhering Tondup marched for Tokpo Karpo early in the morning. Here also they had crossed Shyok river at many places. At the morning water consisted snow pieces, which sometimes hurt severely. Tokpo Karpo is 6 km. from Tangyar, and has grazing fields, therefore, they left their horses for grazing. Then after travelling 9 km. they came at Shyok village. Here they saw 15-20 houses. In late evening arrived at Yurgolok which is 9 km. from Shyok.

In this way they crossed Shyok river 108 times in between Tirit and Yurgolok. Next day from Yurgolok they marched for Saser Kangri Nalla and covered 15 km. distance. Here they dumped their all luggage.

From Sisar Kangri Nalla Hav. Chhering Tondup along with his team members carried some luggage early in the morning for Road Racy to Camp-I. After reaching at Camp-I, they left their luggage there and returned to Saser Kangri Nalla. Unfortunately, when they were returning from Camp-I, one member from Vikas Regiment fall into 30 feet deep crevasses and his back was fractured. Four team members carried him to Base camp. Then through Army Helicopter he returned to Army General Hospital, Leh.

The route between Saser Kangri Nalla and Camp-I was covered by glacier. Here they found 5-6 feet deep snow belt. Next day 15 members of the mountaineering team climbed for Camp-I.

Thereafter, 5 climbers left Camp-I for Camp-II, which was 7 km. from Camp-I. Hav. Chhering Tondup was in this group. They all remained at Camp-II during night. Next day early in morning they climbed for Camp-III and fixed 10 ropes. They took night halt at Camp-III.

From Camp III they climbed for Camp-IV early in the morning. On the way they came across 100 feet snow rock, after fixing 4 ropes they arrived at Camp-IV.

Next day all the five tough climbers tied each others by rope and early in the morning climbed for the summit. Finally at 1 P.M. they reached on the summit of Saser Kangri-I, which is 25,180 feet.

References

1. ITBP : Indo-Tibetan Border Police.
2. T. Samnla : He was born on 14th September, 1957 at village and post office-Tia, Leh-Ladakh. He joined ITB Police in the year 1978 as constable. Soon he showed his interest on mountaineering. Later as a mountaineering career, he took Basic, Advanced and Instructor trainings from the reputed mountaineering institutes. He submitted 26 mountains in India and abroad, of which the most notable are : Stok Kangri-1983, Glob Kangri-1983, Mana (NW)-1984, Indo-Japanese Saser Kangri-II-1985, Saser Kangri-III-1984, Indo-France Saser-IV-1986, Pangong Range-1987, Indo-Japanese Rimo-I-1988, Mana East-1988, Indo-British Kistiwar-1988, Indo-British Kanyazzi-1989, Indo-British Rimo-II-1989, Indo-Japanese Kanchanjunga-1991, Sudarshan-1993. He was one of the first Indian to scale Mt. Everest from the Chinese side from North Col. on 10th May, 1996. He died on 10th May, 1996 while descending from the summit of Mount Everest.
3. N.K. Tsewang Palzor was born on 10th April 1968 at village and Post Office—Sakti, Leh, Ladakh. He joined ITB Police in 1986 as constable. After Basic and Advance mountaineering training he scaled many mountains of National level. He hoisted India's flag atop Mana, Chushul and Chushul-II all in the space of just in 1995. Like T. Samnla, he scaled Mt. Everest from the Chinese side from North Col. on 10th May 1996. He died on 10th May 1996 while descending from the summit of Mount Everest.
4. Dorjee Morup was born at village and post office Skurbuchan, Leh, Ladakh on 1st October 1948. He was enlisted in ITB

Police in 1969 as constable. After completed Basic and Advance Mountaineering Training, he started mountaineering career and scaled Chushul 1973, Stok & Glob Kangri-1974, Stok Kangri-1995 and Mana-1995. He was one of the first Indian to scale Mt. Everest from the Chinese side from North Col. on 10th May 1996. Unfortunately died on the same day while descending from the summit of Mt. Everest.

5. Indian (ITBP) Mt. Everest Expedition 1996 (North Col.), News Magazine.

39

Militant Violence in Zangskar of Ladakh Himalaya

On July 11, 2000 some militants came Rangdun monastery via Doda-Kistawar side and killed three innocent Buddhist monks. This was a well-planned strategy of militants who came Ladakh to turmoil the communal harmony of this region. According to Pushp Saref :

> "In Jammu and Kashmir, ironically, it has been quite fashionable to dismiss the initial occurrences of militancy in any area as routine developments."[1]

As the events unfolded, the situation was much more serious than one could think. The official machinery in Kargil knew the ground reality. There was the possibility to disrupt the harmonious relations among Buddhists and Muslims of Ladakh. But instead to study the seriousness of the killing of lamas, it was apparent that a deliberate twist was being given to the entire situation with two clear objects[2] :

(i) to further sharpen the division between the Buddhists of Leh and the Shias of Kargil.

(ii) to isolate the Buddhists who constitute the overwhelming majority in Leh in the State, where Muslims are in majority.

Not only this some selfish faxed the message from Srinagar to Iran for seeking 'fatwa' against 'kafir' leader of Ladakh Buddhist Association (LBA). Besides it was rumour in Kashmir valley that some militants from Pakistan, Afghanistan and other foreign countries had entered in the valley to assist militant activities in the name of war against Islam.[3]

We came to know that militants first asked monks to stand in a queue and then shot them from point-blank range. What this indicates ? It tells us that militants intention was to destroy the traditional ties between

Buddhists and Muslims. Secondly they would demoralise the Buddhist majority through selective killings.

Thanks to the Buddhists and Muslims of Ladakh region who understood the ground reality and did not disturb the communal harmony of the region.

References

1. Pushp, Saref : 'Warning Shots in Ladakh', 'Yug-Udbodhan', Nov. 2000 : 12.
2. *Ibid.*
3. *Ibid.*

40

Discrimination against Zangskaris in Ladakh Region

On September 1995, the All Party Zangskar Action Committee had taken an unspecified number of foreign tourist 'hostage' to press their demand for 'Justice' to the people of this cold desert region and construction of a link road to Numa in Leh district.[1]

According to official reports, the committee holded the tourists as 'hostage' in the local dak bunglow at Padum, the capital of the sub-division of Kargil division.[2]

The Action Committee had been demanding changes in the recommendations of State Delimitation Commission and 'Justice' to the 18,000 people of the region who remain cut off from rest of the country about nine months every year.[3]

Besides they had been demanding the creation of a separate district, as they allege discrimination by the Kargil Administration.[4]

The District Administration and concern officials of Kargil district had promised to consider their demands. Later foreigners were released.

In 2003, Zangskar people boycotted the Kargil District Hill Council Election, as only three seats were assigned to Zangskar, whereas they wanted 10 seats in the Hill Council. This year Zangskar finally decided to join the Hill Council after some of its demands were met and other promises were made during Chief Minister Mufti Mohammad Sayeed's visit to Zangskar in July 2004.

Thus on July 31, 2004 Hill Council election in Zangskar took place. Sonam Namgyal and Sonam Stobgias were declared elected unopposed from Karsha and Cha constituency. The following table shows the details :

Table 40.1. The Hill Council Election in Zangskar (July 31, 2004)

Sl. No.	*Councillor*	*Constituency*	*Performance*
1.	Sonam Namgial	Karsha	Unopposed
2.	Sonam Stobgia	Cha	Unopposed
3.	Tashi Wangchok	Padum	1,135 votes
4.	Chhewang Gyapo	Padum	819 votes
5.	Mohammad Amin	Padum	26 votes

Source : Compiled from D.C. Office Kargil.

All the councillors were elected as independent candidates, but is said that they had been supported by Congress Party. In this way in the 26 councillors of Kargil Hill Council 6 were from Zangskar. However, they rationalised their demands for 10 seats in the following grounds.[5]

(1) Zangskar formed 62 per cent of total area of Kargil.

(2) It was conferred Tehsil status with Leh, Kargil and Skardo in 1901 during the Maharaja's rule, and

(3) Zangskar never gets its due rights as a sub-division under Kargil district.

However with the boycott called off, the three seats that were left empty have now been occupied. Sources have reported that Zangskar Councillors have decided to support the opposition in the Kargil Hill Council. Three members—Haji Akhoon Hassan from Hardas, Karichu; Aga Syed Mukhtar from Stakchay Khangral and Kacho Gulzar Khan from Shakar.[6]

As a result of this political developments, the ruling National Conference majority in the Kargil Hill Council stands 14 councillors while the opposition has 12 councillors.

References

1. *The Tribune*, Sept. 12, 1995, Vol. 115, No. 252.
2. *Ibid.*
3. *Ibid.*
4. *Ibid.*
5. Ladags Melong, September, 2004 : 32.
6. *Ibid.*

41

King Lodos Chog dan (Tib. blo-gros mchog ldan) : A Ruler Who Ordered to Preserve Buddhist Culture and Religion in Ladakh

Lodos Chog dan was born about 1440, the eldest son of Dragspa Bum dle[1]. He was a brave soldier, conquered Ngaris skor sum[2]. Later he became supreme power after subdued all the vassal chiefs along country side of Ladakh.[3]

After conquering Guge, he received large quantities of presents and tribute from the King of Guge. The following were the important items :[4]

1. Fifty grey ponies
2. Fifty isabel
3. Twenty black and thirty piebald
4. Twenty young yak-cows
5. Twenty light brown yak-bulls
6. Sheep in immense quantity
7. Fifty turquoises of great value
8. Twenty saddles
9. Fifty black ponies
10. Eighteen swords
11. Eighteen *dals*
12. Twenty coloured ponies
13. Valuable Weapons : The resplendent devil-coat-of-mail, the coat-of-mail, devil darkness, the white 'gods' coat-of-mail; the sword 'licking blood off of the sky', the sword 'wild yalk, long

point', the sword 'killer of the red lightning flame', the 'black devil knife'.

Preservation of Ancient Old Culture : King Lodos was very particular to preserve ancient Ladakh culture. He ordered that his subjects will have to wear Ladakhi traditional dress and ornaments.. In this connection he passed a rule, under which every Ladakhi have to wear the following dress and ornaments.[5]

(i) Photib tibi (cap)
(ii) Pichak (knife)
(iii) Sulma
(iv) Yub gyur

It is explained that King encouraged to import *Yubgyur* (or Youbjur) from Mongolia and *Photib Tibi* from Dokyul (Probably Da-Hanu or Baltistan).[6]

Today with the economic development and Tourism, the living standard of Ladakhis have been raised considerably. One can now see the influence of Western and Indian cultural on their day-today life style. Now they often use traditional dress and ornaments during marriage ceremonies and other important occasions.

Took less interest in Religious Activities : King seems to last long. Like his precedessors he didn't take much interest in religious works. Moreover, he supported Likir monastery for its renovation.[7]

Helped Lamas to go abroad for higher Studies : He always happy to see educated or learned lamas, and provided all needed facilities to them to study in Tibet. Phan chen lha cun[8] of Nubra was one of the great learned lama who with his help studied in Tashi lun bu[9] monastery in Tibet, later returned Ladakh and developed monastic order according to Geluk order in Ladakh.[10]

To sum up his contribution, I may stay he was a brave King with strong determination. He subdued all the vassal chief during his regime, extended the boundaries of his Kingdom and conquered Ngari skor sum. In 1470 he passed away.

References

1. Dragspa Bum dle : Tib. grags pa 'abum lde.
2. Ngaris skor sum : Western Tibet.
3. Francke, A.H. : 'History of Western Tibet', Reprinted by Asian Education Services, 1995 : 81-82.

4. *Ibid* and Sonam Phuntsog : 'Ladakh', 2000 : 126.
5. Sonam Phuntsog ; 'Ladakh', 2000 : 126.
6. *Ibid.*
7. *Ibid.*
8. Phan chen lha cun : Tib. Phan chen lha btsun.
9. Tashi lun bu : Tib. bka shis lhun bu.
10. Sonam Phuntsog ; *op. cit.* : 126.

42

King Jamyang Namgyal (Tib. 'ajam dbyangs rnam rgyal) : The Founder of Shia Sect of Islam in Ladakh

Lhawang Namgyal had three sons :

(i) Tsewang Namgyal (Tib. tshe dbang rnam rgyal),
(ii) Namgyal Gonpo (Tib. rnam rgyal mgon po), and
(iii) Jamyang Namgyal.

Tsewang Namgyal was the eldest son, therefore first became the King after the death of his father. He was a strong King and ruled over whole Ladakh, but died unexpectedly without leaving any child. Now quarrels took place between Namgyal Gonpo and Jamyang Namgyal for the throne of Ladakh. Finally Jamyang Namgyal, the youngest one came on throne in 1576.[1]

Disturbances in Lower Ladakh : It is said that after the death of King Tsewang Namgyal, uncertainty took place at Leh palace. Therefore, acknowledging the uncertainty of Ladakh Kingdom and its future, all the vassal Kings along the countryside of Ladakh as a result started to declare them free and escaped out under the control of Ladakh Kingdom. They then ruling their respective provinces independently.

King Jamyang Namgyal's attention towards Purig : When Jamyang Namgyal officially came to know that in Purig region two princes of Chigtan and Kartse changed their religion they became Muslims, declared themselves Sultans of Chigtan and Kartse. It is explained that they became Muslims on the line of Mughal tradition. According to others it is believed that if the above princes would remain in Buddhists, they would hardly control the feeling of their subjects. Therefore, when they became Muslim Sultans could easily control the mob who were suppose to be against their action. According to the Chigtan tradition, Tsering Malik, who then reigned was the first Mohammed Chief in Purig region. Therefore, his interest to capture the Kartse, he, thence invaded Kartse. On the other side Kartse prince also became Sultan of his province got reasonable support by his citizens. Therefore, fought bravely against Tsering Malik. In Leh Jamyang Namgyal did not digesting such changes. He had an opinion, that such practice not only reduce his power, but also effect Buddhism in Ladakh. Therefore, he felt this would be a good chance for him to capture his provinces from them. But instead of attack upon Chigtan or Kartse, he planned to assist Tsering Malik of Chigtan. If he could occupied Kartse, Chigtan later automatically would become a part of his kingdom.[2]

Losar : A New Year Festival Celebration : As king started campaign for the war against Kartse, his advisers said :

> "It would be late if the Ladakhi army marched after Losar festival and if start earlier, it considered to be unlucky. Therefore, king should celebrate Losar festival two months before it actually fell."[3]

King Jamyang Namgyal accepted this advice and celebrated Losar festival earlier to its actual date. Since then it becomes a tradition to celebrate Losar two months earlier in Ladakh than in Central Tibet.

Movement of Ladakh Army and Balti Attack : King Jamyang Namgyal in spite of measure to hasten, got late. On the other side Baltis under the command of Duke Ali Mir had established their bunkers across the passes towards Purig. As soon as the Ladakh army had crossed passes, the Balti force attacked on Ladakh army did not move further, thus Baltis succeeded to hold Ladakhis on passes, until snow fall. As a result Ladakh army compelled to surrender before Baltis.[4]

Baltis Overrun into Ladakh : When Ladakh army surrendered, Balti force rejoined and entered into the countryside of Ladakh. They destroyed Buddhist monasteries, burnt religious books, threw others into the water. Later returned to Skardu.[5]

New Hope for Ending Ladakh Buddhist Kingdom : As soon as King Jamyang Namgyal surrendered, he was taken to Skardu as Ali Mir Sher Khan's prisoner.

Ladakh king was handsome and had attractive personality, so Ali Mir decided to return his kingdom under the following conditions :

(i) that he has to marry his daughter Gyal Katun

(ii) that he has to accept Gyal Katun as his first wife, and to disinherit the sons who had been born by his old queen

(iii) that he has to encourage Mohammedanism in his kingdom.

Gyal Katun was very beautiful girl, king did not hesitate to accept the conditions.

Matrimonial Alliance : According to some historians Ali Sher Khan of Skardu invaded Ladakh and subdued it. As he could remain in Ladakh, he entered into matrimonial alliance with the king. Under the alliance king of Ladakh gave his daughter in marriage to Ali Mir, who in return gave his daughter Gyal Katun in marriage to the king of Ladakh.[7]

Ali Mir Sher Khan Dream : As soon as king of Ladakh accepted the conditions, Raja of Skardu arranged a grant feast in which soldiers and royal dignitaries were present. On this occasion Gyal Katun had put on all her jewels. Later Raja Ali Mir invited Jamyang Namgyal to mount the throne and said :

> "Yesterday in dreamt I saw a lion emerging from the river in front of the palace and jumping at Gyal Katun; he disappeared into her body. At the very same time also Gyal Katun conceived. Now it is certain she will give birth to a male child, whose name ye shall call Sengge Namgyal."[8]

Ladakh Empire Saved : After the completion of marriage ceremony at royal palace in Kapulu. King Jamyang Namgyal, queen Gyal Katun and many musicians from Skardu came in Ladakh. Thus the Ladakhi empire was saved, but its size became smaller than its previous.

King Jamyang Namgyal and Buddhism : After returning to power, King Jamyang Namgyal decided to strengthen Buddhism in Ladakh. He said :

> "I will employ any means that may serve towards the propagation of the religion of Buddha and make it spread. But, as the religion of Buddha for its propagation is entirely dependent on the people, I will, on my part, relieve them from taxation and treat them likes my own children."[9]

Presents to the High Lamas of the principal monasteries in Tibet: In order to keep good cultural and religious relation of Ladakh with Tibet, King Jamyang Namgyal sent a missionary with presents to the important monasteries viz. Sera, Drepung, Gadan, Tashilunbôo, etc. the sons from his old wife now deposed, them became lamas, had to escort them and later on to act as messengers to a high lama.[10]

Repairing of ruined monasteries and printing religious books : During Balti War, Baltis destroyed many Buddhist monasteries in Ladakh. King Jamyang Namgyal rebuilt the destroyed monasteries. The best known ruins of the Balti wars are : Nyizlapug monastery at Saspol; the Kaoche monastery at Spitug (Spituk), and the Lingshed castle and monastery.

Besides, he ordered concerned authorities to print or copied Buddhist text in gold, silver and copper ink.[11]

Chosje Danma in Ladakh : Some Ladakhi historians explained that King Jamyang Namgyal invited Chosje Danma from Tibet. He was a great lama of Drigung pa order. Later King requested him to establish Drigung pa monastery in Ladakh. Accordingly he founded Phyang monastery to Drigung order in Ladakh.[12]

Balti migration into Ladakh : When King Jamyang Namgyal retain power, to know the facts King would help in the propagation of Islam in Ladakh, many Balti families also migrated from Skardu to Ladakh and settled down in various places in Ladakh. At present they have their families in Chushod, Phyang, Thiksey etc.

Singge Namgyal Birth : When queen Gyal Katun got pregnant she went to Timogang palace and stayed there. As soon as Singge Namgyal was born, she returned to Leh palace.

Statues in Monasteries : King Jamyang Namgyal not only repaired Buddhist monasteries also built temples and statues at Basgo, the brass statue of Buddha is one of the important.

King Jamyang Namgyal had two sons from Gyal Katun : Singge Namgyal and Norbu Namgyal. In 1615 Jamyang Namgyal passed away in Nubra. After sometimes, Gyal Katun also died and buried at Hunder. Singge Namgyal then became the King of Ladakh.

References

1. According to Francke : "Why Namgyal Gonpo, was the next, did not become king, is not stated." Cf. Francke, A.H. : 'A History of Western Tibet', Asian Education Services, New Delhi, 1995 : 91.
2. Francke, A.H. ; *op. cit.* : 91.
3. *Ibid.*
4. *Ibid.*, 92.
5. *Ibid.*
6. *Ibid.*, 93.
7. Sumi Tokan, D ; Oki Masato and Fida M. Hussnain : 'Ladakh : The Moonland', Light & Life Pub., New Delhi; 1975 : 7.
8. Francke, A.H. ; *op. cit.* : 94.
9. *Ibid.*
10. *Ibid.*, 95-96.
11. Thupstan Paldan : 'Guide to Ladakhi Monasteries', 1976 : 4.

Bibliography

Bellew, H.W. : 'Kashmir and Kashgar : A Narrative of Journey of the Embassy of Kashgar in 1873-74', Trubner & Co. ; Ludgate Hill ; London, 1875 & Reprinted in India by Asian Educational Services, New Delhi, 1989.

Bergman, Folke : 'Archaeological Researches in Singkiang, Vol. II, Stockholm, 1939.

Bower, Hamilton : 'Diary of a Journey across Tibet', Rivington Percival and Co., London; 1894 : 7-8.

Francke, A.H. : 'Some More Rock-Carvings from Lower Ladakh', Indian Antiquary, Vol. XXXII, 1903, Reprinted by Swati Pub., Delhi : 1985.

Francke, A.H. : 'A History of Western Tibet', Reprinted by Asian Education Services, New Delhi : 1995.

Gompertz, M.L.A. : 'Magic Ladakh : An Intimate Picture of a Land of Topsy-turvy Customs & Great Natural Beauty', Seeley Ltd.; London : 1928.

Heber, A. Reeve & Heber Kathleen, M. : 'Himalayan Tibet & Ladakh', Ess Ess Pub. Delhi ; 1976 (First Print 1903).

Heldin, Seven : 'Trans-Himalaya (Discoveries and Adventures in Tibet), Vol. I, Greedwood Press Pub. New York; 1969.

Jina, Prem Singh : 'Ladakh Aur Paryatan' (Tourism in Ladakh), In Ist National Conference, C.I.B.S., Leh-Ladakh, 1981.

Jina, Prem Singh : 'Ladakh ki Sanskriti per Seemant Sanskriti ka Prabhav', News Letter, New Delhi, Sept.-Oct., 1982.

Jina, Prem Singh : 'Bhagwan Buddha Kaha', Dinman Times of India Pub., New Delhi, 28th Nov.-4th December, 1982.

Jina, Prem Singh : 'Santi Stupa Ladakh Ke', Yojana, Jammu, March, 1983.

Jina, Prem Singh : 'Boudh Biksus of Ladakh', In : Proceed. of All India Conference; Delhi Univ., Delhi, 1983.

Jina, Prem Singh : 'Seet Kal me Leh Ghati', Sheeraja-65, Jammu, March, 1983.

Jina, Prem Singh : 'The Foreign Tourist Traffic in Ladakh', Himalayan Research and Development (Problem Oriented Studies), Vol. 3 (i), Nainital, June, 1984.

Jina, Prem Singh : 'Buddhism in Ladakh and World Peace', in 10th International Buddhist Conference on Buddhism and World Peace, Japanese Temple, Bodh Gaya, Vol. X, 1984.

Jina, Prem Singh : 'Astangik Marg aur Moksa', Prakasitman, Delhi, March, 1984.

Jina, Prem Singh : 'Foreign Tourists and their Impact on Ladakh', in IIIrd National Conference Proceed. Ladakh Prabh (3), 1985.

Jina, Prem Singh : 'A Brief Introduction of Ladakh Gonpas', in : Ladakh : Life and Culture ; K.N. Pandit (ed.), Kashmir University, Srinagar; 1986, pp. 39-50.

Jina, Prem Singh : 'Economic & Cultural Relations between Ladakh and Lahul & Spiti, in Ist All India Conference at Baudh Darshan Mahavidayalaya, Keylong, (Himachal Pradesh).

Jina, Prem Singh : 'A Survey of Buddhist Community in Ladakh Himalaya', in 12th International Buddhist Conference on Buddhism and Social Harmony, Japanese Temple, Bodh Gaya, India, Vol. XII, 1986.

Jina, Prem Singh : Pasturelands of Zangskar and its effects on Ecology, in 1st National Conference, Leh-Ladakh, 1986.

Jina, Prem Singh & Mir A. A. : Pasturelands of Leh and its effects of Ecology in 1st National Conference organised by Indian Army, Trishul Nature Conservation, Leh-Ladakh, 1986.

Jina, Prem Singh : Monasteries in the Economy of Leh-Ladakh, In : All India Conference on Buddhist Monasteries of Himalayan Region : Various Aspect ; 9-13th August, CIBS, Leh, 1988.

Jina, Prem Singh : Bodh Dham Leh-Ladakh, Hindu Chetna, Vol. 7, New Delhi, June, 1988 : 21-33.

Jina, Prem Singh : 'Ladakhi Rajao ka Bodh Dharm me Yogdan' Hindu Chetna, Vol. 10, Sept. 1988 : 19-20.

Jina, Prem Singh : 'Eco-Environmental Study of Tourist Industry in Ladakh Himalaya', in All India Conference, Kashmir University, Srinagar, Deptt. of Centre for Central Asian Studies, 1989.

Jina, Prem Singh : 'Pasture Ecology of Leh-Ladakh', in Wessenschalts Gegschiche and Gegenwarlige Forschungen in Nordwest Indian Saatliches Muslim fur Volkerkunde, Dresden Forschungsstelle, Germany, 1990.

Jina, Prem Singh : Ladakh me Bodh Kala ka Udbhav aur Vikash; Sheeraja, Feb.-March, Vol. 1991: 12-14.

Jina, Prem Singh : 'History & Growth of Education; Himalaya Today, Nov. 1991 : 16-18.

Jina, Prem Singh : 'Ladakh ki Mahila Prashashak Putith Wangmo' Hamara Sahitya, Jammu, 1992 : 104-06.

Jina, Prem Singh : 'Impact of Tourism on Ladakhi Society and Culture', in All India Conference, JNU; New Delhi, 1993.

Jina, Prem Singh : 'Poultry Industry in Ladakh Himalaya', Himalaya Today, Sept., 92-Feb. 1993 Vol. IX, No. 2&3, 1993 : 7.

Jina, Prem Singh : Dasvi Satabdi Purva Lahul me Bodh Dharm evam Sanskriti, Janjati Mela Smarika; 1993 : 60-62.

Jina, Frem Singh : 'Tourism in Ladakh Himalaya', Indus Publishing Company, New Delhi, 1994.

Jina, Prem Singh : 'Tourism Industry in Ladakh', Himalaya Today, Jan.-March, Vol. IV, No. 2, New Delhi, 1994 : 20.

Jina, Prem Singh & Konchok Namgyal : 'Spiti ka Sanskritik Itihas'. Janjati Utsav, 1994 : 70-72.

Jina, Prem Singh : 'Buddhism in Ladakh and its Approach to the Material World; in Buddhism Approach to Material World; Proced. of the 18th International Buddhist Conference, Vol. XVIII; Bodh Gaya, 1993-94 : 51-60.

Jina, Prem Singh : Bhiksuni Sangha Avam Ladakh me Usaki Stithi, Proced. of the National Conference, 1994 : 50-52.

Jina, Prem Singh : Kesar Ka Mahakaviya, Sheeraja, Vol. II, June-July, Jammu, 1994.

Jina, Prem Singh : High Pasturelands of Ladakh Himalaya, Indus Pub. Co., New Delhi, 1995.

Jina, Prem Singh & Konchok Namgyal : Phyang Monastery of Ladakh; Indus Pub. Co., New Delhi, 1995.

Jina, Prem Singh : 'Buddhism in Ladakh', Yug Udbodhan, Vol. I, No. 9, New Delhi, 1995 : 14-16.

Jina, Prem Singh : 'Ladakh : The Land and the People', Indus Pub. Co., New Delhi, 1996.

Jina, Prem Singh : 'Hemis : The Biggest Buddhist Monastery of Ladakh', Yug Udbodhan, Vol. 2, No. 4, New Delhi, 1996 : 15.

Jina, Prem Singh : 'Ladakhi Ganpao me Biksuo ki Pravesh Vidhi', Yug Udbodhan, Vol. 2, No. 6, New Delhi, 1996 : 9.

Jina, Prem Singh : 'Tabo Monastery—A Unique Monument in Spiti Valley', Yug Udbodhan, Vol. 2, No. 11, New Delhi, 1996 : 13.

Jina, Prem Singh (ed.) : 'Recent Researchers on the Himalaya', Indus Pub. Co., New Delhi ; 1997.

Jina, Prem Singh : 'Some Manuscripts and Inscriptions on Ladakh Himalaya', Sri Satguru Pub., New Delhi, 1998.

Jina, Prem Singh : 'Some Monasteries of Drigung pa Order in Central Ladakh', Sri Satguru Pub., New Delhi, 1999.

Jina, Prem Singh : 'Changing Face of Ladakh Himalaya', Om Pub., New Delhi, 1999.

Jina, Prem Singh & Konchok Namgyal : 'Lamayuru Monastery of Ladakh Himalaya', Om Pub., New Delhi, 1999.

Jina, Prem Singh : 'Ladakh Mera Anubhav' (My Experience in Ladakh), Anjuri, 1999.

Jina, Prem Singh : 'History of Education and Growth in Ladakh', International Conference, IALS, Leh-Ladakh, 1999.

Jina, Prem Singh : 'Buddhism and Non-violence', in XXIV International Buddhist Conference, Indosan Nipponji, Bodh Gaya, 1999.

Jina, Prem Singh : 'Ladakh : Past and Present', Gyan Pub., New Delhi, 2000.

Jina, Prem Singh : 'Ladakhi ki Kala Avam Sanskriti', INCA, New Delhi, 2001.

Jina, Prem Singh : 'Varsha Vas Ka Mahatva', All India Conference on 'Trisavara', CIBS, Leh-Ladakh; 2001.

Jina, Prem Singh : 'Buddhism and Science', National Seminar on Role and Contribution of Buddhism and Vedic Dharma in National Integration', Ladakh Phandey Tsogspa, 2001.

Jina, Prem Singh : 'Tibetan Inscriptions in Diskit Monastery Nubra (Ladakh)', 63rd Indian History Congress, 2002.

Jina, Prem Singh : 'Religious History of Ladakh Himalaya, Sri Satguru Pub., New Delhi, 2001.

Jina, Prem Singh : 'Development of Ladakh : Recent Researchers', Gyan Pub., New Delhi, 2002.

Jina, Prem Singh : 'First Hand Tibetan Inscriptions on Rock & Stones of Ladakh Himalaya', Sri Satguru Pub., New Delhi, 2003.

Jina, Prem Singh : 'Tibetan Inscriptions in Chomolagung Temple of Thiksey Monastery of Ladakh Himalaya', 64th Indian History Congress.

Jina, Prem Singh : 'Buddhism and Female Education', XXVIII International Buddhist Conference, Indosan Nipponji, Bodh Gaya, 2003.

Jina, Prem Singh : 'Ladakh Himalaya : Past and Present', in press, Anmol Pub., New Delhi.

Jina, Prem Singh : 'Thiksey Monastery of Ladakh Himalaya', in press, Sri Sat Guru Pub., New Delhi.

Jina, Prem Singh : 'Kesar : A Aetihasik Upaniyas of Ladakh' Sakshi Prakashan, Delhi, 2004.

Jina, Prem Singh : 'History of Education before 1947 in Ladakh', National Conference, CIBS, 2002.

Jina, Prem Singh : 'Buddhism in the Twenty First Century', International Conference, CIBS, 2004.

Knight : 'Travels in Cashmir & Thibet', First Published in 1863, Reprinted in 1992, Vintage Books, Gurgaon, India.

Knight, E.F. : 'Where Three Empires Meet', Longmans, Green and Co., London, 1905 & Reprinted by Asian Educational Services, New Delhi, 1993.

Moorcroft, William and Trebeck, George : 'Travels in the Himalayan Provinces of Hindustan and the Punjab, in Ladakh and Kashmir; in

Peshawar, Kabul, Kunduz, and Bokhara', Sagar Pub., New Delhi, Vol. I, 1971 (Reprinted).

Richardson, H.E. : 'Tibet and its History', Oxford Univ. Press, London, 1962.

Shaw, Robert : 'Visits to High Tartary Yarkand and Kashgar', Oxford University Press, 1984. First published by John Murray, London, 1871.

Sonam Phuntsog : 'Ladakh', 2000.

Sumi, Tokan, D., Oki, Masato & Fida M. Hussnain : 'Ladakh : the Moonland', Light & Life Pub., Delhi, 1975.

Thupstan Paldan : 'Guide of Ladakh Gonpas', 1974.

Index

D

E

F

G

H

I

J

K

L

T

U

W

Y